16.95

THE SHA
OF 1917

Robert Manne is senior lecturer in politics at
La Trobe University and editor of *Quadrant*.
He is a frequent contributor to newspapers
and magazines, and speaks regularly on radio.

BY THE SAME AUTHOR:

The New Conservatism in Australia (editor)
The Petrov Affair
Shutdown (co-editor with John Carroll)

THE SHADOW OF 1917

COLD WAR CONFLICT IN AUSTRALIA

ROBERT MANNE

THE TEXT PUBLISHING COMPANY
MELBOURNE AUSTRALIA

The Text Publishing Company
A division of the Text Media Group Ltd
171 Latrobe Street
Melbourne Victoria 3000
Copyright © Robert Manne 1994

First published 1994
Typeset by Parkhouse Publishing Pty Ltd
Printed and bound by McPherson's Printing Group

National Library of Australia
Cataloguing-in-Publication data:
Manne, Robert.
    The Shadow of 1917.
    Includes index.
    ISBN 1 875847 03 0
    1. Communism - Australia - History. 2. Australia - Politics
    and government - 1945–1965. 3. Australia - Foreign
    relations - 1945–1965. I. Title.
994.05

Illustration: statue of Stalin displayed at the Paris World Fair, 1937.

This project was assisted by the Commonwealth Government
through the Australia Council, its art funding and advisory body.

CONTENTS

To Anne, Kate and Lucy

PREFACE

BY COINCIDENCE I was appointed sole editor of *Quadrant* on the very day, 9 November 1989, that the world celebrated the end of the Cold War with the overthrow of the Berlin Wall. As the first post-Cold War editor of a journal as deeply rooted in this historical period as *Quadrant*, it was obvious to me that I had to come to terms with a new intellectual landscape, where the old Cold War alignments of left and right were certain to dissolve and where the persistence of that peculiarly embattled tone, which characterised intellectual combat during the Cold War, would be nothing more than lazy mental habit. I was convinced that now new political alignments and new lines of conversation between former antagonists were possible. I was also convinced, however, that if these new political conversations were to flourish they could only do so if at their beginning the subject matter of Cold War conflict—the meaning of 1917 and the dark shadow it had cast across our century—was neither to be fudged nor forgotten. My hope is that this volume will help initiate a genuine debate on the nature of political and intellectual conflict during the Australian Cold War.

The chapters in this book were written during the past fifteen years, often as a direct response to a pressing political issue of the day. Except for the introductory chapter, all have been published, in one form or another, before. It only recently became clear to me that these essays might belong together in a book, representing what I have to contribute to discussion of the meaning of 1917 for Australia.

Apart from the first and last chapters all were written while the intellectual battles of the Cold War were still being fought. Inevitably their tone is influenced by this context. I have thought it important not to soften their urgency and their anger by subtle editorial intervention. From the original essays I have omitted only a few errors of fact. On one occasion, in the essay on the election of May 1954, I have added a short passage on an important new piece of information, of which I was unaware when the original piece was written. All other changes from the original texts are stylistic or trivial.

The most difficult decision was whether this book should be published with or without footnotes. The advantage of footnotes is that they allow others to pursue disagreements over matters of fact to their source. The disadvantage is that they tend to repel general readers. In the end I decided against footnotes. Those who wish to check my sources can go to the place of original publication where copious footnotes are provided. The chapter on Wilfred Burchett first appeared in *Quadrant* in August 1985 and then in a slightly expanded version in a monograph, *Agent of Influence: The Life and Times of Wilfred Burchett*, published by the Mackenzie Institute in Toronto in 1989. I am indebted to Winston Burchett and Stephanie Alexander for permission to quote from material in the Burchett papers in the La Trobe Library, Melbourne. The chapters on Petrov, Evatt and Menzies are extracted from *The Petrov Affair: Politics and Espionage*, Pergamon Press, Sydney, 1987. The chapters on Pol Pot and on the Combe affair first appeared in *Quadrant*, respectively in October 1979 and October 1984. The concluding chapter also appeared first in *Quadrant*, in November 1991, without footnotes.

My gratitude is due to Di Gribble and Michael Heyward of Text Publishing for their editorial intelligence; to my friend Raimond Gaita for his conversation over the past quarter century and for encouraging me to put this book together; and, as always, to my wife, Anne, and to my daughters, Kate and Lucy, for their support and their love.

Cottlesbridge, June 1994

THE SHADOW OF 1917

IN OCTOBER 1917, after more than three years of the Great War, and eight months after the abdication of Czar Nicholas II, the Bolshevik Party—the most radical of the Russian Marxist sects—seized power in Petrograd, the capital of the disintegrating Russian Empire. The Bolshevik seizure of power in Petrograd is probably the single most important political event in our century. At the time it occurred few took seriously the prospect of Bolshevik survival. However, only a little over three years later, the Bolsheviks held power securely in whatever remained of the old Russian Empire. A little over thirty years later all of Eastern Europe and much of East Asia was under the rule of communist party governments, modelled upon the system of politics and economy which had been pioneered by the Bolsheviks. At this time all were unshakably loyal to the Soviet Union and to its towering leader, Josef Stalin. The shadow of 1917 fell upon half of humanity.

It would take almost another fifty years before the European peoples which had fallen under communist rule—every single one—were to rise up against it and shrug it off. Revolution is too strong a word for what happened. The Bolshevik experiment continued now only in the great Asian civilisations where, after the 1940s, it had taken hold—China, Indo-China and on the northern half of the Korean peninsula. The abandonment of the Bolshevik experiment in Europe and its continuation in Asia was symbolised by two events which occurred on a single day, 4 June 1989. On that day the Poles went to their first free election since the end of World War II and delivered a humiliating blow to the ruling communist party. All but one of the available parliamentary seats went to the anticommunist opposition movement, Solidarity. On the same day the Chinese communist rulers alerted the world to their determination to hold onto power by whatever means were necessary by crushing under their tanks the unarmed democracy demonstrators at Tienanmen Square. The destinies of European and Asian communism had parted company.

In Central Europe the countries which had been delivered to communism by the Red Army now set out upon a weary trudge along the road back to the European normality, which had been barred to them in 1945. As usual the jokes expressed it best. Socialism was the long way between capitalism and capitalism. Those who could still tell jokes were fortunate. In the former Yugoslavia and the former Soviet Union the quest for Europe and normality looked likely to turn rather into a hellish descent into economic catastrophe, primitive nationalism and barbaric war. In the former Yugoslavia socialism was the long way between civil war and civil war. In the former Soviet Union the even longer way between chaos and chaos.

In Europe at least it was by now possible to assess the costs of the Bolshevik experiment. In building the communist future—the realm where Lenin and his party sincerely

4

believed class oppression would be destroyed, humankind would be redeemed and history would end—millions of innocent human beings had been torn from their families, transported in cattle trucks to frozen wastes, worked pitilessly to death in concentration camps, starved to death, and executed as enemies of the people. How many hundreds of thousands had died in the Red Terror under Lenin which accompanied the savage Civil War of 1918-21? How many millions had perished in the frozen wastes of the Gulag Archipelago or, with distended bellies, died agonising deaths from starvation in Ukrainian villages or on the Kazakh steppe as the price that was paid for the collectivisation of agriculture? How many millions amongst those nations to which Stalin took exception—the Baltic peoples, the Volga Germans, the Tatars? How many millions in the Great Terror which continued, uninterruptedly, from the murder of Kirov in 1934 to the death of Stalin in 1953? The scholars are still arguing over the figures. Their enormity is not in dispute.

To grasp even a part of this catastrophe you must read historians like Robert Conquest or survivors like Nadezhda Mandelstam and Evgenia Ginsburg or, better still, the epic secret history of the wracked and wretched victims of the Bolshevik experimental table, Aleksandr Solzhenitsyn's masterpiece *The Gulag Archipelago*—one of the great works of our century. And, when you weary of all this, turn to the less well documented but not less hair-raising stories of those who tell us about what happened to human beings during the Great Leap Forward or the Cultural Revolution of Mao or on the killing fields of Pol Pot. In absolute terms the victims of Mao outnumber even those of Stalin. And in proportional terms even Stalin and Mao must cede precedence to Pol Pot, in whose honour a somewhat imprecise but nonetheless telling neologism was coined—autogenocide. By the time you arrive at the histories of the forced Bolshevik experiment in Eastern Europe after 1945, where the victims of the executions and the concentration camps can be measured in the tens or hundreds of thousands rather than tens of millions, the crimes of the communist regimes have arrived at a more humanly imaginable scale. By now these crimes, which are far vaster than anything seen in the history of Europe during the nineteenth century, may seem almost petty by comparison.

It would be wrong to think that the cost of the communist experiment can be measured only by counting the numbers of innocents who were delivered to what Solzhenitsyn calls, with characteristically savage irony, the Bolshevik 'sewage disposal system'. In order to assess its cost one has also to consider the swift political death, under bolshevism, of the democratic revolutionary movement of the workers' and soldiers' soviets which had, already by 1918, become the decorative facade of totalitarian single party rule; or the only slightly more gradual transformation of the revolutionary proletarian *citoyen* into the Stalinist cipher, the outwardly enthusiastic and inwardly trembling *automaton*; and the metamorphosis of this automaton, inside the Gulag, into the *zek*—that abject and cunning body of bones, standing in the shadowland between life and death.

One would have, too, to consider the process whereby the Soviet worker and peasant experienced a level of exploitation under Stalin's system of 'primitive socialist accumulation' more radical and cruel than anything even Karl Marx had imagined possible through his theory of 'primitive capitalist accumulation'. One would have to consider how, in the interests of the emancipation of humankind, the arts, history and the sciences were reduced to propaganda. Or how the revolution so swiftly crushed the idea of the rule of law or of the autonomous institution—the family, the church, the circle or the club—which might stand between the naked individual and the state. One would have to consider how a revolution devoted to a single idea—equality—so swiftly reproduced in its stead a privileged and largely hereditary caste, the *nomenklatura*. And one would have, finally, to consider why in every strictly comparable case—Germany, East and West; Korea, North and South; mainland China and Taiwan; Hungary and Austria—the heirs to the Bolsheviks delivered to the societies on which they were able to conduct their experiments not, as some of their more cynical supporters claimed, bread if not freedom, but rather neither bread nor freedom.

II

The shadow of 1917 was cast not only across the societies which fell to communist rule. It also fell more palely over all western societies. The chief mechanism was the Communist International—the Comintern. When the Bolshevik Party came to power in 1917 not one of its leaders believed their revolution could survive unless it sparked socialist revolution in the countries of advanced capitalism. And yet, even in the chaos of postwar Europe, and after the collapse of the political structures of the German and the Austro-Hungarian empires, no revolution worthy of the name socialist (with the exception of Hungary's, which lasted three months) ignited spontaneously. In their absence the Communist International was instituted in Moscow.

The Comintern was the school in which the leaders of revolutionary socialism—both in the countries of advanced capitalism and in the Third World—learnt the rudiments of bolshevism. The parties joining the Comintern were obliged to change their names to Communist Party of...They were obliged to purge themselves of all ideologically suspect

7

elements—reformists, pacifists, patriots—which had infiltrated the socialist movement; to accept the discipline of the executive branch of the Comintern; and to replicate within their own branch offices the fundamental organisational principle of the Bolshevik head office—democratic centralism, a euphemism for 'iron discipline'. They were obliged, too, to conduct revolutionary propaganda in the armed forces of their country and to create—no matter how liberal their domestic political culture—an illegal underground apparatus capable of continuing revolutionary struggle under conditions of civil war.

During the 1920s and beyond, the communist parties of the Comintern underwent a somewhat more elaborate process— Stalinisation. Once Stalin had outmanoeuvred his rivals for the Lenin succession—Trotsky, Zinoviev, Bukharin—there was not the remotest possibility that the Comintern (one of the most significant institutions of the revolution) or its members (the communist parties of the advanced capitalist world) could avoid being contaminated by the grotesque political culture of Stalinism.

Throughout the era of Stalin—that is to say, from 1930 until 1953—the communist parties of the western world accepted as an unquestioned given that Stalin was the greatest political leader, the greatest Marxist theoretician, the greatest military genius and the greatest humanitarian the twentieth century had produced. Some went even further. These communist parties defended each and every domestic action of the Soviet state, no matter how insane—the prolonged hate session directed against the diabolical Trotsky, the show trials of 1936-38 where Stalin's Politburo colleagues of the 1920s confessed to lifelong service for British intelligence or the Gestapo before being shot. Under Stalin the western communists defended each and every intellectual fad and perversion produced by Soviet culture—the biology of the charlatan, Lysenko; the socialist realism of the philistine thug, Zhdanov; the linguistic banalities of the great master himself. With exuberance they defended, too, each and every twist and turn of Soviet foreign policy no matter how machiavellian—the Nazi-Soviet pact, the Winter War in Finland, the brutal takeover in Eastern Europe, the damnation of Tito. And throughout the era of Stalin the western parties played their part in the orchestrated campaigns directed against defectors like Krivitsky or Kravchenko or against ex-communists like Koestler or Borkenau who, in the words of George Orwell, had grasped the essential truth that there was something fundamentally wrong with the project of building socialism upon a foundation of corpses.

To accusations of religious persecution, slave labour in the forests of the north, mass starvation in Ukraine, terror throughout the Union or shootings at Katyn Wood, the communist parties of the west answered—depending on the era—with a single voice: Reactionary, Bourgeois, Fascist, Yankee; Whiteguard, Trotskyite, Hitlerite, McCarthyite.

To point out that the western communist parties of the pre- and post-Comintern period (the Comintern was dissolved in 1943 but its spirit survived until the mid-1960s) injected Stalinist corruption into the political cultures of advanced capitalist countries is true but incomplete. For the western communist parties were heirs to not one but two traditions—Stalinised bolshevism and Enlightenment radicalism. The ironies of the merging of these two traditions ran deep. Revolutionary socialists flocked into the communist parties in the belief that they were struggling against capitalist wage slavery only to discover at the end of their lives that what they had supported was not socialism at all but the most radically exploitative of all the forms assumed by modern industrial society. Sons and daughters of the bourgeoisie entered the communist parties as bohemians and libertines only to discover that what was required of them was obedience and puritanism. Writers and painters squandered their talents in trying to find meaning or depth in socialist realism. Philosophers devoted their intelligence to teaching the dull mysteries of dialectical materialism. Sceptics became moist-eyed when the name of Stalin—one of the most cynical despots in history—came to their lips. Free thinkers expounded the Stalin gospel. Democrats came to confuse politics with conspiracy. Humanitarians devoted their adult lives to apologies for mass murder. In its dual heritage—to Stalin and the Enlightenment—much of the tragedy and the comedy of western communism can be discovered.

III

The communist parties of advanced capitalism were created for a single task: to destroy bourgeois class rule and to bring about socialist revolution in their homelands. In this task they failed utterly. In the short chaotic period at the end of World War II the Soviet revolutionary model was exported only to those countries which were liberated from the Nazis or the Japanese by the Red Army (Eastern Europe east of the Elbe; Korea north of the 38th parallel) or to those countries where communist parties had led resistance armies against foreign occupiers and anticommunist rivals (China, Yugoslavia, North Vietnam). In the advanced capitalist countries no communist revolution in 1945-48—not even in France or Italy—seriously threatened.

In the absence of a plausible revolutionary prospect what were the communist parties under western capitalism to do? It was Franz Borkenau in his classic study of 1938, *World*

Communism, who first identified a precise answer to this question. While never abandoning the ultimate ambition to revolution or the conspiratorial style which the Comintern had taught as its prerequisite, the western communist parties in the 1930s stumbled upon a new task: the defence of Soviet interests abroad. From that time until the death of the Soviet myth in the 1960s this was to prove their most significant contribution to the political culture of the west. The western communists failed dismally in the field of revolution. They succeeded brilliantly in the art of propaganda.

During the 1930s and 1940s the communist parties of the west waged campaign after campaign in the Soviet foreign policy interest. In 1933 and 1934 the focus of the propaganda was on the barbarism of Nazism. To dramatise this threat, the Comintern chose as its key theme the burning of the Reichstag and the heroic performance at his trial before the Nazi courts of the 'Lion of Leipzig', Georgi Dimitrov. Between 1936 and 1938, when the Soviet Union was trying to construct an anti-fascist democratic front, communist propaganda focused on the Spanish Civil War and the struggle being waged there supposedly between democracy and fascism. And so it went on. In 1938 the propaganda of the networks concentrated on the Munich betrayal of Neville Chamberlain; in late 1939 and 1940 on justifications for the Nazi-Soviet pact; in 1942 and 1943 on the heroism of the Red Army and the moral-strategic imperative of the Second Front; between 1946 and 1949 on the corruption and brutality of Chiang Kai-shek's Kuomintang; after 1948 on the many betrayals of Tito, the Anglo-American hireling.

As the Cold War deepened, communist propaganda in the west came, not surprisingly, to be dominated by a single theme: the threat to peace posed by American imperialism and McCarthyism at home. To dramatise US aggression in Korea the networks invented the allegations of germ warfare. To dramatise the threat to peace posed by NATO they invented the myth of West Germany's neo-Nazi revanchism (always revanchism). To dramatise the evil of McCarthyism the energies of the communist networks focused on the executions of the atomic spies, the Rosenbergs. Throughout the 1950s they orchestrated the peace petition campaign which took as its premise the Soviets' singular championship of the cause of world peace.

The impact of the propaganda of the communist parties on western consciousness went deeper than a catalogue of these particular campaigns might suggest. For two generations the communist parties conducted an unceasing battle to capture the sympathy, or at least the neutrality, of enlightened opinion in the west, and in particular to win the hearts and minds of the intellectuals. For two generations they delivered, in one way or another and in one context after another, the following simple message: The Russian Revolution of 1917 represented an epochal event in the history of human progress. After 1917 the world was divided into two camps. One was the camp of socialism and progress led by the Soviet Union and joined after 1945 by the new democracies of Eastern Europe and East Asia. The other was the camp of imperialism and reaction which had been led in the 1920s by the British and French, in the 1930s and early 1940s by the Germans and Japanese and, after 1945, by the Americans. The socialist camp stood for democracy, equality, colonial liberation, science and peace. The imperialist camp stood for class rule, bourgeois privilege, colonial oppression, religious obscurantism and war. From the point of view of the western communists those who seriously opposed this manichean vision—like the émigrés who fled Eastern Europe or the unbending anticommunist intellectuals like Orwell, Arthur Koestler, Raymond Aron or Sidney Hook

—were nothing more than the puppets of imperialism and nothing less than the enemies of mankind.

Throughout the Cold War the battle between the communists and their anticommunist enemies was waged fiercely. Without some grasp of this battle the history of western democracies after World War II is incomprehensible. This was a bitter struggle, fought roughly on both sides. During its prosecution truth and complexity were frequently, and on both sides (although not equally so), sacrificed. Both sides inflicted heavy casualties. From time to time a famous enemy general defected, to delight on one side, dismay on the other.

Many of the intellectual observers of this battle were repelled. A very large number, perhaps even a majority, refused to support the communists but refused to tolerate the anticommunists. These took up the position of anti-anticommunism—roughly speaking, a plague on both your houses, but especially on yours! The rise of anti-anticommunism—the neutralisation of western opinion on the question of 1917— was, paradoxically, probably the most substantial achievement in the west of the camp of progress. As a consequence of this achievement many Cold Warriors who had become uncomfortable or bored, deserted their posts during the 1960s and the Vietnam War. Others, however, joined battle belatedly. I was one such.

IV

I discovered in 1969, in my final undergraduate year at Melbourne University, that I had become an anticommunist. This discovery did not take the form of a conversion so much as a recognition of where my thinking had led me. Nor had it anything to do, at least at first, with any conscious drift towards conservatism. In 1969 I still thought of myself as a leftist and a democratic socialist and would have been as likely to vote for the Liberal Party as to aspire to a career in real estate. Neither did the recognition that I had become an anti-communist have anything directly to do with the debate about the Vietnam War which was raging at the university at the time. Concerning that war I was divided. On the one hand I opposed Hanoi's war aim (military unification, irrespective of the wishes of the South), saw through the myth of the independence of the NLF, and had read a great deal about the totalitarian system in North Vietnam and the atrocities of their southern branch, the Viet Cong. On the other I did not support the American war effort and was repelled by the methods—in particular the indiscriminate bombings—it was using to fight it. Before leaving Australia in 1970 to study abroad I marched in one of the Vietnam moratoria with a handful of friends. As one of these friends, Raimond Gaita, reminded me recently, we gravitated to a banner which read: 'Neither Washington nor Hanoi'. This gives a fair indication of my position on that war or, if you will, of my confusion.

Why, then, did I become in 1969 an anticommunist? I think as a consequence of three things: who I was, who I met at the university, and what I began to read.

Who I was was a young Jewish man of Central European parents—one from Berlin, the other from Vienna—who had arrived, separately, in Australia in 1939, as refugees from Nazism. Neither set eyes on their parents again or, so far as I was told, discovered the exact circumstances of how they died during the catastrophic historical event we now call the Holocaust.

My parents did not often discuss these events with me. Perhaps it was too painful. Perhaps they simply wanted me to be happy and feared that I might come to dwell too much on the horrors which had destroyed our family's and our people's

recent past. If indeed they had consciously tried to shield me
from these events they were unsuccessful. When I discovered
that the Nazis had embarked systematically upon the murder
of an entire people, this fact shook me so deeply, seemed to me
so radically terrible, that it began naturally, as it were, to set
the shape of my life. In part, brooding on the Holocaust drew
me to the study of history and politics—in the hope that I
might come to understand that way how such an evil event,
and soon after, how such evil events, could have occurred. In
part it developed in me a profound suspicion not only of racial
but of all ideological thinking—that is of all the dreams for the
reconstruction of human society on the basis of logically expli-
cated first principles. And in part, in a curious way, it both
deepened my admiration for the Australian political system
and distanced me from serious participation in it. For, in
comparison with Europe's recent past, my family's recent past,
even the most bitterly contested political argument in
Australia had come to seem to me both thoroughly benign and
relatively trivial. I do not record any of this with pride or
regret but simply as matters of fact.

Before arriving at the University of Melbourne in 1966 I
had not read seriously about 1917 or its consequences. It now
became an issue for me. By the mid-1960s no-one at the
university, or almost no-one, still spoke of Stalin as all communists had before Khrushchev's denunciation in 1956—as,
in the immortal words of Frank Hardy, 'the humble and self-
effacing' genius who had led his people 'from ignorance, illit-
eracy and industrial poverty to universal education ... and a
standard of living generally ahead of any in the world' and
who had not committed, in thirty years, a single error. And yet
many *bien-pensants* at the university did share the view put
by Manning Clark in his *Meeting Soviet Man* of 1960, that the
Stalinist aberrations—'the purges, the murdering of one's

15

political opponents, the restrictions on discussion, the low standard of living'—belonged to an era 'which was fast disappearing'. Many would also have agreed with the sentiment if not the tone of Clark's vision of Lenin as political genius and secular saint, the man who, when faced with 'the prospect of people loving and trembling for one another, of people really caring for one another ... was as excited and as lovable as a little child'.

Many of these *bien-pensants* believed that the crimes of 1917 and beyond were the inescapable penalties of progress. One frequently heard it put about that 'you can't make omelettes without breaking eggs'. Most were convinced by the conventional Whig-Marxist view of 1917, propagated in the books of E. H. Carr or Isaac Deutscher, and taught at the university by Lloyd Churchward, that the Bolshevik Revolution and the societies to which it gave birth represented, on balance, the most significant recent chapters in the long story of mankind's progress from darkness to light and from slavery to freedom. Most, in short, believed that what 1789 had been to the nineteenth century, 1917 was to the twentieth.

It was under the influence of two brilliant teachers—the Czech Jewish social theorist Frank Knopfelmacher, at the time the most controversial and effective Cold Warrior at Melbourne University, and the Australian-Irish poet Vincent Buckley—that I learned to distrust and then to despise this Whig-Marxist version of 1917. What I learned from them was that the unfortunate aberrations of Stalin involved the murders of tens of millions, a crime no less terrible than the Holocaust; that the sources of Stalin's rule were to be discovered in Lenin, and that his heirs still ruled in Moscow and Peking. What I also learned, as Buckley once put it, was that if you couldn't make omelettes without breaking eggs, you most certainly could break eggs without making omelettes. Under their joint influence I came to believe that anticommunism was an inescapable, if unfashionable, dimension of a politics of common humanity. And under Knopfelmacher's particular influence I also came to believe—and this was for me the most decisive thought—that the real historical association of 1917 was not with 1789 but with 1933. This recognition transformed the way I looked at politics. It also led me to the authors who were at this time of the greatest political significance to me—George Orwell and Hannah Arendt.

I suspect that Orwell and Arendt got to me so deeply because, in their very different ways, both had theorised the novel political associations—between, on the one hand, socialism and anticommunism and, on the other, Nazism and Stalinism—I was stumbling towards in my thinking. No-one could read Orwell without grasping that it was his socialism— or at least his democratic and egalitarian spirit (he had nothing to say about the economics of socialism)—which had driven him to anticommunism. 'For the past ten years,' he wrote in the Ukrainian preface to *Animal Farm*, 'I have been convinced that the destruction of the Soviet myth was essential if one wanted a revival of the Socialist movement.' At the time this mattered to me a great deal; it was only later that I would be more interested in the conservative undertow of his writing. It was Orwell the socialist who, in 1969, taught me that there was a great deal wrong 'with a regime that needs a pyramid of corpses every few years' and with a left-wing intelligentsia that could not grasp that 'human society must be based on common decency whatever the political and economic forms'. For better or worse Orwell's assault on the left-wing intelligentsia of his age—his attack on their moral blindness and cowardice, their thinly disguised snobbery and power worship, their remoteness from the common people, their uncomely embarrassment before the emotion of patriotism, their unseemly embrace of all things Soviet—altered at once the way I looked at the left intellectuals of my own generation. Certain passages stayed with me forever. 'It is a most encouraging thing,' he wrote of Franz Borkenau's *World Communism*, 'to hear a human voice when fifty thousand gramophones are playing the same tune.' And here of the distance between Henry Miller and the literary milksops of the 1930s British left.

> It was a time of labels, slogans and evasions. At the worst moments you were expected to lock yourself up in a constipating little cage of lies; at the best a sort of voluntary censorship ('Ought I to say this? Is it pro-fascist?') was at work in nearly everyone's mind. It is almost inconceivable that good novels should be written in such an atmosphere. Good novels are not written by orthodoxy-sniffers, nor by people who are conscience-stricken about their own unorthodoxy. Good novels are written by people who are *not frightened*.

And, it seemed to me, not only good novels.

The influence of Hannah Arendt or rather of her *Origins of Totalitarianism* was quite different. This was an abstract and, in some ways, a strange book. And yet in it I thought I had encountered, for the first time, an historical framework profound enough to make sense of the central event—the Holocaust—on which I had been brooding for many years. Arendt argued here that Nazism and Stalinism were expressions of a single political essence, totalitarianism; that totalitarianism was a form of politics, unique to the twentieth century, which had built itself upon certain pathologies of modernity; that it represented an expansionary form of radical evil; and that, at its institutional heart, was the concentration camp, where a fundamental experiment—for the creation of a new kind of human being from whom all traces of individuality and spontaneity had been erased—was being conducted.

It was Hannah Arendt who convinced me of the irrelevance, in the age of totalitarianism, of the old political labels. Again, for better or worse, one passage in the *Origins* was for me a kind of call to arms.

> The fear of concentration camps and the resulting insight into the nature of total domination might serve to invalidate all obsolete political differentiations from left to right and to introduce beside and above them the politically most important yardstick for judging events in our time, namely: whether they serve totalitarian domination or not.

In the world after the defeat of Nazism, this passage had for me only one possible political meaning.

The making of my anticommunism was not yet complete. In the early 1970s I read the first two volumes of Aleksandr Solzhenitsyn's *Gulag Archipelago*. Unlike Orwell and Arendt, Solzhenitsyn had experienced the world of the concentration camp on his skin. Unlike Nadezhda Mandelstam or Evgenia Ginsburg—the finest memoirs I had read concerning the Stalin terror—he knew that the enormity of the Gulag could not be captured by individual portraits, no matter how finely painted, but required a vast and sprawling canvas. Unlike Arthur Koestler in *Darkness at Noon*, Solzhenitsyn was uninterested in the ideology which had led to the show trials and the Gulag. For him it was simply the operational code of gangsters, to be treated with ferocious sarcasm. His eye of pity fell far less than in the previous literature on the party faithful who had been swept into the Gulag in 1937; and far more on its unknown and inarticulate inhabitants—peasants, workers, Christians, women, children. Hannah Arendt convinced me abstractly of the centrality of the concentration camp to the totalitarian experiment. I learned of its concrete reality from Solzhenitsyn. It was a lesson I would never unlearn.

19

V

I read the extraordinary second volume of *The Gulag Archipelago* at a single sitting—on a flight between London and Melbourne in early 1976. Whether or not the events were clearly connected I am not sure, but shortly after I threw myself, for the first time in my life, into a form of anti-totalitarian political activity.

By early 1976 stories had been appearing for several months in the western press of terrible atrocities being committed inside Cambodia, which had fallen to the communists in April 1975. The first such stories came from journalists who had witnessed deaths during the forced march of the entire population of Phnom Penh to the countryside. Shortly after, as Cambodian refugees made their way across the border into Thailand, tales of mass killings, and of generalised conditions of slave labour, starvation and disease, became increasingly common. As the refugee numbers continued to rise the Thai government began to threaten forcible repatriation.

I began writing letters to the newspapers, pointing to the inevitable consequence if repatriation occurred. As a result of one of these letters a two-man 'Committee for Cambodian Refugees' was formed. And as a result of this 'committee' being formed, I was asked by the priest, Father Jeffreys Foale, to help establish the Victorian branch of the Indo-China Refugee Association, a group which had been formed to lobby the Fraser government to provide homes for some of the hundreds of thousands of Indo-Chinese refugees from communism who were by now stranded in an archipelago of harsh camps throughout South-East Asia.

During the course of this lobbying I encountered a group of intellectuals who were enthusiastic about the Cambodian revolution (or what was called at the time Democratic Kampuchea), who scorned the stories of suffering of the Cambodian refugees on the Thai border and who regarded those who took them seriously as CIA propagandists or dupes. For someone who had read fairly extensively in the literature on Stalin apologetics all this was dreadfully familiar. The most illustrious figure associated with this group was the American linguist Noam Chomsky; among the Australian intellectuals or apprentice-intellectuals, Ben Kiernan, Michael Vickery and Gavan McCormack.

In the summer of 1977-78 a conference on the theme of human rights in Asia was held in Hobart under the sponsorship of the Australian Council for Overseas Aid. Although there were hundreds of participants I was the only one who spoke of the crimes of the communist regime in Cambodia. Ben Kiernan defended Pol Pot. A member of the audience where Kiernan and I debated called on me to apologise publicly for a photograph of forced labour in Cambodia which had been used in the western press and which he assured me was fake. Another Cambodian member of the audience advised me that I was unwelcome in Democratic Kampuchea. Shortly after I left the conference in disgust.

Within a year of the Hobart debate Hanoi invaded Cambodia and drove the Pol Pot regime from Phnom Penh. Everything which I had read about the left intelligentsia before, during and after the Nazi-Soviet pact ought to have prepared me for what was to come: the sudden conversion of the pro-Pol Pot intelligentsia to the fiercest enemies of Pol Pot, the Asian Hitler. And yet this process—what I call the epistemology of the tank—came to me as something of a shock. The essay I wrote on this occasion, 'Pol Pot and the Intellectuals', which appears in this book, was my response.

The cold shoulder I had received in Hobart from a number

of people who were by no means committed to Pol Pot sharpened my interest in the phenomenon of anti-anticommunism. In 1983 I observed its power, under more objective circumstances, during what was to turn out to be the first great political battle of the Hawke government—the Combe affair. The background to this affair was straightforward. During 1982 and early 1983 ASIO was watching closely the activities of Valeriy Ivanov, a Soviet embassy official known to be KGB. During the course of this surveillance ASIO discovered the far from unpromising cultivation by Ivanov of the man who had for several years been the federal secretary of the ALP, David Combe.

Since the attack which had been launched by Dr Evatt on ASIO thirty years earlier during the Petrov affair, relations between the ALP and ASIO had been turbulent and tense. During the government of Gough Whitlam, when the attorney-general, Lionel Murphy, had conducted a raid on ASIO headquarters, they had almost altogether broken down. From ASIO's point of view the investigation of Ivanov's cultivation of David Combe, which coincided with the election of the first Labor government since the fall of Whitlam in 1975, had the capacity for creating considerable mischief. ASIO faced the appalling prospect that the cultivation of Combe might assume in their relations with Hawke the kind of spoiling role that the Murphy raid had played in their relations with Whitlam and the Petrov defection with Evatt.

The director-general of ASIO, Harvey Barnett, met Mr Hawke shortly after the 1983 election to brief him on Combe. As it turned out, it was not only Barnett who was keen not to allow Combe's apparent indiscretion to sour, once again, the relations between ASIO and the ALP. Hawke and the security committee of Cabinet acted swiftly on ASIO's advice. They expelled Ivanov and advised the Labor ministry not to have dealings with Combe's new lobbying business. On 10 May these details leaked to the press. For the next five months a fierce battle between, on one side, Hawke and ASIO and, on the other, Combe and the nation's media, raged. This was the last major political struggle of the Australian Cold War. It was also a revelation about how deeply anti-anticommunism had entered the mainstream. My analysis of this political battle and of its cultural significance appears as the penultimate chapter in this book.

By the time the Combe essay was finished my curiosity about earlier phases of the Australian Cold War had been aroused. In 1984 an essay appeared in a left-wing magazine, *Australian Society*, on the journalist Wilfred Burchett. The article was written by an academic whom I had encountered during the Pol Pot debate, Gavan McCormack. For him Burchett was both martyr and hero—Australia's Dreyfus, and a brilliant reporter of 'uncommon moral passion'. For me Burchett was a crude apologist for the most criminal aspects of the Stalinisation of Eastern Europe and an unrelenting propagandist on behalf of the communist side during the Korean and Vietnam wars. When McCormack interpreted the silence which had greeted his hagiographical article in *Australian Society* as meaning the bankruptcy of the enemies of Burchett, I felt no alternative but to enter the fray. The essay which resulted is the first chapter of this book.

Of all the chapters in this book it was the Burchett essay which provoked the most extended public controversy. On one side were ranged old opponents of the Pol Pot days, McCormack and Kiernan, and older communists like Laurie Aarons and Alex Carey. On the other side some of Australia's leading anticommunists—like B. A. Santamaria and Frank Knopfelmacher. The only unexpected intervention came from a politically disengaged filmmaker, Edwin Morrisby, who had worked with Burchett during the Vietnam war and who now recalled the time when he had seen a North Vietnamese communist cadre at Phnom Penh airport handing Burchett a wallet of $100 travellers cheques. They were, he had heard him say, 'a gift from your friends at Starigrad'—a reference, as Morrisby understood, to Moscow.

The controversy on Burchett in the newspapers of 1985 and 1986 became increasingly nasty, narrow and arcane. It ended by concentrating almost exclusively on the credibility of two witnesses—the KGB defector, Yuri Krotkov and the US pilot in the Korean War, Paul Kniss. Krotkov's evidence was critical to the question of Burchett's relations to the KGB and Kniss's to the question of how deeply Burchett was implicated in the process of extracting by force the germ warfare 'confessions' of the US pilots in Korea. By this time all the genuinely interesting questions raised by the career of Wilfred Burchett had been lost. A searching debate on Burchett—that is to say, on the subject of intellectuals, communism and the Cold War in Australia—had not even begun.

If Burchett was by far the most influential communist (in the cultural if not the card-carrying sense) that Cold War Australia was ever to produce, the Petrov affair was equally obviously the most important political episode of the Australian Cold War. While the dust was settling on the question of Combe, the Hawke government agreed to the public release of the vast ASIO and Royal Commission archive on the affair. I threw myself into a study of it.

At the time of this release the left-wing myth of the Petrov affair was still alive. The left believed that the defection of the Soviet spies, Vladimir and Evdokia Petrov, in Australia in April 1954 had been manufactured by the Menzies government in order to ensure victory at the elections in May. It also accepted that Dr Evatt was right in believing that certain of the documents Petrov had brought with him—most famously Document 'J'—were forgeries which had been uttered to damage Dr Evatt and through him the ALP. It was, indeed, Dr Evatt's convictions on these matters which explained the savage attack he had launched in October 1954 on those ALP members associated with B.A. Santamaria's 'Movement', which was, in turn, critical for an understanding of how the ALP split and the long Menzies hegemony over Australian politics had come to be.

At one level the purpose of the Petrov book I wrote—two extracts of which appear here (the book has long been out of print)—was to dispel these myths. In contrast to the reception of the Burchett essay, the conclusions I reached—concerning the emptiness of the Evatt myth—were at the time of publication broadly accepted by the left. *The Petrov Affair* had to run the gauntlet of anti-anticommunist reviewers like Brian Toohey, Richard Hall and James McClelland. It survived pretty much unscathed. At that time at least, no-one seriously challenged McClelland's view that it had 'killed the Petrov conspiracy theory stone dead'.

Oddly enough by the time I had completed the Petrov work a bit of Cold War starch had been washed out of me. What really interested me more than the revisionist destination I had reached by the end of the Petrov journey were some of the unanticipated surprises I had encountered along the way. Before beginning research I had thought of Dr Evatt's Petrov performance as having within it, despite its fundamental wrongheadedness, elements of tragedy. What I discovered, as readers will see, was purest farce. How Evatt could have retained the Labor leadership not only through the Petrov affair but even for six years after it seemed a major mystery. Before I began research I had thought of Petrov in morally conventional anticommunist terms as a kind of 'I Chose

Freedom' hero. What I discovered was that Petrov was a drunk, a womaniser and a minor black marketeer (although also a simple and rather endearing man) who had defected not through a love of freedom but from an animal fear of reprisal in the uncertainty of the post-Beria era.

The Petrov story was more complicated and, indeed, funnier than either the left-wing or right-wing versions had imagined. I had long understood that 1917 had cast a tragic shadow over Europe and Asia in our century. Over Australia, I now belatedly realised, it had often assumed more comical shapes. In this sense, writing on the Petrov affair became for me a kind of homecoming.

VI

In recent years the shadow of 1917 has finally lifted from the west. The decisive events were the overthrow of communist party rule in Eastern Europe in 1989 and in the Soviet Union in 1991. It was plain by now that the experiment in building socialism begun by the Bolsheviks in 1917 in the old Russian Empire would be continued only in the Asian countries where communism had come to power and even there only in a modified and marketised form. The events in Eastern Europe and the Soviet Union of 1989-91 had a profound although still not properly appreciated impact on the intellectual climate of western societies.

It is important to be precise here. The lifting of the shadow of 1917 did not mean that Marxism had died off in the western academy. On the contrary, especially in cultural studies, the influence of Marxism remained extraordinarily pervasive. Nor did it mean that certain habits of mind which had formed among western intellectuals over a half-century of struggle had passed. Reflex anti-Americanism where foreign policy questions were concerned and reflex anti-anticommunism on matters historical—the cultural sediments of the Cold War— somehow lingered on despite everything that had happened.

The lifting of the shadow of 1917 involved something quite different. Before the late 1980s—despite all the admissions of crimes and mistakes which had been committed in the name of communism; despite all the swings in cultural fashion, from Stalin to Mao, and from Mao to Castro or Ho—the left-wing intelligentsia in the west had kept alive the idea that the 'really existing' communist societies of Europe or Asia were, however problematically, still finally connected with that better world of which they dreamt. By the late 1980s this hope died. An illusion—central to an understanding of the history of the left intelligentsia in our century—had been, at long last, quietly abandoned.

It is far from clear to me that the consequences of the collapse of this illusion have yet been fully grasped. For the anticommunist right the lifting of the shadow of 1917 has been more complex than might have been imagined. At one level, of course, the ignominious collapse of the communist experiment in Europe represented an unambiguous vindica- tion. For intellectuals during the Cold War anticommunism was the cultural equivalent of halitosis. For those who had been willing to bear this stigma for so long the desire to have their rightness on the communist question acknowledged by their former enemies ran deep. There was, here, a temptation to an unseemly form of triumphalism, a mood which, to some extent, Francis Fukuyama's essay 'The End of History', expressed. Beneath the surface things were, however, more complicated. For many individual anticommunists the sudden and unanticipated collapse of the communist illusion—that is to say, of both a culpable enemy and a clear and present danger—proved oddly disorienting.

For the left, following the lifting of the shadow of 1917, the challenges were far sharper. Its great temptation was towards the fudging of history; its great hope a general forgetfulness or indifference. Thus far the left in Australia has not resisted temptation. There has been virtually no attempt by the left to come to terms with the compromised strand of its history. Given the current temper of Australia nothing remotely resembling an honest left-wing history of the Communist Party of Australia or of intellectual apologetics for Stalin or Mao is imaginable. An astonishing complacency survives.

Let one example suffice. Recently in the ABC's magazine *24 Hours* the historian, Humphrey McQueen, launched a wild attack on *Quadrant* for the role it had played in Australia during the Cold War. The centre of his charge was the well-known fact that in the late 1950s and early 1960s *Quadrant* had received funds whose ultimate source was the CIA. It obviously did not seem to McQueen even pertinent that on the question of Stalin and Mao and of their tens of millions of victims it was *Quadrant* alone among the intellectual magazines in Australia which had been on the side of the victims and not their tormenters. So far as I knew McQueen has never discussed publicly his own former allegiances to Mao and, through Mao, to Stalin, whose glory Mao celebrated even after the Soviet leadership had disowned him. It is a very peculiar culture which has not called McQueen to account and which is enthusiastic about his assault on the only intellectual magazine in Australia whose record during the Cold War on the question of communist totalitarianism is not one of folly and shame. It seems that the complacency of part of the left still runs so deep that it believes that it was right to be wrong about communism and that the right was wrong despite being right.

Nor does it seem as if the political mainstream in Australia yet knows what to make of this aspect of the history of the left. When Frank Hardy died recently his funeral service dominated the front page of the *Age* and was broadcast in full on the ABC. Hardy's support for the Aboriginal cause in the latter phase of his life was remembered by all. His service in support of Stalin in an earlier phase was passed over in an unembarrassed silence. Of his obituarists only P. P. McGuinness thought fit to raise this uncomfortable fact. A letter to the editor from the writer Barry Dickins soon appeared. With disarming frankness Dickins put the case for historical and moral amnesia. So what, he asked, if Frank Hardy had once been a Stalinist. 'Who cares?'

These essays are my answer to those who think like Dickins. I hope they will prompt some reconsideration of the ways in which the shadow of 1917 was cast across Australia's political life during the Cold War. Even more deeply I hope they might whet the curiosity of a younger generation of Australians who did not live through the Cold War and persuade them that there is something at stake in this history worth caring about.

HE CHOSE STALIN: THE CASE OF WILFRED BURCHETT

IN AUGUST 1984 *Australian Society* published a long article on the Australian journalist, the late Wilfred Burchett, written by the La Trobe University historian Dr Gavan McCormack. Burchett was portrayed by McCormack as the innocent victim of a longstanding right-wing campaign which had been waged against him since the early 1950s. In this campaign, McCormack claimed, Burchett had been falsely accused of betraying his country, chiefly through his activities in the Korean War, and of betraying his vocation, by acting throughout his life as a propagandist and agent of the communist movement. The Australian government had participated in this campaign by depriving Burchett of his passport in 1955 (without giving him even the benefit of a trial) and thus of his Australian citizenship. 'If Australia has a Dreyfus,' he argued, 'it is Wilfred Burchett.' In McCormack's view Burchett was not a traitor but 'an outstanding Australian'; not a propagandist but 'a journalist inspired by an uncommon moral passion'.

McCormack's article went unanswered. In May 1985, again in *Australian Society*, he returned to the fray. Commenting on an article on Burchett in the *Australian* by Peter Samuel, McCormack noted that:

> The attempt by sections of right-wing opinion in Australia to denigrate Burchett is one of the longest-running campaigns in Australian political history, evidently not to be suspended despite Mr Burchett's death in 1983. My own analysis of the weakness and contradictions of the anti-Burchett case has been greeted with deafening silence.

Dr McCormack was, I think, right to complain about the lack of response to his initial article. The case he made ought not to be allowed to pass in silence. The reputation of Wilfred Burchett has great symbolic significance in the Australian political culture. To remain silent in the face of various present endeavours to lionise Wilfred Burchett (which include a promised posthumous anthology) is to accede, without quarrel, to the caricature of the history of Australia in the Cold War and to a neo-Stalinist reading of postwar Asian history being taught in our universities by academics like Dr McCormack. More deeply still it is to allow a time to come when propaganda can with impunity be called independent journalism and treason honour.

There is, however, only one way to answer McCormack and that is to attempt a fresh assessment of Burchett's career, on the basis of old evidence on him (which so far as I know has never been systematically reviewed) and new evidence which has emerged since his death—most importantly his own correspondence (deposited in the La Trobe Library, Melbourne) and from the ASIO files on Burchett, held in the Australian Archives and released in 1985 under the thirty-year rule. Whatever weariness the present author might feel at the prospect of refighting the old battles of the Cold War; however repelled he might be by his subject—a journalist without the power of social observation and an ideologue without the saving grace of imagination; however useless he might realise it to be to try and convince the Dr McCormacks of this world of anything they don't wish to see—nevertheless this piece is written because anger at the doctoring of history is deeper still.

THE MAKING OF A STALINIST

When precisely Wilfred Burchett embraced the communist cause it is not possible to say. His earliest political opinions most likely came from his father George, a progressive-minded lay preacher and autodidact who raised a left-wing family at Poowong in southern Gippsland. One local gossip reported to the authorities during the war that on Anzac Day 1934 George and son Wilfred had appealed to the local Methodist congregation 'to show tolerance of that great country Russia'. Clearly the Depression played some role in moulding Wilfred Burchett's mind; but probably not so large a role (if his own testimony is to be believed) as the dramatic circumstances surrounding the arrival in Australia in late 1934 of the Czech Comintern agent Egon Kisch. Kisch's leap to shore and his protracted legal battles (which included the solemn discussion of the legality of administering to him an immigration entry test in Gaelic)—where Kisch made complete monkeys of the Australian political establishment—had a profound effect on the young Burchett.

In 1936 Burchett set out to experience the world for himself. In London he learned languages, landed a job in the tourist business with Thomas Cook and offered himself to the British Communist Party as a volunteer for Spain. Turned down here he was however able to secure a job with the new Soviet travel agency, Intourist. Through Intourist he met the family of Paul Robeson and listened with great attention as Robeson told a huge rally in the Albert Hall in 1937 of racial persecution in the United States and racial equality in the Soviet Union. The Robeson lesson was underlined for Burchett by Victor Gollancz who told the audience at the summer school he attended of the Society for Cultural Relations with the Soviet Union that there 'for the first time I felt what it was like to move in a society completely free from anti-semitism'.

To its honour the Burchett family in Poowong was involved in the late 1930s in the settlement of German Jewish refugees. Wilfred Burchett himself had met and married a German Jewish woman in London and, through her and his work now for the Palestine-Orient line, had come to see for himself the truth about the Jewish condition in post-*Kristallnacht* Germany and arranged for the emigration of some German Jews. Before war broke out, however, Burchett had quit Europe and brought his new family back to Poowong.

Here he aroused the interest of the local police because of a 'constant correspondence with the Commonwealth Investigation Branch' in Melbourne and because he was passing himself off as a Commonwealth Investigation Officer. When war broke out Burchett immediately offered his services to Australian Military Intelligence—an odd choice of work for a young left-ist—but eventually had to make do with a translation job in Melbourne for the Department of Information, monitoring foreign broadcasts.

During the early months of the war Burchett drifted into journalism, beginning what would be a lifelong career with occasional articles in the Melbourne press on Nazi Germany and consolidating it with on-the-spot reports of political developments in New Caledonia. After 1941 he finally became a fully fledged war correspondent, working in the Pacific for several newspapers including the London *Daily Express*. In this work he quickly developed a reputation amongst his peers for physical courage, initiative and industry, but also for unscrupulous behaviour in what was a fiercely competitive trade. Stories circulated of the tricks he had played on colleagues to advance his career, of Don Juan sexual adventures and of occasional black marketeering. Although fellow journalists were not made aware by Burchett of his political leanings, his wartime books—from *Pacific Treasure Island*, which is an account of the anti-colonial struggles in New Caledonia, to *Democracy with a Tommy Gun*, which ends with a procommunist, anti-Kuomintang chapter—all have a clearly 'progressive' political dimension.

Burchett, however, did not completely commit himself to the communist cause (at least in public) until the Cold War. Between 1946 and early 1949 he reported from Germany, chiefly for the *Daily Express*. His book from this period *Cold War in Germany* shows him now a convinced, credulous and often vicious Stalinist. *Cold War in Germany* combines attacks on American warmongering in Germany (where they were said to be planning their own Pearl Harbor), attacks on the emerging democratic leadership of West Germany (the Social Democratic leader in West Berlin, Ernest Reuter, is, for example, described as a 'renegade', 'neo-Nazi' and American lickspittle) and a description of West Germany as a land in the grip of a Nazi revival, of cultural decadence (of whores, black marketeers and white slave-traders) under the dominance of industrial barons and feudal landlords. By contrast Soviet policy in Germany is portrayed as staunchly for peace and the Soviet sector as a haven of genuine culture and nursery of progressive land reform. It was not for nothing that *Cold War in Germany* was nominated for a Stalin prize.

While in Germany, Burchett (and his father who joined him there) struck up a friendship with a member of the Soviet Information Bureau, Yuri Krotkov, who was in the employ of Soviet intelligence. According to his own account, while in Berlin he travelled into the Soviet sector on average three times per week. A story reached the head office of an American newspaper he wrote for, the *Christian Science Monitor*, from sources it regarded as completely reliable, that during his Berlin period he was engaged in selling automobiles to Soviet officials. Whether or not this story was accurate I do not know; certainly, however, he was involved in the German automobile trade, sending home to Melbourne a late 1930s Mercedes Benz registered in the British zone.

In early 1949 Burchett moved his base from Berlin to Budapest where he reported enthusiastically for both the *Daily Express* and *Times* the trial and conviction of Cardinal Mindszenty, a man whom he described in a letter home as a 'miserable, intriguing, ambitious little man'. Burchett was completely convinced of the guilt of Mindszenty and the gravity of his plot against the Hungarian Republic. Indeed so engaged was he by the details of the trial that he wrote a play about it, *The Changing Tide*, in which Cardinal Feudalics (Mindszenty) and Count Easterberry (Esterhazy) are shown to be involved in a plot with the United States (aided by an army of Deutsch Volk recruited in the Displaced Persons Camps) for the restoration of the heir to the Habsburg throne, Otto. At one moment in this play a Hungarian priest, representing the forces of darkness, lurches at a young peasant girl and in fury tears from her hands a copy of the book she has her nose buried in—Lysenko's *Theory and Practice of Plant Breeding*. All, however, to no avail. As a result of the policies of the new people's government the peasant girl makes her way to university to study Lysenko and returns to her home village at the climax of the play, to announce that she has learned to grow 'tomatoes which have potatoes for roots and potatoes that grow tomatoes on their tops…cotton in half a dozen different colours and maize cobs eighteen inches long'.

Burchett, however, was not concerned merely with publicising the plots of clerical reaction in Eastern Europe; he also reported in 1949 (and extensively in his book *People's Democracies*) on the Tito conspiracy to establish an empire of the Danube in the Anglo-American interest, whose primary aim in Hungary was the murder of the communist leadership—Rakosi, Gero and Farkas—and whose chief co-conspirator, the longtime imperialist agent—and leading communist—Laszlo Rajk. The details of the Tito plot revealed at the Rajk show trial, which Burchett earnestly reported, are too ridiculous to be worth recounting. The tone, however, of his reports can be discerned from his concluding remarks on the affair in *People's Democracies*.

> They were a miserable collection of plotters without a human ideal between the lot of them…Rajk and his gangs were disclosed as miserable, bloodthirsty adventurers who would not hesitate to plunge the country into a ferocious civil war, to destroy everything of the new life which has been so painfully built up, to hand the country lock, stock and barrel to a foreign power…There were no regrets except from a few of the dispossessed and Horthy hangers-on, when the chief culprits were condemned to death and speedily executed.

In 1950 Wilfred Burchett quit Eastern Europe and Fleet Street and toured Australia for the communist party front organisations, the Australian Peace Council and Democratic Rights Council, his ultimate destination being China where he would be joined by his new Bulgarian wife. In his Australian tour Burchett, with characteristic energy and vulgarity, promoted the current lines of the Australian Communist Party—the Soviet Union as the bastion of peace and socialism; the United States as the camp of war and imperialism; Menzies as an American lackey, warmonger and fascist. Although many town halls were closed to him, Burchett spoke to several large gatherings of provincials—communists, trade unionists and fellow travellers eager to hear, from the local boy who had made good, news of the socialist experiment in Eastern Europe.

Burchett assured his Australian audiences that conditions in the people's democracies were 'paradise' in comparison to those prevailing before the coming of communist rule. There was plenty of trade union freedom in Eastern Europe, although, of course, no need to strike. (For workers there to go on strike would, he pointed out, be illogical—a strike 'against themselves'.) Workers now enjoyed paid holidays in the old villas of the rich and had tasted butter for the first time. Under the old regimes they had eaten 'maize mush'. The peoples and governments of the Soviet bloc were peace-loving; to return from there to the west was 'like entering into a mad-house'.

In February 1951 Burchett travelled to China. If anything the revolution in progress there affected him even more deeply than had the socialist experiments he had witnessed in Rakosi's Hungary or Dimitrov's Bulgaria. In mid-April 1951 he wrote thus to his father:

> There is such humanity and beauty in life here, such tolerance and understanding that I feel very small and conscious of my inability to express in print just what is going on…You know I have lived in many lands and my emotions have been correspondingly toughened but I have never experienced anything as moving as here in China where a new life designed to eliminate every tiniest injustice is being built.

Although he had been in China for only two months in April his book in praise of the Chinese Revolution, eventually to be published under the title *China's Feet Unbound*, was well under way. Moreover, and this is of considerable significance, Burchett was by this time a financial dependant of the Chinese Communist Party. As he explained to his father:

> I don't have to worry about finances here. I am treated on the same basis as a local writer although you need not spread this news outside our own circle. In other words I am relieved of financial cares and given facilities to see what I want to see, travel where I want to travel, interview who I want to interview...Luxury needs are not catered for but basic needs are. Most government employees live on that basis. What I need, for example, comes to me, from food and writing paper and typewriter ribbons. I sign for it and it's a book entry somewhere. That's how all artists and writers operate here and I am treated as an honoured foreign guest writer.

I do not wish to be misunderstood here. Burchett obviously did not decide to work for the Chinese Communist Party for monetary gain. As a talented journalist he could have fared far better financially if he had remained in the west. The question of his financial relationship with the Chinese communists bears only on the claims concerning his independence from all governments and the allegations concerning his Korean War treachery. The evidence of his own correspondence makes clear that for ideological reasons by April 1951 Burchett was financially dependent upon, and had decided to serve to the best of his abilities, the Chinese Communist Party. 'I would,' he wrote to his father, 'do anything at all for their people and their government.' When he wrote this Chinese troops ('volunteers') had already been despatched to fight in a war against a

United Nations force which included an Australian contingent. On 13 July 1951 Burchett followed the Chinese volunteers across the Yalu River into Korea.

KOREAN WAR REPORTER

The Yalu was Burchett's Rubicon. Burchett's reputation as a communist agent and as a traitor to his country centres on what he did—or is believed to have done—in the two and a half years he spent in Korea after the summer of 1951. What, then, did he do?

The first thing of course he *did* was that he *wrote*—three books (two in partnership with Alan Winnington, the British communist) and endless journalism. His journalism in particular was important, disseminated worldwide through the networks of the communist movement, distributed in the prisoner-of-war camps and broadcast over Chinese and North Korean radio. An analysis of Burchett's Korean War journalism is an essential part of any serious attempt to discover whether Burchett in Korea acted as a journalist or a propagandist. Moreover, as we shall see, if Burchett had been brought to trial for treason in Australia his journalism and in particular that broadcast over enemy radio or distributed amongst POWs would certainly have been tendered as Crown evidence.

Of Burchett's Korean War journalism Dr McCormack offers no analysis. He does, however, make the following claim:

> Burchett was a journalist inspired by an uncommon moral passion...an honest man who tried to tell the truth, who was almost alone in seeing the war primarily from the viewpoint of the suffering Korean people rather than the great powers or his own *or any other government.* [my italics]

The first months of Burchett's Korean War journalism from

August to December 1951 (at least to judge by the regular despatches from him released in English by the New China News Agency which form the basis of my analysis) were dominated by the progress of the armistice talks at Kaesong. On 3 August he reported the doubts in the Chinese and North Korean camps that the Americans 'really entered the talks in good faith', and added that 'the Americans are now resorting to more intensive atrocity bombing and shelling daily to bring pressure on the conference table'.

After an incident on 22 August, in which the communists claimed that an American aircraft had deliberately bombed near the communist headquarters for the talks at Kaesong, Burchett and his Korean War offsider, Alan Winnington (who reported the war for the British communist newspaper the *Daily Worker*) offered a joint statement beginning: 'We, the undersigned correspondents...disgusted at the monstrous lies that have been issued by the Americans regarding the August 22 bombing raid on Kaesong...'

When, because of Kaesong (which was behind communist lines and close to the fighting), the Americans raised the possibility of a new conference site further from the front, Winnington wrote of 'the sinister American demands for a new site' and Burchett that 'the cunning methods of their assassins make it clear that these are adaptable to any circumstances and any geographical area'.

And so it went on. Time and again over the next months, Burchett reported, the Americans were stalling the armistice agreement through their hatred of peace. Their press chief, General Nuckols, was 'acting on Goebbels' principle that, if the lie is big enough and is repeated often enough, it will be accepted'. The Americans 'by the simple device of leaving corpses on the battlefields and listing them as "missing" ...hoped to get away with a terrific propaganda scoop'.

Instead they 'had been caught in one of the most flagrantly dirty tricks in history'.

On the other hand the Chinese and North Korean delegations in these early talks were 'patient and reasonable in their attitude'. Two statements of the Chinese and North Koreans on 16 November 'cut like a ray of sunshine through the mists and shadows of American propaganda distortions'. Communist draft proposals were 'workmanlike'; American proposals 'motivated more as headline catching propaganda'. When agreement between the sides was reached it was due to 'the firmness, patience and responsible attitude towards peace taken by the Korean and Chinese negotiators'. When they broke down, 'the extraordinary antics of the Americans, ranging from colossal bungling to criminal negligence, spiced by master race arrogance', were 'alone responsible'. Burchett did not even try to disguise the remorselessly partisan quality of his reporting of the armistice talks. In referring to communist positions in the talks he frequently wrote of 'this side'. His despatches, published on occasions in the Peking *People's Daily* and regularly released by the New China News Agency, had a quasi-official status.

In the first six months of his Korean reporting Burchett engaged in a certain amount of atrocity-mongering. He reported, for example, the opinion of a Polish communist journalist that the Americans' 'destruction of Korea was worse than anything the Nazis did during their advance and retreat through Poland', and that when Syngman Rhee's 'hangmen and firing squads' went to work, US General Van Fleet rubbed 'his blood-stained hands together'. From January 1952, however, atrocity stories became the major focus of Burchett's journalism.

The turning point for communist propaganda in Korea and for Burchett appears to have been the American decision to demand, on humanitarian (and no doubt also propaganda) grounds, the application of a principle of voluntariness in the exchange of prisoners of war. Although the horrors that had accompanied the forced repatriation of Soviet POWs to the USSR after 1945 could never be undone, American armistice policy now prevented the risk of a repetition of that tragedy.

The communist delegations for many months flatly refused to accept the principle of voluntary POW repatriation. As General Li Sang-cho pointed out, in a truly Orwellian inversion, 'voluntary repatriation' was 'coercion, intimidation, retention and massacre'. From the first Burchett threw his weight into the communist campaign against the voluntary repatriation of POWs. In a despatch broadcast over Peking radio on 8 January 1952, he asked:

> What is the professed purpose of the American plan of 'voluntary repatriation'?...It is mighty difficult to convince a single Korean or Chinese soldier or civilian of one scrap of humanitarianism on the part of the Americans, after their monstrous slaughter of scores of thousands of Korean civilians in cold blood.

Communist propaganda soon had a firm answer to Burchett's question. Under the cover of the principle of voluntary repatriation, the Americans intended to intimidate patriotic Chinese and North Korean prisoners of war into refusing to return to their homelands. In early 1952, in order to dramatise their propaganda against the principle of voluntary repatriation, the Chinese and North Korean military commands activated those POWs still under their control in the Koje Island camp to mount a fierce and sustained resistance to their captors. When the Americans and their allies used military force to quell these riots the 'proof' of the sinister intentions of the Americans in insisting on the principle of voluntary repatriation was provided. It was time for their propagandists to get to work. On 24 February 1952 Burchett reported thus:

> The brutal massacre of at least 69 Korean prisoners of war and the wounding of 152 others, has brought into the open the ghastly methods being used by the Americans to force prisoners to accept 'voluntary repatriation'. American troops turned machine-gun fire on the demonstrators and hurled hand-grenades into their midst, in a wholesale slaughter of unarmed war prisoners. An additional 221 have thus fallen victim to American 'humanitarianism'.

By the summer of 1952 Burchett's writing concerning the conditions on Koje Island—which of course was not based on observation but on the resources of Chinese and North Korean propaganda and intelligence—had arrived at a state of pure propaganda:

> When discussions on POW exchange got under way at Panmunjon and the Kuomintang and Syngman Rhee officers, who acted as American agents in running the camp, were ordered to force the prisoners to become traitors, then the torture-rooms, the gas-chambers, the steam-heat rooms, the branding irons and the tattooers' needles and the gallows were kept busy...Tanks and flame-throwers...were brought to bear on these prisoners when the torture chambers failed to do their work. There is little need for me to deal further with the horrifying conditions in these American concentration and extermination camps.

To describe Wilfred Burchett as an objective and honest reporter of the Korean War (as Dr McCormack does) is the equivalent of calling Julius Streicher a commentator on German Jewish affairs or Horatio Bottomley a student of

Wilhelmine foreign policy.

Wilfred Burchett's activities at communist headquarters at Kaesong were not, however, limited to writing and broadcasting war propaganda. There was, in addition, important extracurricular work a completely trustworthy English-speaking journalist could perform for the Chinese and North Korean military. During the ceasefire talks at Panmunjon Burchett was able to maintain regular contact with western journalists reporting the war from the United Nations side and to use these contacts to try and influence the way in which they reported the progress of the talks.

A vivid account of this process was given by the Korean War *Daily Mail* correspondent, Lachie McDonald, to Australian security on 28 October 1953:

> During breaks in the [Panmunjon] talks [in April 1953] I saw Burchett and Winnington enter the annexe to the communist half of the talks building where the communist delegates retired for private discussions...When delegates returned to the conference table after these talks, Burchett and Winnington would reappear from the communist annexe and tell UN correspondents the communist story of the reason for each break, and how talks were progressing. I listened several times to Burchett and Winnington answering questions from American correspondents.

By feeding information supplied to him by the communist delegation concerning American arguments at the secret sessions of the ceasefire talks to a hungry press corps, Burchett sought to embarrass the UN negotiators and to create, wherever possible, rifts between the generals and journalists on the western side. He was obviously delighted when, in February 1952, General Ridgway tried (and failed) to inhibit 'consorting' between the UN correspondents and Burchett. Indeed, in the small rifts which Burchett managed to create between the military and the press on the UN side in Korea one can see prefigured the bitter relationship which was to emerge during the Vietnam War (immortalised in the journalists' neologism 'the credibility gap'). Nor, as Burchett explained in a letter he wrote to his father in December 1951, did those western journalists receptive to his influence go unrewarded:

> Today, when prisoner of war lists were released, most of the American press were virtually crawling on their hands and knees on the road to us, begging for crumbs of information. We were in the lovely position of ignoring all those who had tried to injure us and handed priceless information to the few who had written honestly about the talks.

AMONGST THE PRISONERS OF WAR

Amongst Burchett's activities at Panmunjon in early 1952 was the placing in western newspapers of photographs of American prisoners of war 'playing football, baseball and leading as normal a life as is possible'. In May 1952, however, he began to tell the world of what he had seen with his own eyes about conditions in the communist-controlled POW camps.

On 18 May, in what must rank as a classic statement of its kind, Burchett reported thus from a POW camp in the north: 'This camp looks like a holiday resort in Switzerland. The atmosphere is also nearer that of a luxury holiday resort than a POW camp.' Burchett also reported that the men in the POW camps were fed so well that he himself could not finish the 'standard portion of meat and eggs' he was offered. (This was not surprising for the meat ration alone was 'several times higher than the ration in England'.) A British prisoner, selected 'at random', told him, 'we are all getting fat and brown'. Prisoners lazed around during the day with 'swimming, fishing, sports, reading, writing'. The British in particular were avid readers; Burchett discovered that their overwhelming favourite author was not Tolstoy or Steinbeck— but Willie Gallacher of the communist party. The camps were run on strictly democratic lines. (On the morning he arrived at Camp No. 5 the prisoners were holding a meeting to discuss the previous evening's soup which had been 'below standard'.) Religious observances and the traditional dietary laws of the prisoners were 'scrupulously respected' by the camp authorities. 'Scores' of POWs had told Burchett 'with tears in their eyes' of Chinese doctors and nurses 'who worked 24 hour shifts to save them' or sold their 'tobacco rations to buy tomatoes for a specially sick American'. The communists were so kind-hearted that an American pilot was greeted on landing by the fighter pilot who downed him with a slap on the back and a portion of bread and sausage. Within the camps there were no special prisons or punishments for ungrateful POWs. 'If a prisoner merits a gaol sentence he is merely confined in another house away from the rest of the prisoners, quite similar to the house in which he normally lives.'

By June 1952 Burchett pointed out in a broadcast over Peking radio that he had spoken to every single British POW (no mean feat given that there were over nine hundred of them) and to hundreds of Americans. The 'overwhelming consensus' was that no group of POWs had been so well treated in modern history.

I do not know whether there is anyone in Australia, other than Dr McCormack, who believes Burchett's description of communist POW camps in Korea as luxury Swiss holiday resorts to be evidence of the 'greatness' of his journalism or the 'uncommonness' of his moral passion. If so, they would do well to read the British government report of 1955 (which Dr

McCormack has certainly read) on the treatment of British POWs. According to this report in the first year of the Korean War 'food, shelter and medical attention' in the North Korean and Chinese camps was so inadequate that 1600 United Nations POWs died. In June 1951, in one of the camps, 'conditions were appalling, with men dying at a rate of up to twenty a day from malnutrition, beri-beri and dysentery'. While after August 1951 food and medical conditions improved (by the end of 1951 'the staple diet consisted of rice with a few vegetables and a little meat') prisoners 'who had experienced the early days never forgot the fear of not having enough to eat'.

Pace Burchett the report makes clear that the Chinese were essentially hostile to the 'reactionary' practice of religion in the camps, despite the fact that this right was guaranteed under the Geneva Convention. 'Various British prisoners risked their lives to conduct religious services.' The Chinese were, indeed, centrally concerned with the political 're-education' of the Allied prisoners. 'Everything...was tried by the Chinese in pursuit of the desired result: simple psychological pressure, manipulation of welfare conditions, corruption, threats, segregations, force and outright torture.'

To men, 'suffering from starvation, disease and neglect' incessant propaganda in favour of communism was frequently sufficient to gain submission. But the Chinese also used a wide net of informers to intimidate prisoners; manipulated prisoners' desire for mail to and from home to achieve political results; and used their control over the provision of food and medicine as a means of rewarding 'progressive' prisoners and punishing 'reactionaries'. 'Sizes of rations...varied and "progressive" prisoners were sometimes given more and better food..."Progressives" usually received whatever supplies of medicine were available while the "reactionaries" went without.'

The report also stated that 'when all these methods of inducement had failed...the Chinese had recourse to methods of physical coercion and torture, revolting to the humane mind'. These methods included brutal beatings; solitary confinement for months at a time, often in boxes of five feet by two or three feet, without adequate clothing, food or water; and a variety of more refined and shocking tortures.

It is certainly true that by the time Wilfred Burchett visited the POW camps the worst period of mass death through starvation-induced disease was over. Nevertheless it is perfectly obvious that the account he gave of the conditions in these camps was a shocking travesty of the truth and that the contrast he painted—for example in a broadcast he gave over Peking radio in June 1952—between the saintliness of the communist administration of the POW camps and the hell-on-earth of the American concentration and extermination camps on Koje Island, a not insignificant contribution to communist wartime propaganda.

In some cases at least, prisoners in the POW camps, despite the fact that they were frightened of Burchett (if for no other reason than that he clearly had the complete confidence of the camp authorities), let him know something of the truth about conditions in the camps. Here is the account by an Australian POW, Flight-Lieutenant Gordon Harvey, of a meeting with Burchett at Camp No. 2 in April 1952, given to Australian authorities on 16 October 1953:

> I made no complaints to Burchett because I thought he was on the side of the enemy. There were complaints I would have made to an impartial visitor. I feared the consequences to myself of making complaints about conditions. He did ask me what treatment I had received from the North Koreans and I told him I had received very bad treatment. He seemed

rather taken aback and quickly changed the subject and I don't think he wrote anything in his notebook.

A similar account comes from another Australian soldier, Robert Parker, whom Burchett met (with three other Australians) in Camp No. 5 in 1952. Parker claims to have told Burchett of the terrible conditions in the camps. Burchett merely shrugged his shoulders. Even if Burchett disbelieved Parker did he not have eyes to see the condition of the men he met? Parker's weight had gone from thirteen to six stone. In Sydney in 1974 Burchett said it was hard to estimate POWs' weight because they wore 'loose fitting' clothes, although he admitted the food conditions were 'very bad'. As we have seen in his war propaganda of 1952 he had said that the POWs ate like kings with a meat ration several times higher than in England.

On yet another occasion, a British soldier, Derek Kinne, a man of extraordinary courage, approached Burchett after he had lectured a group of POWs on the peace talks. The following was published in 1955 in Kinne's book entitled *Wooden Boxes*:

> 'You see that hill behind you?' He turned around.
> 'Well?'
> 'That's "Boot Hill". There are hundreds of graves on that hill. The graves of men who died from starvation and neglect.'
> Burchett glanced round again before looking back at me. But his eyes flickered as they met mine and then sought the ground. With all that smooth speech behind him, including a declaration on the goodness of the Chinese towards their captives, he neither attempted to justify nor deny the fact of these deaths. All he could say in a flat voice was: 'Well, what can I do about it?'

Wilfred Burchett has often been accused of 'brainwashing'

POWs during the Korean War. The truth or falsity of this accusation is largely a question of semantics. After the Korean War the term 'brainwashing' came into vogue in the west, and was used rather imprecisely. In its broad usage it referred to the manipulative program of political persuasion employed by the communist side against United Nations POWs. In its narrow usage it referred to a specific and somewhat esoteric communist procedure 'designed' (in the words of the US Department of the Army study) 'to erase an individual's past beliefs and concepts and to substitute new ones'. This study concluded that in the narrow sense of the term not one of the thousands of US POWs—not even the pilots who 'confessed' to germ warfare after undergoing prolonged periods of torment—had been subject to 'brainwashing'. Because of the imprecision of the term the major British study of POWs in Korea did not use it at all while the US Senate Sub-Committee study of the same matter used it only with great reservations. Nonetheless both studies agreed that the overwhelming interest of the Chinese communists *was* the systematic political 'indoctrination' and 're-education' of United Nations POWs.

Under the broader definition of 'brainwashing', that is of a manipulative process aiming at the political re-education of its targets, there can be no doubt of the important collaborative role of Wilfred Burchett. His propaganda articles were very widely distributed among POWs in the camps, formally part of their political re-education. (One Australian POW, Colonel Greville, actually kept a list of the various Burchett articles he had come across while a prisoner in Korea.) On several occasions Burchett also is known to have given political lectures to large gatherings of British and American POWs. (Indeed it was after one such lecture that Derek Kinne approached him.) Such compulsory lectures followed by smaller study groups were, according to the British study, 'the basic means' of political indoctrination. The American study of the same process in the camps concludes that Burchett and Winnington served as 'advisers' to the propaganda leaders in the camps and were 'primarily responsible for the preparation of the Chinese propaganda for the United Nations prisoners and worked actively with English-speaking prisoners to try to persuade them to accept communism and betray their own countries'.

GERM WARFARE

In February 1952 a mass campaign was launched by the international communist movement accusing the United States of deploying in Korea a new and hideous weapon— germ warfare. Naturally enough in this campaign the testimony of journalists behind the communist lines was crucial. Wilfred Burchett threw himself into the task. On 26 February he reported that on eight occasions between 28 January and 17 February American aircraft had dropped cardboard containers of 'flies, fleas, crickets, spiders, lice, midges and mites', infected with bubonic plague, cholera and other epidemic diseases, aimed at destroying human lives and crops. In the following month he joined with five other communist journalists in Korea (which included the Hungarian Tibor Meray, who was later to analyse in painful detail his role in this mendacious campaign) in a joint statement to the world. The journalists claimed to have investigated systematically the evidence regarding the American deployment of germ warfare in Korea and to have found it utterly conclusive. In June, Burchett (over Peking radio) accused the Americans of perpetrating 'the most monstrous crimes against humanity' and asked 'how can one label scientists, generals and politicians who cold-bloodedly draw up plans to launch bacteria-carrying insects, to spread deadly diseases which could ravage the entire Asiatic continent? Yes, and ravage Europe too.'

In germ warfare, Burchett argued, the Americans had launched upon mankind a horror more frightful even than the atomic bomb whose effect he had witnessed at Hiroshima.

In order to 'prove' that the Americans were deploying bacteriological warfare in Korea the planners of the campaign did not rely merely on the testimony of journalists or even the results of the investigations by Chinese communist scientists (who worked, according to Burchett, 'in complex laboratories carved out of the North Korean mountains'). What they wanted was the evidentiary 'real McCoy'—the 'confessions' of American pilots that they had dropped germ bombs.

False confessions to fantastic crimes, extorted by protracted processes of mental and physical torture, were of course a standard feature of the international Stalinist culture. In the Soviet Union engineers had confessed to plots to wreck the socialist economy and leading communists—like Bukharin or Zinoviev—to being lifelong agents of German, Japanese or British imperialism. Burchett himself, as we have seen, had played an important part in publicising the confessions of Cardinal Mindszenty and Laszlo Rajk in postwar Hungary. Now in Korea he was to play a far more important role in publicising to the world the germ warfare 'confessions' of captured American pilots. But not merely publicising. As we shall see the evidence is overwhelming that Burchett was actively involved in the literary production of certain of these confessions. By the summer of 1952, in relation to germ warfare, Burchett was no longer a mere propagandist. Since he had arrived in Korea he had passed rapidly through a series of doors that had brought him to the inner sanctum of the world of totalitarianism, the interrogation cell.

Because the communists released in the POW exchange both those pilots who had confessed and those who had refused to confess, a considerable amount of this whole process is known. In late October 1953 the US representative at the United Nations, Charles Mayo, made the following statement:

> We know that the communists accused at least 107 of our captured fliers of engaging in bacteriological warfare. Of these we know that 40 refused to sign any confession. Of the 36 who did sign, all under duress, some 20 were subjected to what can fairly be called extreme and prolonged physical and mental torture.

An example of a pilot who refused, against the odds, to confess was Lieutenant James Stanley, a copy of whose sworn statement on release from a POW camp I have in my possession. In order to extract a confession from him Stanley was subjected to a four-month process of interrogation and torture which culminated in him being placed before a firing squad and offered a last chance to confess. When even this failed he was given up as a hopeless case and eventually returned to a POW camp. Of the 36 pilots who did confess the four most important and highly publicised confessions, at least in the early stage of the process, were those of Lieutenants Quinn, Enoch, O'Neal and Kniss. These four appeared before the 'International Scientific Commission' (of communists and fellow travellers) who investigated the germ warfare issue in lieu of the Red Cross which had been prevented from doing the job by a Soviet veto at the UN. Their handwritten confessions also appeared as annexes to the ISC report.

On returning to the United States each of these pilots was subjected to searching questioning by US airforce intelligence. The testimony of all four showed that, after their resistance and spirit had been broken by Chinese and North Korean interrogation teams and they had agreed to 'confess', Wilfred

Burchett had become an active participant in one way or another in the production and distribution of their confessions. Enoch, for example, testified that in early May 1952 Burchett had worked with him to prepare the script of a film he was forced to make of his confession:

> Burchett got out his typewriter and filled out a little outline for me summarizing the testimony. From this I answered questions. He also put down that list of things I was receiving, such as inoculation—he mentioned a list of things and I would say yes; yes; yes. Burchett typed the movie script in more than one copy. He told me to memorise this.

Enoch also claimed that in an interview he had with two Frenchmen, Farge and Roy, in the presence of Wilfred Burchett (a meeting Burchett later admitted), he told them his confession was false, for which he was 'threatened repeatedly with drastic measures by Burchett'. Quinn testified that Burchett wrote and edited 'to suit himself' a tape recording of an interview he made with him (broadcast over North Korean radio) and the printed version of his confession published in North Korea.

In the cases of Enoch, Quinn and O'Neal I have seen only those extracts of their testimony which in 1954 were passed by the US military to the Australian government. In the case of Lieutenant Paul Kniss, however, I have seen the entire 180-page transcript of the testimony which he gave in Washington on 19 and 20 October 1953 and which, after giving evidence in the Burchett *v.* Kane defamation action in 1974, he passed on to Denis Warner. The transcript of Kniss's sworn testimony, given a month and a half after his release, provides by far the most detailed and illuminating account of Burchett's role in the editing and propagation of the forced germ warfare confessions.

Paul Kniss was shot down on 31 May 1952. In early June his germ warfare interrogation, first at the hands of the North Koreans, later the Chinese, began. Kniss was interviewed briefly by Burchett in June; he denied to him any knowledge of or involvement in germ warfare. After some weeks, by now in a state of extreme anxiety and suffering from what he thought was dysentery, Kniss was exposed to a week of intensive interrogation, lasting from early morning until late at night, on one day for an unbroken twenty hours. On 7 or 8 July he capitulated, in a state of exhaustion and bewilderment, agreed to confess to participation in germ warfare, and wrote a two-page confession. His Chinese interrogator was delighted. 'He was like a kid with a new toy after he got it, and he grabbed it and translated it real fast and ran out of the room.'

Over the succeeding ten days Kniss wrote and rewrote his confession, under the prodding of his interrogators, until it had grown to some twenty pages. His twenty-page confession was now taken from him and returned in one or two days' time 'typed up and edited and parts slashed up'. Kniss was ordered to write up the new version and sign it. What happened next must be followed in full:

> *Kniss:* After I finished I had to go up and talk with W.G. Burchett, correspondent working for that French newspaper, and he was the one who edited my information.
> *Q:* He told you that?
> *Kniss:* He told me that he personally edited it. He showed me stacks of so-called evidence he had this high (indicating) from others. I learned later that O'Neal had seen him the same day I had seen him. He said he wanted me to change three or four points in my testimony which I refused to change.

The following day Kniss was interrogated once more by his

Chinese interpreter on a number of specific points:

> When he left the room, he left a piece of paper that he had
> been working on—had been reading off of. I picked that up
> and it was typewritten, again, and written in just about these
> words: Suggest that the interrogator ask Kniss the following
> questions…and on the bottom W.G. Burchett, and signed.

In the final handwritten version of his confession Kniss
copied from Burchett's typewritten version.

When his confession was completed Kniss was told to make
a recording of it. He baulked at first, but was given no choice.
He was then taken to Burchett again who presented him with
a list of ten to fifteen questions and answers (taken from his
confession) which he was once more obliged to record. He was
then instructed to memorise his confession for the planned
hearings before the ISC on 4 August. Shortly before these
hearings the Chinese general in charge of the entire operation,
General Wang, approached Kniss and warned him of the fatal
consequences of any indiscretion before the international visi-
tors. Dutifully Kniss played his part in this farce, with
Burchett assisting by translating from English into French.

The Commission recorded in their report that they had had
'the opportunity of extended conversations' with the four
American pilots 'under conditions of free discourse':

> Its members unanimously formed the opinion that no pres-
> sure, physical or mental, had been brought to bear upon
> these prisoners of war…These declarations were made of
> their own free will, after long experience of the friendliness
> and kindness of their Chinese and Korean captors had
> brought them the realisation that their duty to all races
> and people must outweigh their natural scruples at reveal-
> ing what might be considered military secrets of their
> government.

Kniss had now served his purpose. As we shall see he was not to encounter Burchett again until the eve of the main prisoner of war exchange in early September 1953 and, then, not for another twenty-one years.

In 1974 Kniss gave evidence at the Sydney trial where Burchett sued Jack Kane for defamation. His evidence about Burchett's role in the germ warfare confessions was based not on mere memory but on the transcript of his sworn testimony, taken six weeks after the POW exchange. Dr McCormack was of course unaware of this. In his *Australian Society* apologia he recognised the seriousness of the Kniss evidence for Burchett's reputation but confidently and conveniently dismissed it on the grounds of faulty memory or something worse. 'It is curious that such a serious matter was not mentioned in any of the published US studies of the problem, and that the charge was apparently not made until 22 years after the event, in a Sydney court room.' I wonder whether Dr McCormack will *now* admit the truth of the Kniss testimony, whose seriousness he has already acknowledged.

McCormack, incidentally, argues in defence of Burchett's role in the germ warfare campaign that Burchett believed in its truth, in part because he witnessed 'what appeared to be' a germ attack on the Yalu River and in part because he was convinced by the report of the 'distinguished body of scientists', the ISC. The idea that Burchett was convinced by the ISC report is indeed droll. As we have seen he played a role in assembling the confessional evidence for it. If its report convinced him it would represent in precise form the often misunderstood Orwellian idea of 'doublethink'—namely that under the system of totalitarianism the fabricators of fraudulent propaganda material are also required to be true believers in it.

THE QUESTION OF TREASON

As the Korean War ceasefire and prisoner-of-war exchange approached, Wilfred Burchett threw himself into a last Korean War battle. In a letter to his father of late 1952 he had explained the consequences should the principle of 'voluntary repatriation' be conceded. POWs would, he pointed out, be pressured by both sides 'to renounce their country, to turn traitors'. (It was, for someone in his position, an interesting turn of phrase.) Burchett's prediction had about it a self-fulfilling quality. After the communists reconciled themselves to voluntary repatriation Burchett moved amongst American POWs of his acquaintance offering them asylum in a communist country of their choice and spreading rumours of the vile treatment to be meted out to them if they returned to the United States. Burchett told Corporal Dickenson (one of the original non-repatriates) that ex-prisoners of war were being beaten and knifed by FBI agents and that, as soon as they crossed into South Korea, the germ warfare pilots had 'disappeared'. He was also, according to Dickenson, involved in the preparation of a statement released to the press on behalf of the twenty-three POWs who opted not to return to the United States.

While Burchett publicly busied himself encouraging POWs to remain within the communist world, in private he was thinking of returning home. In 1953, perhaps in preparation for his homecoming, a small book was published, called somewhat grandly, *He Chose Truth: The Inspiring Story of Wilfred Burchett*. In April 1953, in a discussion with the newspaperman Lachie McDonald (a New Zealander with Australian connections), Burchett had inquired as to his own present standing in Australia. McDonald thought Australian authorities would have compiled a large dossier of his broadcasts on enemy radio, and told him of a conversation he had had with an RAAF captain who had expressed a desire to drop Burchett from his aircraft onto communist headquarters at Kaesong. Burchett made light of all this but apparently took it seriously. Six months later ASIO was told that Burchett was 'contemplating returning to Australia but is somewhat afraid of members of 77 Air Squadron'. Burchett also wrote home at this time asking that the communist party front organisation—the Democratic Rights Council—be placed on alert to locate any libellous material about him appearing in the Australian press.

Burchett had, of course, more to worry about, in regard to his homecoming, than defamatory articles or air force heavies. He knew that for two years he had—in the classic words of the English treason law—been giving 'aid and comfort' in Korea to the enemies of his country at a time of war. *Perhaps* his conscience was clear; he could, after all, tell himself that he had been serving a just cause—the cause of communism—in which he utterly believed. (In mid-1952, on the very day he was broadcast over Peking radio, he had written to his father advising him to read Stalin's masterly 'Remarks on Economic Questions' in which it was explained how within ten years the Soviet Union would make its transition from socialism to communism.) But nothing in his nature equipped him for the role of martyr in a treason trial. Having crossed the Rubicon, Burchett now tried to find some means of crossing back.

We now come to a strange and hitherto unknown episode in the life of Wilfred Burchett—an episode which, by accident, I stumbled upon in the ASIO files on Burchett released in early 1985. By the first week of September 1953 Burchett had used an intermediary in the press corps, Ed Hymoff, to get in touch with the United States military command in Korea and let it be known that, in return for being offered an amnesty from the Australian government, he would be willing to give useful information to American military intelligence.

The Americans took very seriously indeed Burchett's offer to redefect to the west. The plan for what they called the 'exfiltration' of Burchett had the personal support of no less a figure than the commander-in-chief of US Armed Forces in Korea, General Mark Clark. The details of the proposed deal were communicated—via the Australian embassy in Tokyo— to the Australian government on 8 September 1953.

> The United States Army would willingly agree to joint inter-rogation with the Australian Army if we so desire it and would arrange for interrogation to take place in Korea, or Okinawa if we do not desire that BURCHETT travel to Japan. Please advise urgently:
> (a) Whether BURCHETT would be allowed to enter Australia;
> (b) whether he can be given an assurance that, subject to good behaviour, he will not be liable to proceedings or other action in Australia;
> (c) whether you wish the Australian Army to be associated with the United States Army in his interrogation;
> (d) whether his repatriation would be at the Australian Government's expense or whether we should accept United States Transport authorities in the event of BURCHETT not having funds.
> General Clark hopes we will treat this matter as one of considerable urgency since the opportunity for continued personal contact with BURCHETT through the American press correspondent in the demilitarized zone may be inter-rupted in the near future and any delay in reaching a decision will, therefore, reduce prospects of bringing BURCHETT out at all. Obviously, any leakage to the Communists of BURCHETT's desire to leave North Korea would prejudice

the whole operation. According to the United States Army Intelligence, BURCHETT has a Czechoslovakian wife and one child in China. So far as is known BURCHETT has not raised the question of his family and may not do so.

Interestingly, in the light of current views concerning the servility of the Menzies government to the United States, the instant response of Australia to the American request was negative. They made it known to the Americans that they had no intention of granting Burchett any amnesty. Indeed, as the newly released material makes clear, Burchett's attempt to buy his way back to the west, which had caused the United States to approach Australia on the question of the amnesty, prodded the Australian government for the first time into serious preparations for bringing Burchett to trial in Australia on a charge of treason.

By late September 1953 a legal opinion had been prepared for ASIO on the Burchett case. It was clear that Burchett could not be charged under the treason section of the Federal Crimes Act (section 24) because it had no 'extra-territorial' effect. On the other hand ASIO's lawyers were of the opinion that the English statute and common law on treason could form the basis for an action in the Supreme Court of Victoria of which there was 'a reasonable prospect of a successful prosecution'. What would have to be proved was that Burchett owed allegiance to the Queen; that he had 'adhered' to her enemies, giving them 'aid and comfort'; and that the North Koreans and Chinese could, under law, be regarded as the Queen's enemies. The final of these points would, they believed, provide considerable (but not insuperable) difficulty. There was, however, in their view no doubt that Burchett, the holder at that time of a British passport, owed allegiance to the Crown or that his activities in the Korean War could be proven to have given 'aid and comfort' to the North Koreans and Chinese. His propaganda activities in Korea (broadcasts over enemy radio, his journalism and books); his active engagement in the 'seduction' of prisoners of war on the United Nations side (whether or not Australian POWs were directly involved was not considered crucial) from loyalty to their countries; and his open 'association with the enemy' at Panmunjon—were all considered clear instances of providing 'aid and comfort' to the Queen's enemies.

In mid-October 1953 ASIO discussed the Burchett case with the federal Solicitor-General, Professor Bailey, who in turn discussed the matter with the Attorney-General, Jack Spicer. All agreed that the case against Burchett should be actively pursued and thoroughly prepared and that when the time was ripe Bailey should approach the Victorian Solicitor-General on the matter of the prosecution of Burchett. Bailey handed ASIO the copy of the top secret telegram of 10 September, in which the Australian government had refused the idea of an amnesty for Burchett. He did not know whether the Americans still had hopes of 'exfiltrating' Burchett but said that he would not be surprised if they had. In pursuit of the case it was agreed to despatch two ASIO officers post-haste to Japan and South Korea to collect evidence. It was recognised that this mission might mislead the Americans into thinking Australia was 'reconsidering its attitude of non-cooperation' and therefore considered prudent to inform them of its true purpose. For his part Professor Bailey could see no harm being done in Australia participating in the interrogation of Burchett if the American plan, notwithstanding the refusal of the amnesty, still went ahead.

In early November in Tokyo the two ASIO men made contact with high-ranking American military officers, Major-General Ennis and Lieutenant-Colonel Field, and informed them of the purpose of their visit. As one explained in a letter to Colonel Charles Spry, director-general of ASIO:

> Lt-Col Field informed us of the identity of the person to whom the subject of our enquiry made his original approach—but we will probably not seek to get in touch with that person. At present there does not appear to be any great advantage to be obtained by so doing. Having been informed of the Australian Government's decision in that matter, the US authorities did no more about it and show no disposition to renew the proposal.

Instead of pursuing the defection of Burchett the US military agreed now to hand over to Australia the information their intelligence system had gathered on Burchett's Korean War activities, the first instalment of which was based on interviews with American POWs, thirty-five of whom had spoken to Burchett. Interestingly, the first instalment of their information did not include the testimony of the pilots who had confessed to germ warfare, because action against them was still being contemplated. However in mid-1954 an extremely important US intelligence assessment of the Korean War activities of Burchett, including now extracts from the testimony of the pilots, was passed on to Australia. Although it is unclear from the released material whether or not the federal Solicitor-General ever approached his Victorian counterpart, it is clear that in late 1954 the possibility of prosecuting Burchett on a charge of treason, if he could be had, remained open.

Burchett however was not to be had. In 1954 he had moved from Korea to northern Vietnam, where he had linked up with the Viet Minh armies in time to report their final victories over the French, the Geneva Conference and, then, to accompany their troops into liberated Hanoi. With Ho Chi Minh it was, as Burchett later expressed it, 'love at first sight'.

Burchett may have been aware of the plans in Australia to bring him to trial. In mid-1955 he wrote thus to his father from the Bandung Conference: 'I got here much to the surprise and sorrow of many people. I discovered, as they were quite certain that I would not get past Singapore due to the friendly attentions of the Menzies Government.' At Bandung it is certain that plans were indeed afoot to arrest him (not to confiscate his passport, as Burchett later claimed) should he return via Singapore, and likely that details of these plans reached him. Prudently his Chinese friends who flew him out of Bandung avoided British Commonwealth territory on the flight to Kunming.

Shortly after the Bandung Conference Burchett noticed that his (British) passport had been stolen. His application to Australia for a new one was refused, on the ground that he 'had forfeited any claim he might have had to the protection and assistance' of the Australian government, a ground hardly surprising in view of his Korean War activities and of the government's desire to prosecute him as a traitor. In late 1955 Burchett wrote to his father telling him that the loss of his passport had not yet caused him harm. He had indeed 'been offered a passport…by one of Australia's closest Allies. What a joke if I accepted.' Of course, he did not accept. He intended rather to extract the greatest possible propaganda advantage from the withdrawal of his passport: 'I want it ventilated in the press and parliament. I will blow the whole thing wide open at the International Journalists Conference next month.'

If Burchett had desired to clear his name after Korea he could, of course, have returned to Australia and faced the music, in what would have undoubtedly been, if it had gone ahead, the most important Australian 'political' trial of the century. There were however considerable risks involved. The passport issue, on the other hand, presented him with the possibility of risk-free martyrdom. The Australian government had hoped to place Burchett in the dock on a charge of treason to his own country; Burchett now hoped to place his country in the dock on a lesser charge of having deprived an honourable Australian of his passport and citizenship and on a greater charge of having, alongside the United States, engaged in unjust war against the communist cause in Asia. By the early 1970s—by the end of the Vietnam War—he had more or less succeeded.

WORKING FOR THE KGB: THE KROTKOV TESTIMONY

In Hanoi, where Burchett was based between 1954 and 1957, he and his family lived comfortably. A British journalist friend, Dennis Bloodworth, wrote in April 1956 to Burchett's father from Saigon, assuring him that his son's family 'had a very nice house up there with good servants' and that Wilfred had 'bought an excellent French car recently which goes well'. By 1956, however, Burchett was thinking of leaving Hanoi. One possibility was to return to Peking; another was to set up in the capital of the communist world, Moscow.

In mid-1956, Burchett passed through Moscow briefly. An acquaintance with an old Soviet friend from his Berlin days, Yuri Krotkov, was renewed. Krotkov, a playwright and KGB agent, later defected to the west and outlined in considerable detail to the US Senate Sub-Committee the story of his dealings with Burchett. The Krotkov testimony is, of course, potentially at least, the most important source of information concerning the establishment of Burchett's relations with the KGB. An evaluation of the accuracy of the evidence he gave in Washington is a central element in the understanding of Burchett's career.

First, then, Krotkov's story. According to Krotkov he met

Burchett in Berlin in 1947 when Burchett (at the time a *Daily Express* journalist) accompanied him to the rocket site at Peenemunde in East Germany. After the trip Burchett contacted Krotkov and told him that after going to Peenemunde a representative of the British Admiralty had been in touch with him. Krotkov, who was formally a representative of the Soviet Information Bureau but actually working for Soviet intelligence with a mission to 'sell' himself to western journalists, responded quickly to this gratuitous tip-off. He contacted his MVD chiefs about Burchett. (The MVD was the precursor of the KGB.) At first they were suspicious. Burchett's approach to Krotkov appeared too crude; moreover the MVD had files on Burchett's employment with Intourist in the 1930s and on his German Jewish wife. Why had Burchett not mentioned his previous Soviet connections to Krotkov? Soon these suspicions were allayed. Krotkov was instructed to cultivate Burchett—without, it appears, any great haste—and this he did until November 1947. During that time Burchett intimated that he was a communist, while Burchett's father (who was in Berlin at the time) 'openly declared his Communist ideas' to Krotkov.

Krotkov claims not to have met or heard from Burchett again until mid-1956 when out of the blue he received a telephone call from him. Burchett was calling from the Hotel Savoy, Moscow. Could he meet Krotkov? Krotkov was uncertain how to respond and called his KGB Chief, Krasilnikov. Krasilnikov instructed him to go ahead with the meeting. Here, according to Krotkov, Burchett laid his cards on the table.

> And in that time when I visited him and we went to a restaurant, he openly told me that he is a member of the Australian Communist Party, but for the benefit of party, he is on the illegal underground position, and that he showed me his document, that was a rather strange paper which was issued

in Hanoi, by the North Vietnam Government—but he told me that he hadn't an Australian passport. He told me that the Australian authority refused to give him the passport. Then he told me that he was in Korea, and then he was in China. He worked there as a free lance correspondent but he was supplied, he was paid by the Chinese Communist Party all that period. Then when he came to Vietnam he was under the—all his expenses were paid by the Vietnam Communist Party, by Ho Chi Minh, and he mentioned that he was in a very close relation with Chou En Lai, that's the Chinese, he is now Prime Minister of China, that he was in very close relation with Ho Chi Minh himself. He told me that he visited him many times, that Ho gave him a house in Hanoi, and a car, a secretary, that he was 'equipped' very beautifully by the Vietnamese Communist Party. And then he said that, he had now a new idea—in that time he told me—that he wanted to come to Moscow and to stay in Moscow because now, after the Khrushchev speech, Moscow became the most important place in the world. And he gave me a hint that he wants to be in Moscow in the same position as he was in China and in Vietnam. In other words, to be a free lance correspondent, representing the American newspaper *National Guardian*. It's a small 'progressive' pro-communist newspaper, which could give him accreditation because he still formally needed to be accredited. And then he told me that he could get these papers, he could officially be accredited in Moscow, but money was a problem, because no one would pay him money and he asked money from the Soviet Communist Party. He told me all these directly and said that it would be nice if I would be able to find the right man to discuss all this.

After travelling in Eastern Europe Burchett in 1956 again passed through Moscow before returning to Hanoi. Krotkov was now able to assure him that if he came to work in Moscow everything would be arranged. Some time later (according to Krotkov a 'couple years', in fact it was less than one) Burchett telegraphed that he and his family were arriving in Moscow. At first there was a hitch; Krotkov's KGB chief had changed from Krasilnikov to Churanov and details of the agreed arrangements had been misplaced. From what Krotkov could make out Burchett went in high dudgeon to see a representative of the Australian Communist Party then in Moscow. Matters were, however, soon clarified. The KGB provided Burchett with a handsome flat and Burchett's case was handed over to a former senior and highly decorated secret policeman, Victor Kartsev, who after the Khrushchev 'thaw' had been reduced to part-time work. Krotkov's relations with Burchett now ceased, except for a chance meeting at a petrol station where Burchett complained to him about Kartsev, whose manner and overt anti-semitism offended him. For his part Kartsev told Krotkov that the relationship was progressing satisfactorily. Krotkov learned that Burchett's KGB activities were under the overall direction of Colonel Barsegov, who ran the special section of the KGB concerned with foreign correspondents. Of Burchett's particular operations for the KGB after 1957 Krotkov claimed no knowledge.

When Krotkov's Washington testimony was published Burchett hotly denied the substance of his story, although not the former friendship with him. He knew of course that if Krotkov's evidence was accepted as substantially true then the case against him as a communist agent was closed and his reputation as an independent journalist shattered.

Because an evaluation of Krotkov's testimony is so obviously crucial to the understanding of Wilfred Burchett I have taken considerable pains to check wherever possible from available sources its accuracy. In particular I have tried to discover, in those cases where Burchett denied point blank details of the Krotkov evidence, whether it was Burchett or Krotkov who was telling the truth.

Let us proceed through the instances where the claim of Krotkov and the denial of Burchett can be tested. In his evidence at Washington Krotkov claimed that in 1956, in angling for money from the Soviet authorities, Burchett had told him that in China and Korea, while working as a freelance correspondent, 'he was supplied, he was paid by the Chinese Communist Party all that period'. Burchett in Sydney totally denied this claim:

> *Q:* During that period were you being paid by the Chinese Government?
> *Burchett:* Certainly not.

In China, he had, he said, lived exclusively on his 'substantial revenue from books'. He had not been paid in China for his journalism and while travelling there had paid even for his hotel accommodation. He had 'no relations whatsoever with the Communist Party of China'. As we have seen this was all quite untrue. In April 1951 Burchett had written to his father from Peking telling him that he was 'relieved of all financial cares' and was being treated as an 'honoured foreign guest writer' whose needs, including food and travel, were being supplied gratis by the Chinese communist authorities.

In his evidence at Washington Krotkov claimed that Burchett had told him that he had undertaken a secret mission to Pathet Lao territory under Vietnamese direction. Burchett once more flatly denied this:

> *Q:* Did you say to him, 'I must admit that even I was involved in one special assignment; I went secretly to the Pathet Lao squads twice.'
> *Burchett:* Nonsense...I was involved in no special assignments.

On this question, once more, Krotkov's memory seems accurate and Burchett to have been telling less than the truth. In December 1955 Burchett wrote to his father of an expedition to Pathet Lao territory in the company of a cook, student, doctor, interpreter and chauffeur. On 30 January 1957 he wrote to his father of the formation of a new government in Laos involving Souvanna Phouma and the Pathet Lao leader, Souphanouvong. 'I wish,' he wrote, 'it were true that it was "all my work", but I am very pleased that I did help it along a little.' Although the details here are not identical with Krotkov's memory they do reveal that Burchett was indeed involved in some special assignment involving the Pathet Lao in 1956 and 1957 at the very time Krotkov was acquainted with him.

Krotkov then claimed that at this time Burchett had told him: 'I am deeply involved in this struggle with the Americans, and I am doing my best.' Burchett flatly denied saying any such thing. Again there is every reason to believe Krotkov was telling the truth and not Burchett, for this was precisely the way in which Burchett was speaking of his work in the mid-1950s. In a letter to his father at this time for example, which concerned an extremely successful operation he was involved in against the Americans in Cambodia on behalf of the Vietnamese, Burchett wrote: 'I am feeling extremely happy at having helped put another spoke in America's world domination machine.'

Finally Krotkov remembered that Burchett had told him of some obscure involvement he had in the Petrov affair.

> *Sourwine:* Did Burchette [sic] tell you he had participated in the Petrov case?
> *Krotkov:* Yes, he told me that, it's correct.
> *Sourwine:* Did he tell you what part he played?

> *Krotkov:* It was not clear for me. But he gave me a hint, that
> was the first time, when we wanted to know his ability...
> Then he mentioned that he had his finger in that case, and
> he mentioned that in that case were involved the editor of
> the Communist newspaper Chaplin [sic] and one girl.

Burchett once more denied any such conversation, although
he admitted having introduced Krotkov to Rex Chiplin and to
having given him a broad outline of the Petrov affair. Yet once
again Krotkov's memory is to be preferred to Burchett's denial.
For indeed Burchett *was* involved in one extremely small and
obscure incident in the Petrov affair, which fits precisely
Krotkov's account. Burchett had introduced an agent of
Chiplin's, Mercia Masson (who was also working for the
police), to Ivan Pakhomov, an MVD officer and Tass representative, at a party arranged in his honour during his brief visit
to Australia in 1950. This detail emerged during Mercia Masson's testimony at the Petrov Royal Commission.

Readers may be interested in the level of reliability revealed
in Dr McCormack's contribution to the question of the
Krotkov testimony. According to McCormack Krotkov was a
fabricator of malicious lies aimed at harming Burchett, in
order to buy a haven for himself in the United States. His
charges were not only false but also 'trivial and absurd'.
Krotkov, McCormack claims, had for example invented an
utterly ridiculous story about the communist sympathies of
Burchett's father, who (he informed *Australian Society* readers
who presumably did not know old Burchett from Adam) 'was
a former farmer, lay preacher and sometime National Party
candidate in Victoria, a man whom nobody in Australia had
ever thought to accuse of being a communist'.

Really? Burchett senior published during the Korean War
pamphlets entitled *Will America Dominate the World?*, *That
Rascal Rhee* and *America's Threat to the World*. In mid-1953

he made a broadcast over Peking radio in which he hailed 'the magnificent leadership' of the Chinese Communist Party, congratulated them for a productive capacity which 'far surpassed the output of any highly industrialised nation of the West' and concluded that in the communist world he had seen 'the brotherhood of man in action'. 'The basic motivating force governing the relationship between the Soviet Union, the peoples democracies and China...is their desire to help one another...The greater the need the more generous the assistance.'

Again McCormack claims that amongst the 'more or less trivial or absurd charges' made by Krotkov was that the KGB had provided Burchett 'with an expensive flat and other privileges in Moscow and had paid him well. In fact, Burchett lived in an old apartment block (known locally as "Stalin's Folly")...and drove a second-hand car bought from a departing journalist.'

Here is Burchett's own description of his Moscow flat, taken from his correspondence with his father, a correspondence McCormack has studied: 'We have a very nice apartment of five rooms, wonderfully located in a modern skyscraper and looking out over the whole of Moscow, particularly the river which flows at our doorstep and the Kremlin.'

As for the second-hand car it was a 1954 Chevrolet with 25,000 miles on the clock. Both the flat and the car represented in conditions of mid-1950s Moscow extreme luxuries, beyond the wildest dreams of ordinary people, who lived at the time not in five-room apartments but five to a room.

On every point where they clash, and where a check has been possible, it is Krotkov and not Burchett whose memory is reliable; and, for those who know the evidence, McCormack's account of the Krotkov testimony is a joke. Krotkov as a witness in Washington was not only truthful as far as can be judged; he also revealed a remarkable memory for fine detail of fact and tone. There is every reason to accept his story of how he helped recruit Burchett in 1956–57 for the KGB.

LIFE AFTER STALIN

For many western communists the events of 1956—Khrushchev's 'secret' speech about the crimes of the demigod Stalin and the Hungarian Revolution which was bloodily suppressed by Soviet tanks—were shattering events. Not for Wilfred Burchett. The Twentieth Congress, where Khrushchev had named Stalin as a murderer, *deepened* his faith in the Soviet Union. It had, he wrote to his father, 'cleared up just about all those points which perplexed friends for many years…That is the marvellous thing, that they keep going over the record, admitting their mistakes in a loud, clear voice. That will be the day when Menzies goes back over his record.'

Burchett, moreover, *gloried* in the Soviet Army's crushing of the Hungarian Revolution or 'counter-revolution' as he preferred to call it. He explained the situation, thus, to his father:

> Due to the fact that Hungary was liberated from the Nazis by the Soviet Army and progressive forces came into power as a result of this, there never was a confrontation between the forces of revolution and counter-revolution until now. In the past counter-revolution has always been able to count on armed forces of neighbour states. This time, for the first time in history, it was the reverse…I know that it is difficult for progressives abroad to maintain their positions in such situations. It needs long memories like yours or a good global view of the situation.

Within a few months of Soviet military operations in Budapest the Burchett family had settled in Moscow.

Burchett's Moscow period—from 1957 to the early 1960s—is certainly the most dreary of his career. During this time, apart from whatever assignments he might have undertaken for the KGB, all that is known is that he wrote unreadable books publicising Soviet achievements in space and Siberia, and journalism for the *Daily Express* and the Moscow *New Times*. His reputation amongst Soviet officials and journalists remained, however, high. A Canadian newspaperman who was stationed in Moscow recalled that whenever in conversation the name of Burchett came up 'there was an inevitable ripple of interest and admiration...and a desire not to discuss the topic'. On the other hand, Soviet officials were also aware that Burchett was drinking like a fish.

During the early 1960s the great ideological dispute within the communist world between Moscow and Peking passed to the stage of open conflict. But at the end of his Moscow period Burchett totally (but secretly) supported the Chinese side. In March 1963 he wrote to his father from Peking in the following terms:

> I am very glad that you and Clive [Burchett's communist brother] have been supplied with literature. There is no doubt at all in my mind that this side is right and not just 80-90 per cent right but 100 per cent right. The fact that some high-ranking Australians have been paid to think otherwise...only confirms what I have thought for a long time...In my own position, I have to be extremely careful as you can imagine and you should show this letter only to a few really good friends. And those should not gossip about it.

Twice in this letter Burchett announced that the days of 'papal infallibility' were over and that henceforth communists would be 'forced to think for themselves'. This was as close to an understanding of his own Stalinist past as he was ever to get.

Wilfred Burchett's 'thinking for himself', that is to say his ideological journey from the Sino-Soviet schism until his death, can be briefly sketched. In the early 1960s as we have seen he secretly supported the Chinese line while publicly maintaining neutrality between Moscow and Peking and his valued connections and perquisites (including his Moscow flat) on both sides of the Sino-Soviet line. In the mid-1960s he supported the Chinese Cultural Revolution with, however, just a touch of doubt clouding his enthusiasm. 'There are some aspects of it all that I don't like very much,' he wrote in an otherwise extremely positive appraisal in late 1966, 'but then I am not Chinese.'

By the late 1960s Burchett had begun to see himself not as a covert Chinese supporter but as an independent operator *within* the communist world, and to fancy himself as a kind of honest broker *between* Moscow and Peking, possibly even to help bring them together for discussions after their clash on the Ussuri River.

In the mid-1970s, as we shall see, Burchett finally broke publicly with the Chinese, first by his support of the pro-Soviet elements in Angola and then by giving his full support to the Vietnamese in their invasion of Pol Pot's pro-Chinese Cambodia. (The Vietnamese quarrel with Pol Pot and invasion saved him a considerable embarrassment. In 1976 he had been planning a book on the Khmer Rouge when Cambodia 'opened up'. He thought his old friendship with Ieng Sary, one of the leading members of the Khmer Rouge, made it virtually certain he would be the first western journalist invited in.)

By the late 1970s Burchett was, then, once more a supporter of Soviet global interests, although by now the support he gave the Soviet Union was far more geopolitical and far less ideological in nature than it had been in the 1950s. While his allegiance to the communist movement *as a whole* remained absolute, by this time the only particular regime to have his perfect loyalty was the Vietnamese.

VIETNAM: COMING HOME

In the spring of 1962 Burchett travelled to Hanoi. He resumed his friendship with Ho Chi Minh and his work for the communist forces in Vietnam. The Vietnam War was destined to become the political cause of his life. It was also his salvation. At its beginning it offered him deliverance from the wilderness of Moscow; at its end his reputation—at least among the western intelligentsia—was high and his exile over. Vietnam represented Burchett's cultural homecoming, although (as with Mohammed and the mountain) it was not he who came to the culture, but the culture which came to him.

Burchett produced nine books in support of the Vietnamese communist cause in Indo-China, a vast output of journalism and a number of films. In no modern war had propaganda played so central a *strategic* role as it did in the Vietnam War. From the very early days Hanoi understood the importance of the struggle for the 'hearts and minds' of the American and western public. In this struggle Wilfred Burchett's role was second to no-one. The North Vietnamese understood his *military* value. When during the 1960s Burchett travelled behind National Liberation Front (NLF) lines he invariably travelled with a sizable armed contingent in support. 'The lengths taken to avoid dangers and discomforts,' he explained to his father before a trip into NLF territory, 'are really most embarrassing.'

Burchett's early writing on the political struggles in South Vietnam are no more sophisticated than their Korean counterparts. Take for example his treatment, in *The Furtive War*, of the strategic hamlet program. Burchett describes this plan, drawn up by the American Dr Eugene Staley, as one 'of which a Hitler or an Eichmann would have been proud,' as an 'atrocious attempt to uproot a whole nation'. The program compelled people to choose between living as 'concentration camp slaves' or fighting back. They were herded into the hamlets by the kind of police dogs 'the Nazis used to force their victims to quicken their pace into the gas chambers'. Naturally, 'the whole population opposed the action and the majority resisted it physically...When there were no...witnesses around, people were shot down like dogs'.

President Diem is portrayed as an Asian fascist and antinational puppet; his methods the most barbarous imaginable. 'No peasants in the world had so many dollars lavished on their extermination.' His prisons were 'medieval torture chambers'. They were reserved for all genuine Vietnamese patriots. When the anti-Diem forces revenged themselves on one of his agents 'there was a momentary gasp of horror when they pulled out one large drawer and found it full of human ears, in each case the left ear only, and stapled to each a paper with a name and a receipt for 5,000 piastres'.

Naturally, in these circumstances, 'the people' of South Vietnam decided to resist. His second book *Vietnam: Inside History of the Guerilla War* is a record of its emergence. At first resistance was spontaneous and sporadic. During 1960 it became organised with the formation of the National Liberation Front—an alliance, totally independent of Hanoi, of three equal political parties and all social classes and religious groups in the South. In its social policies the NLF favoured capitalism and modest land reform, with landowners fully compensated. As an administration it was a model of efficiency. Its field hospitals, for example, had a success rate of 98 per cent; people even from Saigon flocked to them. As a military machine it was a model of ingenuity, heroism and of merciful forbearance towards its enemies. Even mass murderers of the people were to be spared by the NLF 'if there was the slightest chance they might mend their ways'. Burchett tells of a case 'in a village of Ben Tre province in September 1961...a group of women talked an entire garrison into surrendering'. After a raid on a Diemist military post, he had been told by a participant, 'people actually wept for joy when we explained who we were'.

One of the specialities of Burchett's Vietnam writing was manichean contrast. The typical strategic hamlet is described thus: 'Houses were hovels, huddled together with no trees or greenery...no garden or fish ponds. A skinny old man, with a figure like an Auschwitz victim, acted as spokesman.'

Contrast the scene in an NLF village. 'The table was piled high with fruit and New Year sweetmeats and red paper streamers from the ceilings...A dignified, tiny old lady appeared...who [had] performed miracles of courage...' Guerillas captured by Diem are 'almost invariably tortured to death immediately'. A captured American tells Burchett how his captors 'patted my back...stroked my arms and generally made signs that I shouldn't worry'. The mental universe of these Americans, Burchett has discovered, is limited to concerns like the heavyweight boxing championships. 'Very different were the interests of the young soldiers and cares of the Liberation forces. Questions ranged over the whole world and discussions lasted far into the night.'

Instinctively Burchett understood that bathos, triumphalism and absurdity are no enemy of the propagandist. In 1966 he reported on how the North was bearing up under the American bombardment. Here is his conversation with a young man badly wounded in a bombing raid.

'What do you think about that?', I asked the lad. 'I would willingly give my leg or my life for my country,' he said so spontaneously and with such a warm smile that it was clear the words came straight from his heart.

When the Politburo in Hanoi speak of their women, 'Their faces take on an ecstatic look, their eyes go moist, their voices husky.' These women manage to remain 'exquisitely feminine...even when engaged in bayonet drill'. In a hotel in Hanoi Burchett discovers a western journalist slumped in dismay over his typewriter. 'I've come to write about their sufferings,' he groaned, 'but all they will talk about is "Victory".' And so on.

In 1965 Burchett's Vietnamese material really began to take off in the west. No longer a communist journalist destined to appear merely in the sectarian publications of the western communist movement or in Russian and Bulgarian translations, Burchett now suddenly found himself being vigorously pursued by the western 'capitalist' media. He had become fashionable. To judge by his correspondence of early 1965 he had arrived at a state of near euphoria. 'This looks,' he wrote home in January 1965, 'like the start of my most triumphal week since I started journalism.' A ten-part series of articles was about to appear in Japan. It was, he had been told, his best journalism ever. Even more importantly a television film he had made for the NLF when he travelled there with the French communist, Madeleine Riffaud, was taking the world by storm: 'The TV film had terrific success. In Paris, New York, Rome, West Germany, Switzerland, Canada, etc. A dozen countries so far and more negotiating. The film is 35 minutes and is really very, very good.' The Japanese alone had paid $3000 for it; and in the enemy capital itself the CBS network had bought it. In addition:

All sorts of picture magazines including Paris Match and Quick magazine of Munich are negotiating for rights for illustrated articles, the Daily Express is making its bid for black and white pictures and in general, things are very brisk. I am enormously pleased for all my friends 'down there' because they all worked hard to make the trip a success.

In 1968 Wilfred Burchett teamed up with a successful Australian film producer, Edwin Morrisby. Their first film was called *The Third Arrow*. As Morrisby subsequently explained the name came from 'a quotation of General Giap—the first arrow is Vietnamese history, the second is the Vietnamese people, the third arrow is propaganda'. This film was sold in Britain, Ireland, the Netherlands, all Scandinavian countries, Canada and the United States. In mid-1969 they teamed up a second time. Morrisby met Burchett at Phnom Penh airport.

> We left the airport terminal and walked to the car park. There the North Vietnamese produced a rather bulky envelope and gave it to Burchett. He opened it in front of me. It contained five bundles of American Express Travellers' Cheques. Wilfred flipped through one of them. They were all of $100 denomination and unsigned in the place where they should have been signed in front of the selling agent. There were between ten and twelve cheques in the bundle I saw. Wilfred didn't seem to mind that my cameraman and I had observed this. He put the envelope into his pocket.

His North Vietnamese companion spoke of 'un cadeau de vos amis' from Starigrad or Tsarigrad. Morrisby understood this to be an oblique reference to Moscow.

Of Burchett's propaganda successes of the 1960s none could outdo the visit of the prestigious *New York Times* journalist Harrison Salisbury to Hanoi in 1966 to report the impact of American bombing on North Vietnam. It is generally understood that Salisbury's reports had a profound impact on the climate of American opinion in regard to the Vietnam War. For some time, moreover, it has been known that in his reports Salisbury passed off officially released North Vietnamese material as if it were his own independent observations. What has not been known is that Salisbury's trip was arranged through the good offices of Burchett and that Salisbury was extremely grateful for what Burchett had done for him in Hanoi. On 7 February 1967 Burchett wrote thus to this father:

> For your *very private information* I will quote an extract from a letter I found awaiting me in Phnom Penh from Harrison Salisbury: 'I need hardly say that I am deeply grateful to you for the aid and assistance that you were able to give me in presenting my case to the Vietnamese authorities'.

Even more interesting is the fact that Burchett looked upon the Salisbury articles as a case of benign plagiarism. He explained to his son:

> Rainer, your suspicions were quite correct in your letter before last but that is not a thing to talk about. The main thing is the result. As you said Harrison said what I have been saying for a long time, but it is much more important that it is said in the New York Times.

Harrison Salisbury repaid his Hanoi debt to Burchett in 1981 by writing the introduction to Burchett's *Memoirs of a Rebel Journalist: At the Barricades*. Salisbury here threw his considerable weight behind Burchett's mendacious self-description (crucial to his work as a propagandist in the west) as a courageous loner, an independent-minded professional journalist, unattached to any government or ideology, fearlessly reporting contemporary history 'from the other side'. Salisbury concluded:

Burchett, thus, can be seen as sui generis, a radical who moves through a changing milieu, lending his sympathy to one cause after another not because of some Marxist doctrine, but because he believes in the underdog whatever the continent, whatever the color, whatever the creed. He is, in short, the iconoclast of contemporary radicalism.

After the Salisbury *coup* Burchett was greatly in demand by westerners wishing to visit Hanoi. The go-between in the exfiltration plans of 1953, Ed Hymoff, asked for his government's clearance before approaching Burchett in Phnom Penh for a Hanoi visa. Others were less circumspect. When Burchett arrived in New York in late 1968 as an observer at the United Nations, the State Department was informed that he had been approached by 'Harris of Hearst, Sheehan of ABC, Topping of NY Times, Foell of Los Angeles Times, Flora Lewis of Newsday'—all seeking his aid in opening the door to Hanoi.

Only one American visit to North Vietnam rivalled that of Harrison Salisbury's in political significance. In 1972 Jane Fonda travelled to Hanoi and there delivered eight passionately anti-American broadcasts over Radio Hanoi. According to a recent biographer, Wilfred Burchett could again claim the credit. Burchett had met Fonda in Paris and had become her Vietnam mentor. Not only did he inspire her trip to Hanoi; he also helped orchestrate the publicity campaign following it. When Fonda returned from Hanoi to Paris, and delivered a diatribe on the wickedness of her country, Burchett was at her press conference. A film released in Paris to coincide with her visit was interspersed with clips of US POWs interviewed by Burchett. When Burchett later in life landed himself in legal troubles in his homeland, Jane Fonda was one of the first contributors to his cause.

Readers will not be surprised that as in Korea so in Vietnam did Burchett take a special interest in the propaganda potential of interviews with American POWs. In 1964 he published interviews with four Americans who had been captured by NLF forces at Hiep Hoa training camp in November 1963. From 1966 he began interviewing, for purposes of journalism and film, US air pilots shot down in the North. These interviews were designed to demonstrate both the desperate criminality of US policy and the extraordinary humanitarianism of its victims. One pilot interviewed by Burchett was Colonel Guarino. After his release he recalled Burchett's role thus:

> One night in April of 1966 the Vietnamese came for me...They blindfolded me and put me in irons. When they took the blinders off me I was in a small room of a large building...I was introduced to a man whose name was given as George Graham, who, after a little while, I knew for sure was Wilfred Burchett. He proceeded to interview me. The entire interview was filmed but only a small piece of it was played in America and no attempt was made to hide his true name. Mr Burchett is a sly one. He is not very direct but asks questions in a manner which is certain to leave the desired impression on the viewing audience. The text of my interview was centred upon the implication that I was a war criminal...In late 1968 the Vietnamese showed us a movie-recorded interview of Burchett and USAF Lt Col Leo Thorseness...The flavor...was such to intimidate viewing aircrews who were involved in flying over North Vietnam. I felt that Thorseness had been tortured to involve himself in this theatrical but didn't know for sure until late '69 when I moved into a cell with him. Thorseness indeed confirmed that he was kept in strict solitary confinement, in irons and was beaten and maltreated until he agreed to the Burchett interview. The entire POWs community lived in constant fear of being selected by the Vietnamese to see Burchett and

others like him. They knew they would have to go through torture and be forced to parrot the commie line of lies and discredit our side and beef up the anti-war movement.

Burchett's links with the POWs were of great interest to the US government. According to information recently released under the Freedom of Information Act, in mid-1966 US authorities decided to make contact with Burchett through some of his western journalistic colleagues, to use him as a go-between in negotiations for POW release with Hanoi. Canberra was informed. As with the US exfiltration plan of 1953, the Australian government was far from enthusiastic. It believed Burchett to be a 'basically unstable and unpredictable person who might well rush into print or otherwise publically [sic] embarrass US and SVN [South Vietnam]'. The US government was determined, however, to press ahead. Unfortunately the released documents do not reveal the fate of their Burchett plans.

As this incident shows, by the late 1960s Wilfred Burchett had acquired a curiously ambiguous status in the west. Newspapers and television networks treated his despatches and documentaries as if they were impartial commentaries on military and political affairs in Vietnam. Governments and intelligence agencies regarded him as an agent or emissary of Hanoi. His interviews with North Vietnamese officials had acquired a semi-official diplomatic flavour. In February 1967, the Soviet premier, Kosygin, referred to Burchett's recent interview with the North Vietnamese foreign minister, Nguyen Duy Trinh, as a sound basis for peace. When Burchett was himself interviewed by western journalists—in 1968 in the *Far Eastern Economic Review* or the Montreal *Star*—the views he expressed were perused carefully inside the State Department for signs of any change of line at Hanoi. In 1971, when the secret talks between Dr Kissinger and Le Duc Tho temporarily broke down, Kissinger actually breakfasted with Burchett at the White House, in the mistaken belief that he might bring with him a message from his friends in North Vietnam. For years to come Burchett would dine out on that story.

In reality, however, throughout the Vietnam War, Burchett was far more valuable to Hanoi as an avenue of disinformation than as a diplomatic emissary. During the political and military struggles in South Vietnam, power on the communist side remained highly centralised. Ultimate power lay with the Politburo at Hanoi. Its immediate representative in the South was the southern branch of the communist or Lao Dong party—the People's Revolutionary Party. The PRP was, in turn, the dominant element in the National Liberation Front (created in 1960) and its successor the Provisional Revolutionary Government (created in 1969). Both were portrayed for public relations purposes (in South Vietnam as well as the west) as genuine, totally independent of Hanoi. In 1968 the NLF itself created the Alliance of National, Democratic and Peace forces, the so-called 'Third Force', as a means of organising the anti-Thieu non-communist intelligentsia in Saigon. It was a principal aim of communist propaganda during the Vietnam War to disguise the genuine power relationships between these political bodies.

As ever, Burchett did his duty. Throughout his Vietnam journalism the NLF and PRG were portrayed as genuine coalitions, quite independent of Hanoi. 'The NLF's leadership,' he told Tokyo *Shimbun*, 'is extremely independent...[It] alone can decide when and where an offensive can be staged.' Time and again he reassured his readers that after the withdrawal of the Americans and the collapse of its puppet, South Vietnam would become a strictly neutral country. Reunification with the north was decades distant. 'Neither the north nor the south

will be allowed to press unilaterally the reunification of Vietnam...It seems certain that both the north and south will
remain as two separate states for a considerable period of time
to come.'

In the new South Vietnam the interests of capitalists and
even landlords would be safeguarded. The socialism of the
north would not be imposed on an unwilling south. The leader
of the southern communists assured Burchett that his party
fought also 'for the interests of the upper class'. The 'Third
Force' was certain, Burchett argued on several occasions, to
play an important role in the future government of South Vietnam. 'On the question of reprisals,' he told the Montreal *Star*
in December 1968, 'I just don't believe there are going to be
any.' The NLF was run by 'very civilized, cultured people'.

Within months of the fall of Saigon all of this proved false.
Burchett now revealed that he had been involved in a decade
of dissembling. He asked a southern cadre about reunification.
Was it a priority? 'Of course it is,' he replied. 'In many
respects it has already been done. The whole country is liberated—we have total independence.' And what about the
imposition of socialism? 'All the elements are at hand to build
socialism...Even the national bourgeoisie and small com-
pradore bourgeoise in principle admit the necessity of taking
the socialist road.' What, then, of the powerful 'Third Force'?
Prime minister Phat told Burchett: 'The Third Force could
exist and have a role only as long as the enemy existed...it was
not very strong, not a real 'force'.'" What, then, of reprisals, of
the estimated 300,000 South Vietnamese who were incarcer-
ated in the horrible re-education camps in 1975 and
held indefinitely? Burchett quotes approvingly the view of a
communist cadre:

> With many of the senior officers, imperialism changed them
> into wild beasts. Our task is to turn them back into human

beings. The families of the junior officers and administrative personnel are very enthusiastic about the results of the courses. [When they return from re-education camps] they are polite and decent—they even give a hand with the housework.

According to a Northern Party historian, 'The Provisional Revolutionary Government was always simply a group emanating from the government of North Vietnam. If we had pretended otherwise for such a long period, it was only because during the war we were not obliged to reveal our cards.' Burchett had for long been one of the key pretenders.

LAST YEARS

As opinion against the Vietnam War hardened in his homeland so did the memory of Burchett's Korean War treachery fade—except amongst soldiers and the small anticommunist intelligentsia. Burchett prepared for a triumphal homecoming. As early as 1968 he was considering the initiation of legal action over his passport. 'When the Vietnam war is over,' he wrote to his brother, 'I'll come to Australia and fight them in the courts with Australia's Far East policy the main accused.' In the late 1960s a Burchett Committee was established in Australia under the auspices of the Soviet front organisation, the CICD. Burchett himself soon staged a sensational passport-less return to Australia, hoping no doubt that his landing might be to the 1970s what Egon Kisch's leap to the shore had been in the 1930s. He was generally pleased with the reception he received.

In fact the majority of the Australian Cabinet of prime minister John Gorton were already by September 1969 in favour of restoring Burchett's passport and only inhibited from so doing by the stubbornness of the then minister for immigration.

On the leader of the opposition Labor Party's famed pre-victory China visit (before Australia had recognised the People's Republic) a friend of Burchett's, Ross Terrill of Harvard, received a firm assurance from Gough Whitlam that when Labor came to power Burchett's passport would be immediately restored.

So it turned out. Within days of the Whitlam government taking office Burchett, the former 'exile' wrote to both Whitlam and the deputy prime minister, Dr Cairns (the leader of the anti-Vietnam War movement and a longstanding associate of Burchett's), offering to use his extensive contacts throughout the communist world for the benefit of Australian trade and diplomacy. At this time Burchett believed there was 'some offer of a job in the wind' with Dr Cairns which, if senior enough, he 'might be inclined to take'. As it happened nothing ever came of this. Some time later, however, the prime minister of Australia wrote to Burchett in the following terms:

> You would be better placed than most Australians to assess the new mood and spirit we have tried to bring to our foreign relations. Indeed, your own vigorous brand of journalism has done much to keep alive a fundamental goodwill towards Australia and ensure that the changed emphasis in our foreign policy is more readily understood and accepted in many parts of the world.

This is one of the more extraordinary letters written by a prime minister of Australia.

With the return of his passport, Burchett began legal proceedings to clear his name. Already in 1969 he had opened a defamation action against a leading critic in Australia—the outstanding journalist Denis Warner. This suit silenced Warner effectively but never proceeded to court. In 1974 Burchett changed tack. *Focus*, an obscure Democratic Labor Party magazine, had published an account of Yuri Krotkov's evidence. Burchett sued, and this time meant it. Krotkov refused to fly to Sydney to attend the case, but detailed evidence from him about Burchett's KGB connection, taken on commission in the US, was read to the court. From all over the world, witnesses—two defectors from the NLF, two captured American pilots who had encountered Burchett in Korea, several Australian POWs from the Korean camps—assembled in Sydney to give evidence about an extraordinary career. Outside the court, one witness, the former British POW Derek Kinne—who had been threatened by Burchett in a Korean camp twenty years earlier—lunged at Burchett and took him by the throat. Onlookers had to separate the two men. When the verdict was delivered it proved a bitter disappointment to Burchett. The court found that he had indeed been defamed by *Focus* but that its report was covered by parliamentary privilege. (Before the Burchett piece had been published, Krotkov's evidence had been read into the record of the Australian parliament.) Burchett lost his case and was responsible for massive costs—upwards of $60,000. Rather than pay, he began a second exile.

Burchett's last years were rather sombre. In 1975 he broke finally and decisively with the Chinese Communist Party (abandoning thus a long balancing act over the Sino-Soviet dispute) and threw his support behind the pro-Soviet forces in Angola. An old friend, the New Zealand pro-Chinese communist, Rewi Alley, thought he needed the money. 'What on earth,' he inquired of Burchett, 'Do you want to go to Angola for?' What indeed? In 1978 Vietnam invaded Kampuchea. Burchett had initially been a Khmer Rouge enthusiast. He had planned a book extolling the virtues of life in revolutionary Kampuchea. Its constitution, he had written, was 'one of the most democratic and revolutionary in existence anywhere.'

Now his 'Asian friends'—as he called them—'were at each other's throats—each waving the banner of socialism and revolution'. Burchett cut his ties with his communist outlet in the US, the *Guardian*, and gave Vietnam his wholehearted support. He became one of the leading publicists in the west of the Hitlerite evil of the Khmer Rouge.

Burchett lived out his final days in Bulgaria. One of his last articles poured scorn on the idea of any Bulgarian secret service involvement in the attempted assassination of the Pope. He also threw himself into the anti-nuclear peace campaign in Europe against NATO's installation of Cruise and Pershing missiles with a book entitled *The Shadow of Hiroshima*. Eventually his body gave way. He died of liver failure in September 1983. Journalist colleagues had rarely experienced a heavier drinker than Wilfred. His widow, notwithstanding, put it about that his death was most probably caused by the radiation he had taken in at Hiroshima, almost forty years earlier. Wilfred Burchett had worked single-mindedly, and with not a little success, for the communist cause over four decades. He would not have begrudged this last service.

CONCLUSION

Wilfred Burchett's postwar career was that of apologist for terror and judicial murder in Stalinist Eastern Europe and fighter for the communist cause in Asia, most importantly in Korea and Indo-China. In Korea his service to the communist cause involved propaganda, disinformation, indoctrination of POWs and collaboration in the creation and dissemination of false confessions. To say of Burchett—whose every syllable in Korea supported the communist side, whose journalism was distributed by them over official channels almost daily, who walked freely in the POW camps run by the communists and at their delegation's headquarters at Panmunjon, and who edited the germ warfare confessions of American pilots—that he was an objective reporter of the Korean War, who saw the war from the viewpoint of the 'suffering peoples' of Korea but reported on behalf of no government (as does Dr McCormack), is a misdescription of unusual preposterousness and gall. Burchett's service to the communist side would have been no less real and considerably less effective (and sleazy) if he had taken a rifle and gone to the front. The pen may not be mightier than the sword, but one pen well wielded is certainly mightier than one sword. Burchett well deserved the decoration which the North Korean Vice-President pinned on his chest for services during the Korean War.

In Korea, however, Burchett not only served the communist cause but also armies fighting in a war against his fellow countrymen. To argue at home against a war one (rightly or wrongly) considers unjust ought never be confused with fighting abroad alongside the enemies of one's country. In giving 'aid and comfort' to the enemies of his country at a time of war Burchett was in the deepest sense of the word a traitor.

At what moment the Australian government's resolve to so try him collapsed I do not know; however it is almost certain that if he had returned home in 1953 or 1954 he would have stood trial. Nor do I know the precise reasoning behind the decision in 1955 not to renew his passport. But how it can be seriously suggested that the Australian government owed him—after his performance in Korea—its protection and good offices abroad I simply cannot understand. In Korea Burchett broke all ties of faith and community with his countrymen. We will have fallen on very bad times when such behaviour can, without opposition, be called honourable and such a man an 'outstanding Australian'.

THE PETROV AFFAIR AND THE ELECTION OF MAY 1954

CERTAIN ALLEGATIONS about the impact on the May 1954 Australian federal election of the defection of the Petrovs form the most fundamental and enduring element in the Petrov conspiracy theory. While the conspiracy theorists may differ on many questions of fact and interpretation none would dispute the proposition that Mr Menzies, with the assistance of ASIO, consciously manipulated the Petrovs' defections for the purpose of achieving a coalition victory at the polls. Insofar as Australian students now know anything at all about the politics of the Petrov affair, what they 'know' is that Mr Menzies cunningly used Petrov to hold onto a political power that was inevitably falling from his grasp. After the Petrov defections and the election loss the Labor Party soon split. The potency of the Petrov affair for Australian political mythology lies in the suggestion that the long period of conservative political hegemony in Australia was only made possible by a swindle.

The electoral dimension of the Petrov conspiracy theory

consists of three distinct claims which can, at least for analytical purposes, be examined separately. The first of these is that Mr Menzies and ASIO saved up the Petrov defection for the election of 1954. While, it is claimed, Petrov would have been willing to defect at any time over a period of many months, ASIO, on behalf of Menzies, delayed his defection until election eve. In this view the director-general of ASIO Colonel Charles Spry and Mr Menzies, not Petrov himself, were the masters of the defection timetable. 'Although the Government had been aware of Petrov's desire to defect for several months,' the *Dictionary of Australian Politics* informed its readers, 'the defection was only announced on the eve of the House rising for the forthcoming elections.' Many years earlier Dr Evatt made the same point even more strongly.

> Petrov was nursed and nurtured over a period of years before his defection…the object of Dr Bialoguski and the Security Chiefs was that his defection was to take place only if and when required. In fact it is reasonably certain that Petrov would most gladly have defected and sought asylum at least twelve months previously.

The second claim about Petrov's role in the election of 1954 concerns the manner in which the Menzies government is alleged to have used the Petrov issue during the course of the campaign in April and May 1954. 'Prime Minister Menzies,' the *Dictionary of Australian Politics* continues, 'announced the defection and imputed the existence of a widespread Communist conspiracy network, reaching the highest reaches [sic] of the Labor Opposition, e.g., the private secretary to the Labor leader, Dr Evatt.' Dr Evatt had himself long ago argued such a view.

> The Zinoviev letter and the political manipulation and propaganda of the German fascists in 1933 *pale into*

insignificance [my italics] before what was done in the name of the internal security of Australia for the purpose of influencing the 1954 general election. Those responsible for the Tory victory in the British elections of 1924 or the Reichstag fire manipulation in the German elections of 1933 had at least some small excuse...because of the period of excitement but in the present case of Petrov the organisation of the affair was...careful, calculating, cold and callous.

The third allied claim concerns consequences, not intentions. According to this extremely widely held view the Petrov defection turned the election tide in 1954 and was responsible for the victory of the Menzies–Fadden government at the polls. 'The spy scare,' according to Professor Russel Ward, 'was sufficient to arrest the swing of popular opinion against the Government.' Earlier historians of the Petrov affair, Nicholas Whitlam and John Stubbs, claim even more precision than Professor Ward in their analysis of the electoral impact of Petrov. In what they believe to have been the last published Gallup Poll taken prior to Petrov's defection, the ALP commanded 52 per cent support. According to them, after the Petrovs' defection another Gallup Poll, held on 1 May, found coalition support to have soared to 57 per cent. 'There can be,' they continue unsurprisingly in the light of these 'facts', 'no question that a strong reason for the return of the Government was the Communist scare, a scare created by the Government itself.'

To assess the Petrov conspiracy theory and to determine the role the Petrovs played in the Australian election of 1954 three separate questions must be addressed. Firstly, did Mr Menzies, either alone or in association with ASIO, save up the Petrov defection until the eve of the election? Secondly, did Mr Menzies or his coalition colleagues use the defections during the election campaign to destroy the political credit of the opposition? And thirdly, did the Petrov defections actually determine the outcome of the Australian election of 1954?

I

The first of these questions can be answered, with least uncertainty, on the basis of the ASIO archives released in 1984. Between the end of 1951 and July 1953 ASIO had employed an agent, the Polish migrant Dr Bialoguski, ultimately with the intention of leading Petrov towards defection. At no time, however, between late 1951 and July 1953 did Petrov and Bialoguski discuss the question of defection openly. In July 1953, primarily as a result of intelligence information which friendly services had supplied to ASIO about unrest in several MVD stations abroad following the demise of Beria, ASIO decided to make an approach to Petrov, with the purpose of inducing him to defect. For this mission they selected not Dr Bialoguski but a more trusted Anglo-Saxon intermediary, Dr Beckett. In July, Beckett broached the question of defection with Petrov. Although he did not rise to the bait, ASIO in July 1953 was not unhopeful that Petrov might change his mind. A second Beckett–Petrov meeting for August was arranged but here Petrov steered clear of any discussion whatever about remaining in Australia. Beckett was now of the opinion that the prospective Petrov defection was a 'dead duck'. The idea, that if in July or August 1953 Petrov had indicated a willingness to defect then ASIO would have advised him to wait several months for the next year's general election campaign, is as implausible as the idea that Mr Menzies might have gone to the polls early if Petrov had defected in the spring of 1953. At this time the Gallup Poll showed that the coalition parties were likely to gain 45 per cent and the ALP 54 per cent of the popular vote.

By September 1953 ASIO clearly no longer held out much hope of a Petrov defection. After Dr Bialoguski went to Canberra, in the hope of being able to complain to Mr Menzies of ASIO's niggardly treatment of him, Colonel Spry summarily dismissed him from ASIO service. ASIO's interest in the Petrov defection was only rekindled in November 1953 when Bialoguski contacted them, in part with the news that Petrov and his wife were about to defect, and in part with the threat that if ASIO was not interested he would take the Petrovs to the newspapers. ASIO quickly decided to offer the Petrovs political asylum at once. Its intentions can be demonstrated by a simple detail. In early December 1953 ASIO rented a safe house for the period of one month as the proposed accommodation for the Petrovs should they decide to defect.

Between December 1953 and February 1954 Petrov, however, moved far more painstakingly slowly towards his defection decision than Dr Bialoguski in November had suggested to ASIO he would. In this period ASIO did all it could to lead Petrov towards defection, supporting two Bialoguski initiatives—one tempting him with the prospect of owning his own farm; the other employing Dr Beckett to encourage him to make contact directly with Australian security. Already in early January, Petrov—in conversation with Bialoguski—had indicated that if he was to defect he would do so in early April, after the arrival of his MVD successor. On 19 February Petrov finally agreed to Beckett's proposal of a meeting with Ron Richards of ASIO, but on 20 February apparently changed his mind. Their first meeting eventually took place on 27 February 1954. Richards offered Petrov political asylum, if he wished on that very night.

Between 27 February and 2 April Richards and Petrov were in frequent contact. The minifon wire recordings of their meetings were amongst the materials released to the general public. Far from revealing an ASIO holding Petrov's defection back, what they reveal is an ASIO increasingly anxious about Petrov's vacillation and fearful that, while he dithered, his freedom of decision might be destroyed by some punitive action against him taken by his colleagues at the Soviet Embassy. The wire recordings also reveal that Petrov's procrastination did not finally end until the night of 31 March–1 April, on the eve of the arrival of his successor. On that night two events—the chastisement of his wife at a party meeting and the raid on his own embassy safe and desk—clinched Petrov's defection decision.

Only if it is believed that ASIO fabricated hundreds of documents after Petrov's defection and destroyed hundreds of others and employed the services of Petrov, Dr Bialoguski, Dr Beckett and Richards (or actors to mimic them) to record a large number of tapes (incidentally containing certain material embarrassing to ASIO) can it now be believed that Petrov's defection was saved up for the election of 1954.

Nor is it possible to believe that Mr Menzies played any role at all in the timing of Petrov's decision to defect. Evidence of Menzies' involvement in the Petrov conspiracy has traditionally pointed to the events of September 1953 when Dr Bialoguski journeyed to Canberra in search of an interview with him. There is no evidence—old or new—that the man Bialoguski saw, Menzies' secretary Geoffrey Yeend, ever informed Mr Menzies of his conversation with Bialoguski. More revealing is the fact that the immediate result of their meeting was an act signifying the abandonment of hope in the Petrov defection—namely the dismissal of ASIO's greatest asset on the Petrov front, Dr Bialoguski.

Recent evidence from the ASIO archives (summarised in an article in the *Sydney Morning Herald* of 14 October 1993) has shown that Mr Menzies was informed by Colonel Spry of the

possibility of a Soviet defection on 3 August 1953, between
the time of the first and second Beckett approaches to Petrov.
Neither in his post-defection parliamentary speeches nor in his
memoir on the affair did Menzies refer to this meeting. Almost
certainly the explanation for Menzies' lifelong silence here was
his fear about how his tenacious political enemies might
exploit knowledge of such a meeting to press home their conspiracy charges. Menzies' reticence here is regrettable. But,
given the charged political atmosphere which accompanied
the Petrov affair, it is also understandable. Although his innocence would have been of little assistance to him if his enemies
had come upon details of this meeting, as a matter of fact it is
certain that Mr Menzies had nothing of substance to hide. It
appears from the new evidence that Colonel Spry did not even
mention Petrov's name at this meeting. It also appears quite
certain that he did not again raise the subject of the defection
with Menzies until 10 February 1954. If Spry's memorandum
is misleading on this point how is his willingness to mention
the 3 August 1953 meeting—an uncomfortable fact for Menzies —to be explained? And, again, if Menzies had been in any
way involved in the Petrov operation between August and
February how is it to be explained that in Spry's internal
memorandum, which he prepared for his meeting with the
prime minister on 10 February 1954, he refers to his task as a
'preliminary briefing'?

Once informed of the likelihood of Petrov's defection in
February, however keen Menzies might or might not have
been for it to occur before the election, it is difficult in the
extreme to see by what means he could have influenced, one
way or the other, the outcome of the delicate discussions which
occurred between Richards and Petrov from 27 February until
2 April. The evidence reveals beyond reasonable doubt that
it was neither Mr Menzies nor ASIO but Petrov himself who

ultimately determined the moment of his defection and that there was no time in 1953 or 1954 when ASIO would not have offered Petrov immediate asylum.

Even if, however, it is conceded that neither Menzies nor ASIO saved up the Petrov defection for the election (as the traditional conspiracy theory had suggested) might it not alternatively be argued that Mr Menzies delayed the election until the last legally permissible date in the hope of an eleventh-hour Petrov defection? In support of this theory a conspiratorial significance might be attributed to the fact that, on 10 February, Mr Menzies received his preliminary briefing on the possibility of the Petrov defection from Colonel Spry and that, two days later on 12 February , the Cabinet determined that the election should be held on the last possible day, 29 May.

Again, however, the sinister construction of these events crumbles on investigation. Firstly the decision to put the question of the election date to Cabinet on 12 February was not taken after but before the Spry–Menzies conversation on 10 February. On 9 February journalists already knew that this was to be an item on the Cabinet agenda of 12 February. Secondly, and more importantly, the 29 May election date was the obvious and logical choice for Mr Menzies and his Cabinet, readily explained without reference to a secret hope in Menzies' heart about an impending salvific Petrov defection. By early 1954, for the first time in two years, economic indicators—employment, inflation and import levels—were beginning to look favourable for the government. If an election had been held at any time in 1952 or 1953 the Gallup Polls suggest that the Menzies government would have been swept from office in a landslide. In February 1954, in a steadily improving economic climate, political logic suggested that the passage of as much time as possible could only improve the once-remote chance that a Menzies–Fadden ministry might be re-elected.

There was, in any case, in mid-February, no possibility of holding an election before, at the very earliest, the beginning of May. The Royal Tour of Australia, by the new Queen and her Consort, was not to come to an end before early April. It was, of course, inconceivable that it should be allowed to coincide with an election campaign, let alone an election. As election campaigns in Australia traditionally continued for three to four weeks, the earliest possible election date by middle February was early May. But as election manoeuvring was difficult to contain to the official campaign period even a date in early May would threaten to undermine the political truce both government and opposition parties favoured for the extent of the Royal Tour. Moreover, ironically as it turned out, in mid-February Cabinet would have been aware that to set an election date for early May, with a campaign beginning at the moment Queen Elizabeth departed Australia's shores, would have exposed the government to the charge of political opportunism. From every point of view 29 May was a sensible election date, irrespective of whether or not Mr Menzies might privately have dreamt of a Petrov defection.

II

It appears, then, clear that Mr Menzies neither saved up the Petrov defection for an impending election nor, alternatively, delayed the election until the last possible moment in the hope of an eleventh-hour Petrov defection. What, however, is to be made of the second charge—namely that once Petrov had defected Menzies and his colleagues ruthlessly used the fact during the election campaign to discredit Dr Evatt and, through him, the Australian Labor Party?

It is certainly true that Mr Menzies was very keen to announce Petrov's defection to the world before the Australian parliament rose for the election on 14 April. It would be naive to consider this keenness unrelated to the possible political advantages the defection might bring to the government parties in the forthcoming election. The Menzies government had twice unsuccessfully attempted—once by legislation which had been rejected in the High Court and once by a referendum which had been narrowly defeated by a popular vote—to dissolve the Communist Party. On both occasions the leading opponent of their attempt had been the present leader of the Labor Party, Dr Evatt. Evatt had also, more recently, led his party in opposition to the government's trade union secret ballots legislation, which many Australians regarded as having been crucial in the struggle against communist industrial power. The Petrov defection and Mr Menzies' revelations of 'systematic espionage and at least attempted subversion' could not but revive in the public mind memories of former battles between the coalition and Labor over the communist issue and were likely to convince many Australians that the government's anticommunist initiatives had been well-founded. On the evening of Mr Menzies' Petrov announcement many gallery journalists believed the government's electoral stocks had risen sharply. In the excitement of the moment one, at least, thought the Petrov announcement had already determined the outcome of the election. Frank Chamberlain wrote in the Melbourne *Sun*:

> The Communist plot now revealed by one of its leading diplomats so completely vindicates the Menzies–Fadden policy that the result of the elections is a foregone conclusion …Labor men are flabbergasted. They thought that Communism was a dead issue. They cannot accuse the Government of arranging the Petrov affair.

Given opinions such as these it would be foolish in the extreme to believe that in mid-April Mr Menzies was either unaware of, or embarrassed about, the political advantages which might be expected to flow to the coalition candidates in the forthcoming elections as a result of the Petrov defection announcement. This, however, is no great criticism. Despite his irritating habit of pretending never to stoop to mere political calculation, Menzies was, after all, a politician. Machiavelli had long ago commanded the Prince not to squander whatever good fortune Fate might throw in his direction.

Political advantage was, then, undoubtedly one motive propelling Mr Menzies towards a rapid defection announcement. It was not, however, his only motive. If Menzies had not announced the Petrov defection in April (as his critics suggest he should not have) it is difficult to believe that news of it would not anyhow have reached the Australian public—via the Soviet Embassy—before the election of 29 May. Earlier that year an MVD officer, Yuri Rastvorov, had defected in Tokyo and been flown to the United States. Within a week of his defection the Soviet Embassy in Tokyo had announced his disappearance, publicly claiming that he had been kidnapped and that he was being held against his will in Japan by agents of American intelligence. If the Soviet Embassy in Canberra had made a similar accusation to the Australian press the Menzies government would have been placed on the defensive and possibly even seriously embarrassed by opposition criticism, during the course of the election campaign, that it had behaved over Petrov in a dishonest and secretive fashion.

In the defection announcement and the establishment of the Royal Commission, Mr Menzies' misgivings about the character and reliability of Dr Evatt also, again, possibly played a part. By establishing the Royal Commission before the election, even if the Labor Party were to be successful at the polls,

Dr Evatt's hands—at least in relation to the broad juridical form of the inquiry into the Petrov material—had been tied. As with the failure to inform him in confidence of the Petrov defection when it occurred or that three members of his staff had been named in the Petrov documents, here again Dr Evatt had some justification for feeling that he was being treated with mistrust. He was certainly, however, not justified in believing, as he came to, that Mr Menzies or his colleagues had ruthlessly used the Petrov defection and the documentary material Petrov had brought with him for political gain in the election campaign of 1954. If anything, the opposite was the case.

By mid-April Mr Menzies was aware that Dr Evatt's present press secretary, Fergan O'Sullivan, was the author of one of the documents Petrov had brought with him, Document 'H', and that his private secretary, Allan Dalziel, had been for many years under study by Soviet intelligence operatives in Australia. Moreover, he was also aware by this time that O'Sullivan, Dalziel and Albert Grundeman, another member of Evatt's staff, had been cited as sources of information in Document 'J'—the document Petrov had told ASIO Rupert Lockwood had composed inside the Soviet Embassy in May 1953. If O'Sullivan's authorship of Document 'H' or the fact that he, Dalziel and Grundeman were cited as sources in Document 'J' had been revealed to the Australian public before the election, Dr Evatt would have had some genuine grounds for feeling aggrieved, if not for comparing the Petrov affair with the 'Zinovieff letter' scandal or the Reichstag fire incident. In fact Mr Menzies' behaviour gave him no such grounds.

A search through the metropolitan press of Sydney and Melbourne in the months of April and May 1954 has revealed only two indirect references that suggest any leakage of information concerning the involvement of Dr Evatt's staff in the Petrov materials. On April 15 the *Sydney Morning Herald* was able to predict, on the basis of what it called 'Canberra sources', that 'people closely associated with politicians would be named in the Petrov case. There is speculation that some members of Parliament may have to give evidence in the inquiry following the disclosure of these names.'

As so often in the mid-1950s, the best informed journalist was Alan Reid. Buried in an article of his concerning the Petrov affair in the *Sun-Herald* of 18 April is the suggestion 'that very important figures are involved—not key in them-selves, but key in that they would occupy if Labor were returned to power, posts from which they would have access to vital information'. Clearly one or two leakages had occurred in the early days of the defection. According to Whitlam and Stubbs, senior journalists in Canberra in the early 1970s remembered them as having come from the camp of Sir Arthur Fadden. Yet in these leaks no names—either of Dr Evatt or his staff—were revealed. The references were, more-over, buried in such a mass of sensational material that their impact on the electorate was almost certainly negligible.

There was, in addition to these vague but generally accurate leaks, one story which appeared in the Melbourne *Sun* and *Herald* on 22 April which suggested (as it turned out falsely) that Labor parliamentarians were directly implicated in Soviet espionage as 'the dupes of Communist agents'. Not surpris-ingly, this story, which both these Melbourne newspapers attributed to the 'North American Newspaper Alliance', par-ticularly angered Dr Evatt. However as no newspaper followed it up it is unlikely, to say the least, to have had any impact on the fortunes of Dr Evatt or his party. Moreover any suspicion that Labor politicians might be directly involved in Soviet espionage was carefully extinguished by Victor Windeyer, counsel assisting the Royal Commission, at its pre-election Canberra sitting. Windeyer told the Commissioners that there were, in the Petrov documents,

> two or three Members of Parliament mentioned. It is said of them that they are, in effect, worth remembering as possible 'in the dark' informants…They are not persons whom the public generally regards as of great importance…to the public life of the country…[They] sit on opposite sides of the Chamber.

The self-denying ordinance Mr Menzies and his Cabinet swore on 13 April concerning the suppression of names mentioned in the Petrov documents was scrupulously maintained throughout the period of the election campaign. When Mr Menzies was subsequently charged by Dr Evatt and his supporters with the most ruthless manipulation of the Petrov defection for political purposes, he not unjustly reminded his accusers of his decision to suppress the names of Fergan O'Sullivan, Allan Dalziel and Albert Grundeman. In October 1955 Menzies told the Parliament:

> I well remember the cynical but wise remark of a former Supreme Court judge…'You may think it is permissible to regard your opponent as a crook; but you must never commit the elementary error of thinking he is a fool.' The right honourable gentleman says…I was a crook. But why should he also charge me with being a fool?…When I made my announcement to the House about Petrov and the royal commission, I would have been, in the ordinary course, well entitled to quote a specimen of the documents Petrov had brought with him. If I had done this, the names of O'Sullivan, Grundeman and others, directly or indirectly associated with the right honourable the Leader of the Opposition would have become public property.

The fact that Dr Evatt eventually came to believe that the role of Petrov in the Australian election of 1954 made the 'Zinovieff letter' and Reichstag fire incidents 'pale into insignificance' showed—given the suppression of the names of O'Sullivan, Dalziel and Grundeman—an extraordinary absence of balance and common sense.

III

Clearly Mr Menzies and his coalition colleagues did not use the Petrov defections in the unscrupulous manner they might have—and in the manner Dr Evatt and his defenders have always suggested they did—in the election of 1954. What impact, however, did the Petrov affair in fact have in the 1954 election?

As the official campaign opening approached, Australian newspapers began speculating about the likely role of the Petrovs in the coming election contest. Political journalists were generally of the opinion that party-political argument about the Petrov affair was almost inevitably destined to become a major and possibly even the main issue of the coming election. The editorialists, however, had warned the parties not to allow the Petrov defections to become an election issue. Already both Dr Evatt and Mr Calwell had been chided for introducing a partisan note into the nation's Petrov discussions.

At the official opening of the coalition's campaign by Mr Menzies at Canterbury Memorial Hall on 4 May both the curiosity of the press gallery and the piety of the editorialists were to some degree satisfied. Everybody noticed that in his speech the name of Petrov had not passed Mr Menzies' lips— as it was not to do for the entire extent of the campaign. On the other hand, in offering the prime minister a vote of thanks, the treasurer and deputy leader of the government parties, Sir Arthur Fadden, rhetorically asked the audience whether, at the time of the Petrov Commission, they would prefer to see Mr Menzies or Dr Evatt in charge of the nation's affairs. According to the Melbourne *Age* after Sir Arthur's remark Menzies looked 'momentarily uneasy'.

Whether or not this was the case, on the following evening two senior coalition ministers again made passing reference to the Petrov affair. In Sydney, Sir Eric Harrison, the minister for defence production, criticised Dr Evatt harshly for representing communist trade unionists in the courts. 'This man,' he added, 'with this record now asks you to let him take charge of the Royal Commission into communist espionage.' On the same night, speaking in Hamilton in support of a young, obscure Western District grazier (Malcolm Fraser), Sir Arthur Fadden—while claiming that he did not wish to deal with the Petrov case—reminded his audience of Dr Evatt's record of appeasing the communist enemy and warned it that 'only the present Federal Government could be trusted to carry out with the rigour of the law the findings of the Royal Commission on espionage'.

Sir Arthur's hypocritical disclaimer made him an easy target for editorial criticism. Fadden was now chastised, as Evatt and Calwell had been before him, for introducing party politics into the Petrov affair. The *Sydney Morning Herald* was ironical about his performance; the strongly anticommunist Melbourne *Herald* openly censorious:

> When Mr Menzies opened his Government's election campaign, he refrained from making political capital out of the circumstances which have led to the setting up of a Royal Commission on the allegations of Soviet-inspired subversion in Australia. His colleague, Sir Arthur Fadden, would be well advised to follow the same line.

On the weekend prior to the election campaign Mr Menzies had advised Liberal Party state branches not to permit any mention of the Petrov affair to appear in their election material. Politically speaking, a partisan use of the Petrov defections would not only be unfair but might be seen by the electorate to be so. Legally speaking, after the executive council had agreed to form a Royal Commission on espionage, Mr Menzies evidently believed all discussion of the Petrov affair would involve breaching the rules of *sub judice*.

After the Fadden–Harrison remarks of 5 May it appears that Mr Menzies acted to enforce a Petrov gag on all coalition candidates. In October he told parliament :

> Early in the campaign it appeared that some reference had been made on a public platform. I at once communicated with every Government candidate in Australia—as everybody here can confirm—and said that as this matter would receive judicial investigation, I wanted it kept out of the political campaign. I have every reason to believe that this request of mine was scrupulously observed.

And indeed it was. Although a defensive Sir Arthur Fadden denied to the press that his Petrov reference at Hamilton had infringed any coalition agreement, he never again returned directly to the Petrov theme. Nor, after 6 May, did any other coalition candidate. Extraordinarily enough, even the anti-communist crusader W.C. Wentworth more or less held fire on the Petrov front.

Given that the coalition had determined not to refer to the Petrov affair on the hustings it was not, of course, surprising that the opposition also generally kept silent about it. Dr Evatt was almost certainly privately convinced that the Petrov defection had been timed for the election. Some advice, indeed, came to him—in particularly from a conspiratorially minded confidante, R. F. B. Wake, a former prominent ASIO officer with a deep grudge against Colonel Spry—urging him to seize the initiative on Petrov and campaign on the theme of a 'frame up', the theme that dominated the Petrov propaganda being produced in April and May by the Communist Party of Australia. Fortunately for the Labor Party Dr Evatt declined this advice. On 2 May Alan Reid claimed that Evatt had consulted widely in his party on the implications of Petrov and had come to the conclusion that 'he should watch his public statements most carefully'. Like Mr Menzies Dr Evatt did not mention Petrov during the course of his campaign.

To show that the Petrov defections and their implications went almost entirely undiscussed during the course of the 1954 campaign is not, of course, to show that it played no role in influencing the outcome of the election. While coalition candidates after 5 May avoided the Petrov affair altogether in their campaign, it is also true that they played the communist issue very hard in the election of 1954. Labor, the electorate was told time and again, had successfully frustrated the coalition's attempts to have the Communist Party banned and unsuccessfully tried to frustrate coalition legislation for trade union secret ballots. Nevertheless despite this Labor opposition, under Mr Menzies' anticommunist regime Australian industry and the Australian nation had prospered. Under Mr Chifley and Dr Evatt the Communist Party had almost, during 1949, brought the nation to its knees. One of the Liberal Party advertisements in Victoria argued that 'THE COMMUNIST CONSPIRACY WAS THE GREATEST CHALLENGE TO PROGRESS AND SECURITY DURING THE EIGHT YEARS OF FEDERAL LABOR GOVERNMENT ...DON'T GIVE THE REDS A SECOND CHANCE.'

The coalition not only played the communist issue hard, it also played it very personally. Dr Evatt might not be, it was argued, a communist himself or even a communist sympathiser but he was certainly the most powerful asset the communist cause had ever had in Australia. The electorate was asked to judge Dr Evatt by consequences not intentions. The central moment in coalition anti-Evatt propaganda came when Sir Arthur Fadden launched the Country Party's campaign. Fadden addressed to Dr Evatt a list of '13 questions'. His list began uncontroversially by asking Evatt whether he had been appointed Attorney-General on 7 October 1941 and ended by asking him whether he had opposed the government's secret ballots legislation, 'the most potent weapon yet placed in their hands to combat Communist domination'. In between it inquired of him whether he had released well-known communists from wartime internment; whether he had paid for an overseas trip for the communist leader Ernest Thornton 'out of taxpayers' funds'; whether he had represented communist trade unions in the High Court; and whether he had campaigned 'vigorously against the Menzies Government's constitutional referendum designed to provide safeguards against Communist espionage, sabotage and subversion'.

In general the superior metropolitan press—the *Sydney Morning Herald* and the *Age*—steered clear of endorsing the more strident aspects of the Fadden–Wentworth anticommunist campaign, finding (as we shall see) other grounds on which to base their support for the coalition. On the other hand, the more popular press of Sydney and Melbourne, the *Daily Telegraph*, the Sydney *Sun*, the Melbourne *Herald* and *Sun*, all strongly and indeed enthusiastically supported the Fadden tone. In the final week of the election campaign the *Daily Telegraph*, evidently fearing a coalition electoral defeat, even (this was unusual) briefly gave the communist issue a pre-eminent place in the case for the return of the Menzies government.

Clearly Dr Evatt and the Labor Party were deeply concerned about the role the communist issue might play in determining the election outcome. On the day after Fadden's challenge to him Dr Evatt—in one of those characteristic public storms where emotion overcame prudence—made an impassioned broadcast over national radio in which he spoke of his opponents as the 'vilest liars', 'smearers and slanderers' in the world. His voice, according to the *Age* report, was 'trembling with anger'. On this evening Evatt almost broke his self-imposed Petrov taboo. 'Very odd things,' he told an audience at Dandenong, 'have been happening in the Australian Parliament in connection with the timing of important events.'

In general, in order to answer the charge of frustrating Mr Menzies' anticommunist program, the ALP adopted for the 1954 election a very strongly anticommunist line of its own. While the coalition merely talked of opposition to communism, the Chifley-Evatt Labor government, it claimed, had acted. Under Menzies, Dr Evatt pointed out, no communists had been arrested or imprisoned, whereas under his Attorney-Generalship several had been. Why, Arthur Calwell asked on numerous occasions, had the Menzies government issued passports to communists to allow them to travel to China during the Korean War? Why was a well-known communist leader, Laurie Aarons, even now meeting with other communists in Indonesia? When, Stan Keon continued, would Casey clean out the 'nest of traitors' in the public service he had spoken of two years earlier? The most effective weapon against communism in the trade union sphere, Labor claimed, had not been secret ballots but the long, persistent organisational struggles of the ALP's Industrial Groups, which had been formed in order to break communist influence in the trade unions. The coalition might pretend to oppose communism but they, in fact, secretly needed to preserve it, in order to have it on hand for election campaigns. All communists knew that the greatest destroyer of communist hopes in Australia would be a strong and effective Labor government—a government of the workers. As the campaign drew to a close ALP anticommunism was an increasingly frequent aspect of its advertising. In his final remarks to the electorate Mr Menzies actually made no reference to the communist issue, while Dr Evatt reminded voters that 'the Labor Party fights and has always fought Communism'.

Communism was, then, an issue in the election of 1954 as it was in every Australian election between 1949 and 1969 and as it certainly would have been in 1954 whether or not the Petrovs had defected. It is, of course, likely that the Petrov defections gave it a greater prominence and sting than it might otherwise have assumed in the campaign, although, as we shall see, it was certainly not the most important 1954 election issue. It is also likely that when in 1954 the politicians cried communism the people thought Petrov and that, to some degree, thinking of the Petrov affair and its implications aided the coalition with its strongly anticommunist rhetoric and program and harmed the opposition with its more ambiguous record on the issue.

It can, of course, have done no harm to the government's electoral prospects that in the middle of the penultimate week of the campaign the newspapers were again dominated by the Petrov affair, this time by reports of the first three days' hearings of the Royal Commission on espionage, held in a specially redecorated concert hall in Canberra before a tense and expectant audience which included a large part of the diplomatic corps and sixty Australian and foreign journalists. It would, again, be naive to believe that Mr Menzies and his colleagues were unaware of the possible political advantages of a pre-election sitting of the Royal Commission. On the other hand, in fairness to them, it must be pointed out that the government, in the latter half of April, came under considerable newspaper pressure to convene the Royal Commission with the least possible delay. In the week following Mrs Petrov's defection the Melbourne *Herald* ran what amounted to an editorial campaign on the need for an early Commission and, even before that, a press interview with the Petrovs. 'For the peace of mind of our own people,' it editorialised on 20 April, 'the start of the Commission's tasks should be expedited.' On 23 April it ran a front-page editorial hostile to the government entitled 'End All This Secrecy'. Three times in the week following Mrs Petrov's defection in Darwin the *Age* editorialised on the same theme. 'There should not be,' it argued, 'a moment of avoidable delay in telling the people in broad outline what it was that Mr Petrov disclosed to the Government.' On 23 April even the most 'left-wing' political commentator to be found in the metropolitan dailies, Peter Russo of the *Argus*, argued for all haste in convening the Petrov enquiry. 'The sooner the Royal Commission gets down to business the sooner shall we be able to see the Petrovs in correct dimension.' It is perhaps, in the circumstances, unreasonable to have expected Mr Menzies to forgo the political advantages of an early Commission sitting in order to run the risk of serious editorial and possibly even opposition criticism.

It is certainly true that, in the pre-election hearings of the Commission, evidence which might have embarrassed the government was withheld—most importantly that Petrov had been paid £5000 on his defection. (Whether it was withheld for that reason is another matter.) But it is also true that material which would certainly have damaged Dr Evatt and Labor—the names of the author of Document 'H' and the sources of Document 'J'—was likewise deliberately withheld. Moreover, as we have seen, in these hearings Windeyer made a point of assuring the Commissioners and through them the public that no Labor parliamentarians were implicated in Soviet espionage. The fairmindedness, the solemnity, even the dullness of the first days of the hearings (where the Petrov couple had not been called to give evidence) more than satisfied even the strongly anti-McCarthyist Melbourne *Argus*, which supported Labor during the campaign.

> There was an air about the opening session of the Royal Commission on espionage yesterday that should have done Australian hearts good...In some hands, this investigation *could* become a heresy hunt...Australia is lucky that its judicial system is modelled on the British system, which is about as decent and honest an instrument of justice as any that mankind has yet devised.

In the election campaign of 1954 it cannot be emphasised too strongly that it was not communism, let alone Petrov, that was the dominant issue. The overwhelming issue, which in reality swamped all others, was Dr Evatt's startling proposals—made in his campaign opening on 6 May—for the extension of the welfare state in Australia. In brief Dr Evatt promised, if Labor were elected to office, to abolish the means test on old age pensions within the life of a single parliament, to increase at once the rates of old age, invalid, widow and repatriation pensions and child endowment, to provide a form of universal medical insurance, to increase commonwealth finance for road building and to provide, through the Commonwealth Bank, housing loans at 3 per cent repayable within forty-five years. He pledged to cut sales tax on certain items (in particular home furnishings) and even to make certain cuts in direct taxes. His program, he claimed, could be financed through eliminating government 'waste and extravagance', from an expected budget surplus, through loans raising and by diverting the cost of the commonwealth works from annual revenue to the Loans Fund. In his campaign opening Dr Evatt did not offer any overall cost estimate of his program, let alone an itemised account.

Shibboleths of the past—in particular all discussions of socialism and all undertakings to nationalise certain industries—were carefully avoided. (He signalled clearly, for example, that bank nationalisation would not be revived.) In pledging the abolition of the means test and arguing that it penalised thrift, and in appealing to the needs of the home buyer, Dr Evatt was both employing Liberal rhetoric and attempting to outbid the coalition in the quest for the 'middle class' electorate. In his campaign Dr Evatt tried to move his party from the Age of Chifley to the Age of Whitlam in a single stride. His program of 1954 was a bold and dramatic gamble.

With the metropolitan press of Sydney and Melbourne Dr Evatt's basket of promises went down like a lead balloon. Almost with one voice (if not one tone) the editorials argued that the Evatt program was little more than a cynical attempt to bribe voters. Australians no longer believed in Father Christmas. How were the costs of Dr Evatt to be met? Was Australia now destined to return to the inflationary spiral from which it had so recently and so painfully escaped? The Sydney *Sun* thought Dr Evatt's 'fairy floss' proposals would drive Australia into a 'bottomless pit of inflation'. The Melbourne *Herald* compared the Menzies–Fadden 'business-like management' with Dr Evatt's 'wild cat finance'. The *Sydney Morning Herald* thought Evatt's election speech 'the most irresponsible ever delivered to Australian voters'. The *Age* spoke in the *lingua franca* of the metropolitan dailies when it commended voters to ask themselves 'whether it is wise to risk a growing stability and prosperity...for a shadowy future in which the prospect of a return to inflation looms large'.

Dr Evatt's campaign speech provided Mr Menzies with the opening he needed. Dr Evatt's proposals were, he announced, 'the most disgraceful' he had encountered in twenty-six years of political life, an insult to the character and intelligence of Australians, certain (if implemented) to plunge the nation into economic ruin. A high official of the Treasury had, on his instruction, made an estimate of the cost of Evatt. The figure he had arrived at, Mr Menzies told an audience in Brisbane, was £357,800,000. Three days later Sir Arthur Fadden, in his campaign opening, provided a rather devastating critique, from the Treasury point of view, of what he called 'Dr Evatt's crack-pot financial revolution'. Evatt's pledges would cost the people an additional 40 per cent to 'the total tax revenues in the present year'. The money would have to be raised either by credit expansion, the use of the printing press and consequent inflation, by diverting loan funds from the states, or by vast increases in direct or indirect taxes.

Labor, through Calwell and Senator McKenna, naturally promptly provided alternative costings to the coalition's 'faked figures' and attempted to demonstrate the fiscal responsibility of their leader's strategy. Nevertheless for coalition candidates Dr Evatt's welfare state program provided the most promising line of attack. Some, taking their lead from the prime minister, linked Dr Evatt's profligacy with the anticommunist motif by suggesting that communism would feed upon the inflation and economic ruin Labor would visit upon the nation. Alternatively, Sir Eric Harrison told an audience of seven, which gathered to hear him at Mitcham, that under Labor living standards would fall to those of Russian peasants, while W. C. Wentworth thought Dr Evatt might prove the Australian Kerensky.

There is also, however, no doubt that certain government members and supporters feared the electoral impact of Dr

Evatt's promises. As the campaign neared its end one pro-coalition newspaper—the *Sunday Telegraph*—panicked and called upon Mr Menzies to 'get in and fight', that is to say to offer the electorate something more tangible than his record of steady and responsible economic management. The prime minister refused to join in what he called a public 'auction'. He could not help it 'if the Australian electors care to abandon solid prosperity and security for a wild-cat policy which will eventually destroy them'.

IV

On 29 May Australians went to the polls. Some 50 per cent of the electorate supported the Labor Party and some 47 per cent the coalition.* (A little over 1 per cent voted communist and a little under 2 per cent for independent candidates.) Because of the closer concentration of Labor voters the coalition was returned to government although with a reduced majority. After the election of 1951 the coalition had sixty-nine seats in the House of Representatives and Labor fifty-two seats; after the election of 1954, sixty-four and fifty-seven respectively. If five additional coalition seats had gone to Labor, Dr Evatt would have been prime minister with a majority of two in the lower House.

It has long been an article of faith of Dr Evatt's supporters and Labor stalwarts that the result of the 1954 election was

* According to the final result 50.03 per cent of valid votes were cast for the ALP. In fact, this figure slightly exaggerates the real level of Labor support. In 1954 six constituencies were uncontested, five of them 'belonging' to the coalition and one to Labor. Moreover in three contested constituencies there were no coalition candidates, only independents and communists. If the potential coalition voters had not been, as it were, statistically disenfranchised, Labor would have polled slightly less than the magical 50 per cent.

determined by the Petrov defections. In 1974 Nicholas Whitlam and John Stubbs, in their *Nest of Traitors*, attempted to prove this faith was not unfounded by reference to the Gallup Polls. According to them, following the Petrov defections, there occurred 'a complete reversal of the drift of public opinion'.

> Before, the Labor Party had every chance of forming a new government...the last published opinion sample had shown the Opposition party commanding 52 per cent of the vote. Now a Gallup Poll published in the *Sydney Morning Herald* on 23 May showed a remarkable switch in popular sentiment. The survey, which had been completed on 1 May, indicated that the Menzies Government had the support of 57 per cent of the voters.

If the facts indeed were as outlined by Whitlam and Stubbs the case about the role of the Petrov defections in the election of 1954 could be closed. In reality their case rests upon two obvious errors. What they claim to have been the last Gallup Poll taken before the Petrov defection announcement was taken in mid-February 1954. It revealed support for Labor (including, as Gallup always did, the communist vote) at 52 per cent and support for the coalition at 47 per cent. In late March 1954 (apparently unbeknown to Whitlam and Stubbs) Gallup polled the nation again. It now discovered that support for Labor (including the Communist Party) had declined to 49 per cent, while support for the coalition had actually increased to 49 per cent, with 2 per cent of the voters preferring independent candidates. In late March 1954—before the announcement of the Petrov defection—support for the coalition (at least as measured by the usually accurate Gallup) was actually considerably higher than it proved to be at the election of 29 May.

Even if Whitlam and Stubbs are wrong, then, in their first contention—that the ALP had a clear electoral lead until the Petrov defection announcement—what is to be made of their second contention, namely that after the Petrov defections a Gallup Poll taken on 1 May showed coalition support to have soared to an extraordinary 57 per cent of the popular vote? Surely this, by itself, should constitute proof that the Petrovs swung the election. The trouble here is that the 57 per cent claim is sheer fiction, based upon a misreading of a Gallup Poll finding, published not (as the authors claim) in the *Sydney Morning Herald* but the *Sun-Herald* of 23 May 1954. What this article showed was that in fifteen city electorates which had voted solidly Liberal in 1951 (seven with a poll of less than 55 per cent, eight with a poll of between 57 and 61 per cent) 57 per cent of the voters on 1 May and 56 per cent on 15 May intended to vote Liberal in the coming election. This level of support, Gallup estimated, would be sufficient to return the government to power. Apparently either Whitlam or Stubbs took the headline of the article ('Gallup Poll Favours Return of Government') and glanced at its statistical table but omitted to read it. From this misreading the Petrov myth was proved for a new generation of students!

The following statistical table—which combines electoral results and Gallup Polls—may help begin to chart the ebb and flow of opinion between the Representatives election of 28 April 1951 and that of 29 May 1954.

	Liberal-Country Party	ALP*	Others
April 1951—Election, H. of R.	50	49	1
August 1951—Gallup	49	50	1
October 1951—Gallup	45	54	1
February 1952—Gallup	47	52	1
May 1952—Gallup	43	56	1
October 1952—Gallup	40	59	1
February 1953—Gallup	39	60	1
May 1953—Election, Senate	44	54	2
June 1953—Gallup	45	54	1
September 1953—Gallup	45	54	1
December 1953—Gallup	48	51	1
February 1954—Gallup	47	52	1
March (late) 1954—Gallup	49	49	2
May (early) 1954—Gallup	50	49	1
21 May 1954—Gallup	48	51	1
29 May 1954—Election, H. of R.	47	51	2

From this table the following (necessarily tentative) conclusions can be drawn. During the second half of 1951, following the so-called 'horror budget', coalition support declined sharply, although it had improved slightly by early 1952. In late 1952 and in particular in early 1953, in an extremely serious economic climate (with unemployment, inflation, taxation increases and import restriction only the largest

* All ALP statistics here include the communist vote. This was the Gallup practice of the 1950s, based on the fact that at this time the Communist Party invariably directed their preferences to the ALP.

problems) coalition support declined to probably the lowest level—39 per cent—experienced by the non-Labor parties since the Great Depression. By the May 1953 Senate election coalition support was beginning to pick up, although not yet sufficiently to save the coalition from landslide defeat at a general election. This remained the position in the spring of 1953.

By December 1953, for the first time in more than two years—as the austere Menzies–Fadden economic policies began to bear fruit—the coalition appeared to have some real chance of success at the next general election. This possibility was made clear to the nation by the more solid Country Party victory at the Gwydir by-election, where the coalition vote almost returned to its 1951 general election level. In February 1954 the Gallup Poll recorded a slight swing back to the Labor Party. (On this poll the entire statistical base of the Petrov-turned-the-election case rests.) However, in late March 1954, at the climax of the triumphal Royal Tour, coalition prospects looked extremely good—with the conservatives and Labor both polling at 49 per cent, enough to secure a comfortable government victory. After the defections of Petrov and his wife the Gallup Poll of 1 May showed a marginal (1 per cent) increase in support for the coalition, although no percentage decline at all in Labor support. Possibly—and this is as much as can be ventured—the dramatic events were responsible for delaying the drift back to Labor of some of the support the coalition had gathered during the Royal Tour. It appears that during the official election campaign of May some support did move back to Labor, although, as it happened, not quite sufficient for it to secure victory. Perhaps the number of swinging voters attracted by the Evatt program was larger than the number of those fearful of its consequences. Perhaps the passage of time dulled the temporary pro-coalition effects of the Royal Tour and the Petrov dramas, with the electorate returning, roughly, in May 1954, to the position of December 1953.

In the rise of the coalition from the dismal 39 per cent of February 1953 to the 48 per cent of December 1953, a level of support which more or less held until the election of May 1954, clearly the dominant underlying factor was the perceived success of government economic policy. By late 1953 and early 1954 all the major indicators—inflation, unemployment and import levels, trade and budget balances—were looking favourable. (On the eve of the general election even the pro-Labor *Argus* felt compelled to congratulate what they hoped would be the outgoing Menzies–Fadden Ministry on its economic achievements.) The movement of opinion to the coalition in March and April 1954 appears, at least on a survey of the polls, to have begun not with the Petrov defections but with the Royal Tour. The standard case, that these defections were solely responsible for turning a certain Labor victory into a narrow defeat, is at best a vast and misleading oversimplification.

THE SELF-DESTRUCTION OF DR EVATT

ON 13 APRIL 1954 Mr Menzies had in his possession the knowledge that Dr Evatt's press secretary, Fergan O'Sullivan, had been the author of Document 'H'. He also knew that Evatt's private secretary, Allan Dalziel, had been the subject of MVD study over many years and that another staffer, Albert Grundeman, had been cited as a source of information in Document 'J'. His private resolve that these names would not be revealed before the election had on that day been translated into a binding Cabinet commitment. It is not necessary, of course, to believe that the motive for the self-denying ordinance Mr Menzies took in Cabinet on 13 April was solely or even mainly one of political honour. Menzies was probably highly conscious that any appearance of manipulation of the Petrov defection for party-political gain exposed him to censure not only from his opponents but also from his friends, for example from the conservative moralists who wrote editorials for Australian newspapers in the mid-1950s. Sometimes in the life of politics, honour and prudence may dictate the same course of action.

Not everything that occurred in Cabinet on the morning of 13 April appears to have been quite so honourable as the decision to suppress the names mentioned in the Petrov documents until after the election. By the late afternoon of 12 April Mr Menzies had decided that the Soviet ambassador would be officially informed of the Petrov defection at noon on 13 April and that he would make his announcement to the parliament, during the course of question time, at 2.30 p.m. As late as 11.30 a.m. on 13 April External Affairs cabled this timetable to Moscow. For some reason, however, around lunchtime on 13 April the decision was taken to delay the parliamentary announcement of the defection from 2.30 until 8 p.m. Why?

On the morning of 13 April, before Cabinet, Harold Holt, who was acting leader of the House, was informed by Arthur Calwell, the deputy opposition leader, that Dr Evatt would not be in Canberra for the parliamentary sitting that evening, having agreed to attend a function held by his old school, Fort Street High. It appears that the impending absence of Dr Evatt from the House, of which Holt no doubt informed Menzies, determined the change in timetable. As planned the Australian Embassy in Moscow was informed of this change at noon on 13 April. However, before Dr Evatt's departure from Canberra at 5.30 p.m., the government had given the opposition no warning that an important announcement was to be expected that evening. Shortly before the announcement was due, Evatt's office was phoned. As expected the caller was told he was in Sydney. In Evatt's absence Calwell was informed of what was to take place. Dr Evatt himself did not hear of the Petrov defection until an hour after Menzies' announcement to the House. He was caught badly off balance.

At the best of times Dr Evatt was a prickly and suspicious

character. It boded ill that from the first moment of the Petrov defection announcement he felt, not unjustly, that he had been treated dishonourably. While later defenders of Mr Menzies would struggle valiantly to find an innocent explanation for his failure to inform Dr Evatt of the announcement to be made in the House, one of Menzies' close friends and colleagues, Percy Joske, knew that Evatt had 'some justification for regarding himself as ill-used' over the events of 13 April. As for Evatt himself, although he was not aware that the defection announcement had actually been delayed for five and a half hours apparently on his behalf, he never forgave Menzies this original discourtesy.

Already by the morning of 14 April a divide between the position on the defection Dr Evatt felt obliged to adopt for the public realm and his private bitterness about the defection and its timing had appeared. The morning newspapers carried his brief press release of the previous evening in which he offered his party's full support for a thorough judicial investigation. On the other hand the commonwealth driver, Gordon McPherson, who took him to Mascot that morning revealed to someone (who was an ASIO informant) that on the way 'Dr Evatt had given the impression that he regarded the "Petrov disclosures" as a lot of bull'. In parliament on 14 April Dr Evatt repeated his support for the Royal Commission, especially one that could lead to the prosecution of traitors, and stressed the importance of a 'non-party' approach to the matter. Only the expression of his irritation at not being informed of the announcement before going to Fort Street revealed his inner tension. Yet when he phoned Colonel Spry to request an immediate interview on the affair his explosive mood was clear. Dr Evatt complained bitterly about the previous day's events. Spry explained he had been instructed to pass all requests for information to the prime minister. Evatt paused and then banged down the telephone. It was the last time Spry and Evatt spoke.

Deep mistrust of Dr Evatt's character (whether justified or not is another question) explains at least in part why he was not told in confidence about the Petrov defection when it occurred; why he was not informed before the election of May 1954 that the names of three members of his staff had been found amongst the documentary material Petrov had brought with him; and why Mr Menzies instructed Colonel Spry not to deal with him directly over the defection. It can, of course, never be known whether the leader of the opposition would have been briefed more fully on the Petrov defection if Mr Chifley had been alive at the time or if Mr Calwell and not Dr Evatt had succeeded him. No doubt being treated as an untrustworthy character and in one instance with pointless discourtesy rankled Dr Evatt deeply. Even more importantly for the future politics of the Petrov affair, in a psychology such as his, personal grievance was rapidly converted to dark suspicions of a conspiracy directed against him.

On 16 April the tension between Dr Evatt's public and private selves was rather startlingly revealed when on the basis of Mr Menzies' utterly innocent exposition to a journalist of the principles of parliamentary privilege (in answer to a question about whether Australia had any equivalent of the American 'Fifth Amendment'), Evatt compared Menzies unfavourably to Joe McCarthy.

> Mr Menzies had...made the sly insinuation that members of the Parliament might be called as witnesses...It resembles the 'smear' technique employed by some of Menzies' supporters...[He] disclaims McCarthyism in his background statements to the Press. But this much must be said for Senator McCarthy. At least he makes his own charges...under his own name.

Not surprisingly or unjustly Mr Menzies characterised Dr Evatt's complaints as 'curious', 'hysterical' and 'meaningless', and added: 'If Dr Evatt's statement is a fair sample of what he regards as a non-party contribution, then the election should be a pretty lively one.'

Although Dr Evatt quickly reined himself in, his outburst of 16 April was the first public sign of the storm that was to come after the election of 29 May.

II

For a fortnight after the Canberra hearings in May of the Royal Commission on Espionage, Dr Evatt's press secretary, Fergan O'Sullivan, kept secret from his employer all knowledge of his authorship of Document 'H'. Only on 3 June 1954, five days after the election, did he pluck up the courage to make his confession to Evatt. Why, one of the Commissioners would later ask him, had he not confessed to Dr Evatt sooner? Confession to a man like Evatt, O'Sullivan replied, no doubt truthfully, was not an easy matter. Dr Evatt's reaction to O'Sullivan's news was predictably and characteristically explosive and violent. He dismissed O'Sullivan from his service at once. A letter from him formalising the situation, which was sent on 4 June, reveals the spirit in which the leader of the opposition received the intelligence of his youthful press secretary's even more youthful indiscretion.

> The statements made by you to me late yesterday afternoon in my office and repeated this morning, in the presence of your father, Mr P.G. Evatt and myself, have amazed and disgusted me as they obviously did your own father. Although the matter disclosed by you related to a period when you were on the staff of the 'Sydney Morning Herald' at Canberra, and before you became Press Secretary on my

staff, I have no alternative but to treat you as immediately suspended from the performance of all duties.

The shattering news Fergan O'Sullivan brought on 3 June 1954 could not have come for Dr Evatt at a less propitious time. His psyche seemed peculiarly unable to cope with setback and peculiarly vulnerable in the face of failure. On 3 June he was still reeling from the shock of the election loss, particularly severe because it was unexpected. (An eleventh-hour *Argus* poll had predicted a comfortable victory.) Dr Evatt's post-election press release of 30 May was bitter and graceless.

> The Government did not win the election fairly...Throughout the campaign it resorted to the smear and hysteria technique adapted from the police states of Germany and Russia. In spite of that, Labor outnumbered Government votes by more than 250,000. Yet Labor did not win the election.

The same mood dominated a lunch he took with the editor of the *Sydney Morning Herald*, J. D. Pringle, towards the end of the week following the election. Pringle recalled:

> I was appalled by the deterioration of his mind. He blamed his defeat on a conspiracy...At one moment he accused Menzies and the Australian Security Intelligence Organisation who, he firmly believed, had timed the defection of Petrov...so that Menzies could use it against him...At another moment Evatt blamed 'certain forces' in the Labor Party which were plotting against him...His mind seethed with plots and conspiracies.

It is, unfortunately, uncertain whether this lunch occurred before or after the O'Sullivan news. It cannot therefore be known whether Dr Evatt's frame of mind at his lunch with Pringle reflected the consequences of his interview with

O'Sullivan or the mood in which it was to be received.

Certainly, however, this much can be said. Before O'Sullivan had come to him, Dr Evatt was convinced that the Petrov defections had determined the election result. Now on 3 June he discovered that a member of his own staff was to be centrally implicated in the Petrov inquiry. Dark questions and sinister possibilities surfaced in Evatt's mind, demons from whose grip he would not be freed for the remainder of his life. Who after all was this Fergan O'Sullivan? Who had prompted him to apply to join the Evatt staff? What was his connection with Evatt's coalition political opponents? What was *Fergan O'Sullivan*'s connection with 'Catholic Action'? What was his connection with the Petrovs and ASIO? Had he been planted upon Dr Evatt by his enemies in order to destroy him? Over the next few weeks Dr Evatt's mind turned these questions about O'Sullivan into possibilities and the possibilities into established facts. He now came to see with a terrifying certainty the connections between apparently unconnected persons and events. Progressively from this moment, Dr Evatt, a man whose life had been devoted to justice, reason and scholarship, abandoned himself to the darkest suspicions concerning real and imagined enemies and to an absolute faith in his powers of intuition. Psychologically speaking, O'Sullivan's confession to him of the authorship of Document 'H' appears to have broken through some dam which held back the flood waters of his paranoia. Politically speaking, this is the turning point of our story. Without Dr Evatt there would have been no Petrov affair.

III

On his second appearance before the Royal Commission Fergan O'Sullivan confessed to being the author of 'H'. The

131

portraits of the gallery journalists contained in 'H' had been given to Pakhomov, the Tass correspondent, he claimed, to help Pakhomov place pro-Soviet articles in the Australian press. Why would information about journalists' extramarital affairs or drinking habits assist Pakhomov here? O'Sullivan was not sure. What had he meant when he described certain journalists to Pakhomov as 'politically reliable'? He had meant, O'Sullivan answered, reliable from the point of view of the ALP. He was shocked to discover that Pakhomov was an intelligence officer and that his little typescript had been despatched to the MVD Centre at Moscow.

Precisely because O'Sullivan had been appointed as Dr Evatt's press secretary in April 1953 this case seemed, from the espionage point of view, far more serious than the case of Rupert Lockwood, the communist who the Petrovs had claimed to be the author of Document 'J'. Petrov gave evidence that a Party 'talent scout', Rex Chiplin, had recommended O'Sullivan to Pakhomov. The Moscow letters revealed that MVD Centre had been extremely interested in him in 1952, while in April 1954 Mrs Petrov had heard from Kovalenok (Petrov's successor) that for Moscow the cultivation of O'Sullivan had the highest priority. In the case of an Evatt prime ministership the Soviet intelligence service might have an agent at the heart of the Australian government.

It was with such considerations in mind that the Commission turned, late on the afternoon of 15 July 1954, to the question of the appearance of Fergan O'Sullivan's name in the list of 'sources' at the end of Document 'J'. Under Windeyer's examination O'Sullivan admitted that he had drunk with Lockwood at the Kingston Hotel. He was certain, however, that it had not been in May 1953 but sometime after July. O'Sullivan was then shown page thirty-five of 'J'. He had been, he now discovered, listed as a source for certain information about difficulties Dr Evatt was supposed to have experienced in acquiring a visa for the United States and about big business donations to the ALP election fund. O'Sullivan denied possessing such information, let alone passing it on to Lockwood. Mr Justice Owen pointed out that O'Sullivan had also been named as a source in 'J' for a story about a security file photograph of another Evatt staffer. Windeyer added that a third member of the Evatt staff—one Albert Grundeman—had also been named as a source in Document 'J'.

Shortly before the Commission adjourned for the day Mr Justice Owen returned to the question of Document 'J' and the Evatt staff.

> We think it is right that we should say that we do not find anything in this document which reflects on the Leader of the Opposition. What disturbs us is that the document quotes as sources on various matters, some of which are of a confidential nature, three members of the secretariat of the Leader of the Opposition, including, in that three, O'Sullivan.

As it turned out these were probably the most consequential words to be uttered by Mr Justice Owen during the course of his distinguished life in the law.

Ever since the fateful interview with Fergan O'Sullivan on 3 June Dr Evatt had known that his name was certain to be involved in the Royal Commission on Espionage. Soon after it he had revealed to Victor Windeyer that O'Sullivan was the author of Document 'H' and had inquired of him whether any other associate of his was likely to be called as a witness to the Commission. 'Perhaps wrongly,' Windeyer later confessed, 'I told him that that was so.' Now, on 15 July, the expected had happened; the Commission Chairman had indicated that three members of the Evatt secretariat were listed as 'sources' in Document 'J'. Not surprisingly, the radio news on the evening of 15 July and the morning headlines of 16 July were dominated by this new sensation.

Dr Evatt, who had been on an exceedingly short Petrovian fuse since early June, now exploded into action. At once he telegrammed the prime minister demanding his rights as leader of the opposition to be supplied with all the information 'adversely affecting my staff'. On the same day he prepared a statement for the press and radio which denounced the Commission in the strongest terms. 'At the commencement of the enquiry,' he wrote, 'the Commission boldly nailed its colours to the mast of just procedures and no McCarthyism.' But was not this singling out of 'one or two members of the staff of the leader of one political party' (one of one hundred names listed as sources in 'J') 'the quintessence of McCarthyism'?

Within the Evatt camp there were certain tactical differences about how best to answer the 'charge' that Dalziel and Grundeman had supplied information to Lockwood. Dr Evatt's younger brother, Clive, wanted to accept the Commission's invitation, to fly to Melbourne at once and to represent there the 'injured parties', Dalziel and Grundeman. To judge by his later account of the matter Dalziel favoured this approach. Dr Evatt, however, would have none of it. He intended to represent them himself. Faced with the determination of his 'boss and political chief' Dalziel felt no option but to 'defer'.

Despite his frequent public declamations about the McCarthyist smearing of his staff, in reality in mid-July Dr Evatt's overwhelming interest was not in their vindication (which of course could best have been achieved by an immediate Melbourne appearance) but in the exposure of what he now understood to have been the true meaning of the Petrov defections. The naming of Dalziel and Grundeman gave him an opportunity to place himself at the centre of the inquiry and to transform it from an investigation of espionage into an investigation of political conspiracy. For this he needed evidence and time. On 21 July the solicitors he was instructing wrote to the Secretary of the Commission requesting access to Document 'J' (which Evatt was by now convinced would provide the clue to the conspiracy which had been mounted against him) and the deferral of the appearance of Dalziel and Grundeman for a further five weeks.

As it turned out, Dalziel, who, if Clive Evatt had had his way, might have been called on 19 July and cleared his name in a matter of minutes, found himself compelled—because of Dr Evatt's deeper concerns—to wait until 13 September before being invited to take the stand.

IV

In the first fortnight of August 1954 the Royal Commission was in the process of transferring from Melbourne to a permanent home in Sydney, and in recess. Temporarily the focus of the Petrov affair moved to Canberra where the parliament elected on 29 May had at last assembled. Here, in the second week of August, the Petrov affair emerged unambiguously as the central issue of Australian politics. The precipitant was the revised 'Act relating to the Royal Commission on Espionage' which Mr Menzies brought into the parliament on 11 August.

On 12 August Dr Evatt rose in parliament to speak on the Royal Commission on Espionage Act. Unbeknown to his Caucus colleagues he intended to use the occasion to begin his public exposé of the Petrov conspiracy. For the most part this new Act, he argued, merely replicated legal powers of existing legislation. Why then had it been introduced? 'One of the reasons,' he suggested darkly, 'may be that the question asked of Lockwood was about his authorship of a document known as

Exhibit "J".' At once, the Speaker, Archie Cameron, stopped
Evatt in his tracks. Cameron ruled that there could be no
debate on any matter at present being heard before the Royal
Commission. Dr Evatt had been robbed of his chance to begin
in parliament his exposure of the Petrov conspiracy.

Blocked in the parliament, Dr Evatt resorted to the press
release. For the first but by no means the last time, the nation
now learned the outline of the Petrov conspiracy theory which
had taken possession of the leader of the opposition. One of
the keys to the Petrov affair, Evatt argued, was the payment—
in advance of the delivery of any documents—of £5000. These
documents had been 'bought for the purpose of unduly and
improperly influencing [the] people of Australia at the general
elections'. Why had Mr Menzies not informed the parliament
of this payment on 13 April? Why was 'this vital fact' suppressed before election day? Had any intermediaries bar-
gained with Petrov 'during 1953'? What moneys were, even
now, being paid to the Petrovs? Evatt concluded: 'I believe
that when the tangled skein of this matter is finally unravelled
the Petrov/Menzies Letters case will rank in Australian history
as the equivalent to the notorious Zinoviev letter or the
burning of the Reichstag which ushered in the Hitler régime
in 1933.'

Dr Evatt's press release was too much for Menzies to bear.
Late on the evening of 12 August he rose to speak in the
adjournment debate. The Evatt production was, he said, evidence of a 'grave state of panic' and closely reminiscent of the
communist line on the Commission. One by one Mr Menzies
answered Dr Evatt's charges. He had not told the House of the
£5000 payment on 13 April because he knew nothing of it
then. He had not in fact learned of it until 9 May. He reminded
Dr Evatt that many facts had not been publicly revealed
before the election. If he had revealed what he knew of

O'Sullivan and Dalziel, Dr Evatt would not be in the House now. Menzies said he did not know whether or not ASIO had used an intermediary in the Petrov defection. But how did 'people suppose the Government is to fetter Communist activities unless it has secret agents'? Of course the government was now supporting the Petrovs financially. It would have to be 'half-witted' not to do so. As for Dr Evatt's theory that the Petrov defection had been used to influence the election, had he not personally ordered every government candidate to refrain from Petrov comment? 'I say to the House and the country'—and with these words Mr Menzies landed himself in much later trouble—'that the name of Petrov became known to me for the first time on Sunday night, the 11th April, I think, or the preceding Saturday night.'

And as for Dr Evatt's theory that the Petrov documents were forgeries Mr Menzies asked Hansard to record the eloquent and embarrassed silence of the opposition benches. By the time he arrived at the Zinoviev letter and Reichstag fire analogies Menzies was positively crowing with the pleasure of the chase.

As he rose in his place Dr Evatt seemed relieved to have finally provoked a Petrov confrontation with the prime minister. 'At last,' he began, 'the oracle has spoken.' As Dr Evatt repeated his conspiracy charges he was continuously taunted from the government back benches in what the *Sydney Morning Herald* called 'one of the most merciless spectacles the House of Representatives has ever seen'. According to the *Age* the adjournment debate on the evening of 12 August was 'probably the most bitter personal debate' that had ever taken place in parliament 'between a Prime Minister and an Opposition leader'. The uneasy Petrovian political truce, which had sealed the lips of Menzies and Evatt in May, had at long last formally ended. Between the prime minister and the leader of the opposition—between whom there existed an utterly genuine and fully reciprocal passion of loathing—the Petrov affair would now be an open fight and, most likely, a fight to the finish.

V

Following the Menzies–Evatt clash of 12 August rumours circulated freely about the possibility that Dr Evatt might personally represent his staff before the Royal Commission when it resumed its sittings on 16 August. Dalziel told journalists that the decision rested not with himself but with his solicitor, Mr Barkell; Barkell told them that thus far he had certainly not engaged Dr Evatt. On 13 and 14 August the press carried stories of the deep concern within the parliamentary party about the possibility of Dr Evatt's appearance at the Commission and of the failed attempt, mounted by the anticommunist right, to convene an extraordinary Caucus to debate the matter. Obviously Dr Evatt was determined to do whatever he could to conceal his intentions from his Caucus colleagues and to prevent them from making moves to bar his passage to the Royal Commission. Only on the actual morning of his appearance did he despatch to all members of the Caucus an explanatory telegram. Caucus was not asked for a decision but presented with a *fait accompli*.

On the morning of 16 August the nation—perhaps by now becoming somewhat addicted to the dramas that almost inevitably followed Dr Evatt—turned its eyes to the Darlinghurst courtroom in Sydney. From the moment of his arrival at the Commission, until the moment of his involuntary departure on 7 September, Dr Evatt totally dominated its proceedings.

In order to grasp the meaning of Dr Evatt's strange and

often obscure three-week performance at the Royal Commission it is necessary to understand what it was that he had already come to believe about the Petrov affair. In mid-August Dr Evatt was unshakably convinced that there had been a conspiracy—involving Petrov at one end and the Menzies government at the other with ASIO in between—to harm him and the party he led in the election campaign in May 1954. Petrov had sold, and the government through ASIO had bought for £5000, certain documents amongst which were to be found some malicious forgeries. Already it was clear to him that the central document in the conspiracy was 'J'. As the world had discovered in mid-July, three members of his staff had been named as 'J' sources. Evatt believed that 'J' had been brought into existence, and bought and sold, in order to damage him. For this purpose the names of two loyal members of his staff—Dalziel and Grundeman—had been wickedly inserted into it. The third (disloyal) member—Fergan O'Sullivan—had been not a victim but an active participant in the conspiracy. At his most charitable he was willing to believe that O'Sullivan had been blackmailed by Petrov (on the basis of his authorship of 'H') into inserting the names of Dalziel and Grundeman and details about the affairs of the Evatt camp into Document 'J'. At his least charitable he believed that O'Sullivan was a conscious anti-Evatt agent planted upon his staff by ASIO.

For all these core beliefs Dr Evatt in mid-August as yet possessed no evidence. He entered the Royal Commission with a dual purpose: to expose the conspiracy and to acquire the evidence by which its existence could be proved. Until the early hours of each morning during his Commission appearance Dr Evatt perused the documentary material he had prised from the Commissioners with an attention to detail worthy of Sherlock Holmes. Unlike Holmes, however, his reasoning was not empirical. For three weeks he threw himself into the evidence in a feverish hunt for clues which might confirm a truth which had already been revealed to him.

On 20 August Dr Evatt was granted access to Document 'J' in its original form and in its entirety. At the commencement of the next sitting day, 24 August, he announced in triumphant mood that a weekend of study had led him to the inescapable conclusion that 'J' could not possibly be, as the Petrovs had claimed, the work of Rupert Lockwood. Unlike Lockwood's polemical writings, which displayed a certain felicity, 'J' was full of 'gibberish and rubbish', a 'literary monstrosity'. Dr Evatt—whose literary essays had won him several prizes while at university—informed the Commissioners that style was to the scholar what the fingerprint was to the policeman. In 'J' moreover certain 'historical howlers' appeared and certain phrases were used for which Lockwood could not conceivably have been responsible. As his examination of Lockwood later that day made clear, the historical howler the author of *Rum Rebellion* had in mind was the description of D'Arcy Wentworth as a 'sexual pervert'. The phrase he believed Lockwood could not conceivably have used was 'right wing *clerical* group'. Not surprisingly, Lockwood was more than happy to accede to the propositions Dr Evatt put to him about his fine style, historical integrity and vocabulary. He agreed that without evidence he would never have described W. C. Wentworth's ancestor as a 'sexual pervert'. He had indeed noticed that 'J' was not in his style, had a 'different swing' to it. 'A man at least,' he proposed, 'gets to know his own style.' And for the word 'clerical'—although it might perhaps 'slip' into his writing on occasions—it was certainly a term foreign to him.

By now Dr Evatt appeared to believe he was well on the way to having proven 'beyond doubt and peradventure' that the whole of 'J' could not have been the work of Lockwood.

His submission was that there had been 'a deliberate conspiracy to injure the Leader of the Opposition by defaming his staff' through their appearance in 'J'. He submitted, moreover, that Fergan O'Sullivan had been the author of at least part of 'J'. On the morning of 25 August Dr Evatt declined the persistent invitation of the Commissioners to indicate who, besides O'Sullivan, had participated in this anti-Evatt conspiracy. Everything would soon 'unfold'. He asked Their Honours to be 'patient'.

In order to test Dr Evatt's 'two hands' theory of 'J', Inspector Rogers, the most experienced handwriting and typewriting expert in the New South Wales police force, was recalled to the Commission on 25 August. He had spent the last four days examining 'J' and typewriting specimens from Lockwood and O'Sullivan. Rogers had arrived at three main conclusions. The uniform nature of the paper on which the whole of 'J' had been typed and the persistence throughout of certain idiosyncrasies of typing style—the use of the double-dash, the irregularity of paragraph spacing, a repetitive apostrophe error and the abundance of parentheses—had convinced Rogers that 'J' had been typed by one person. When he compared the typing in 'J' with other pieces of Lockwood's work he had discovered these same characteristics. None of them had appeared in the specimens of O'Sullivan's typing which Dr Evatt had supplied to the Commission. Moreover, as he had previously testified, in his view the handwriting in the margins of 'J' was the same as that which had appeared on Lockwood's passport application, hotel registration form and customs declaration. His conclusions were clear. One person had typed 'J' and that person was Lockwood.

On 26 August Inspector Rogers was due to complete his evidence but was ill. The Commission might have adjourned for the day had not Dr Evatt asked for Richards of ASIO to be recalled to the stand. Apparently that night Dr Evatt—who was reported to be working on 'J' until three each morning—believed he had made a discovery (concerning the width of the staple or pin marks on J35) which might prove to be the turning point in the Commission's investigations. The matter, he told the Commissioners, could not wait. 'The reason why the urgency is so great,' he said to the complete bewilderment of everyone present, 'is to protect the condition of evidence—physical evidence.' The matter on which Dr Evatt interrogated Richards concerned the precise manner in which 'J' had been stapled when it had been passed to him by Petrov. Richards thought that the sections concerning America and Japan had been stapled separately. Four of the five pages of sources had, so far as he could remember, been stapled together. One was loose. J35 was attached to nothing…But it had the appearance of having been 'attached to something'. 'It had what?' Evatt enquired.

When exactly had the document been handed to Richards? At whose house? ('Dr Evatt!' Owen exclaimed.) When J35 had been handed over was the present tear on it? Dr Evatt's suspicions were now aglow. He feared that Richards might be tampering with the crucial clue to the conspiracy—the staple/pin marks at the head of J35—even as he stood in the witness box. 'Are you touching portions of the original?' 'DR EVATT!' On the morning of 26 August Dr Evatt proposed formally to the Royal Commission that J35 had been torn from some other document and fraudulently inserted in 'J'. To his 'two hands' theory he had now added his 'ring in' refinement.

On 27 August Dr Evatt was let loose upon Inspector Rogers. At first he sought Rogers' assistance over the staple/pin marks on J35. Rogers could not offer him an opinion one way or the other. He was not, he pointed out, a staple expert. 'There must be,' Owen warned, 'less laughter in the court room.' With little satisfaction on the staple front and perhaps disturbed by the fact that all of Rogers' typewriting and handwriting evidence pointed to Lockwood as the sole author of 'J', Dr Evatt now raised a new possibility—forgery. If someone had in his possession specimens of Lockwood's typing and writing would it not have been a relatively easy matter to give 'J' the appearance of Lockwood's work? Meagher, O'Sullivan's counsel, rose to his feet. Was his client now being charged with forgery? If so, he demanded a trial by jury. In front of Evatt the Commissioners speculated about what was in the doctor's mind. Owen thought the logic of his position entailed the allegation that O'Sullivan was the forger. Philp thought that he might merely be talking of some 'hypothetical forger'. The trouble was, Meagher suggested, that Dr Evatt would not 'come out into the open and say what...' He was cut short. 'I will come into the open, and I am not going to be intimidated by anybody.'

There were many bizarre moments in the Evatt performance at the Royal Commission but none so bizarre as his exchanges with Inspector Rogers during his attempt to prove 'J' a forgery. Let one example suffice. Dr Evatt thought the side-letter 'Y' in Document 'J' was uncharacteristic of Lockwood's hand. Lockwood's Y's were tailed 'U's; this looked more like a tailed 'V'. Did this not point inescapably to forgery? Rogers begged to differ. In his view the 'Y' in 'J' bore the mark of Lockwood, but even if Evatt was right why would a forger make such an obvious error as this? Because, Evatt returned, he had no example of a Lockwood 'Y' to forge. There was an 'AX and an 'AZ' later in the document but no 'AY'. Was it not clear that towards the end of his labours the forger had lost his nerve?

> *Rogers:* I do not agree with you, Doctor.
> *Evatt:* What do you mean, you do not agree?

> *Rogers:* I understand that you had been putting to me for the last quarter of an hour that he was a very shrewd, cool, calculating forger.
>
> *Evatt:* And he is a very wicked man if he is a forger.
>
> *Rogers:* If he is, by the time he reaches 'AX' he says to himself, 'I have made a possible mistake in using that "Y"', and it seems to me he would have enough brains not to use the 'Y' again, but to remove the 'Y' he had made.

Touché!

Lost in the mysteries of staple marks and forged 'Y's, Dr Evatt was now proposing parallel theses concerning the authorship of 'J'—the older 'two hands–ring in' thesis and the newer 'forgery' thesis. No-one—neither he, nor the Commissioners, nor the counsel assisting—had noticed the simple fact that Dr Evatt's theories were not only equally implausible but also mutually contradictory. If the whole of 'J' was, as Dr Evatt had maintained, a forgery, how could he also maintain that J35 was a 'ring in' page which had been torn from somewhere else and wickedly smuggled into it? Everything was, by late August, getting out of hand.

On the morning of 1 September Mr Justice Owen's patience with Dr Evatt was finally exhausted.

> You were permitted to appear here, Dr Evatt, for two persons, and you are entitled to ask such questions as we think proper. We are not prepared to allow you to ask questions the relevance of which to your clients we are unable to see. My colleagues and I wish to know from you, after the lunchtime adjournment at half past two, what is the conspiracy to which you have made many allusions, and who you allege are the conspirators in addition to O'Sullivan.

After the luncheon break Dr Evatt pronounced his conspiracy charges formally. Document 'J' was not Lockwood's work but a concoction and a forgery. There had been a 'foul and most serious conspiracy' to insert the names of Dalziel and Grundeman into it in order to damage their master, the leader of the opposition, and, through him, the Labor Party. The forgery had been produced, Dr Evatt now made explicit for the first time in the inquiry, in order to influence the outcome of the May federal election. He introduced to the Commission the two evidentiary jewels in his political conspiracy crown. Had not B. A. Santamaria's 'Movement' newspaper in Melbourne, *News Weekly*, boasted in its 28 April 1954 edition that as early as 28 January 1953 it had tipped its readers off about the coming Petrov defection? His plans were 'an open secret' then (at least in certain circles!), fully fifteen months before their implementation on the eve of the election. And had not the *Sydney Morning Herald's* parliamentary correspondent written on 16 April that, if Mr Menzies hoped to win the coming election, he would have to pull one or two rabbits from the hat he had worn with such aplomb during the Royal Tour? The Petrov affair had been, Dr Evatt claimed, 'one of the basest conspiracies known in political history'.

But who precisely, the Commissioners asked Evatt, did he allege had been involved in this conspiracy? The 'centre' of it was, of course, Evatt replied, Petrov himself. Fergan O'Sullivan, who had been blackmailed by Petrov, was his main assistant. Mrs Petrov, while perhaps not a main initiator of the conspiracy, had nevertheless supported it. Mr Justice Ligertwood was not satisfied that Dr Evatt's list of conspirators was yet complete. 'You suggested that it was a conspiracy for political purposes.' Dr Evatt knew where Ligertwood was heading. Did he refer to security? Evatt was strangely cautious now. While he would not allege that anyone in ASIO was involved in the political conspiracy he did charge Richards with having been 'negligent' in not testing for forgery the documents he had bought from Petrov from £5000 and of having 'uttered' them untested to the government. Questioned on the point Dr Evatt declined to charge Colonel Spry even with negligence. He was never to be asked whether his charges extended to Mr Menzies.

Dr Evatt was far from discouraged by the confrontation of 1 September. On the following day he made application to call a new witness—Dr Charles Monticone, a New South Wales government interpreter and part-time handwriting expert—to give evidence on the question of the side-lettering in 'J'. There were, he maintained, grave objections to Inspector Rogers' evidence. On 3 September, however, Mr Justice Owen turned down Dr Evatt's Monticone request. While the question of the handwriting in the margins of 'J' might be crucial to Dr Evatt's conspiracy allegations, it seemed to Owen to be assuming an undue importance in his Commission's hearings. Had not Lockwood himself even admitted that the side-lettering closely resembled his handwriting? In the end, no matter what expert opinions were presented, the Commissioners would have to make up their own minds on the Lockwood handwriting question. In reality the refusal of the Monticone request was the first clear sign that the Commissioners were determined to retrieve their inquiry from Dr Evatt's control.

The inevitable crisis between the Commissioners and Dr Evatt arrived almost at once. On Friday 3 September the Sydney *Sun* unexpectedly broke the story of the arrest and repatriation—on the basis of the Petrovs' evidence—of an attractive, western female diplomat, a reference to the Second Secretary at the French Embassy, Madame Rose-Marie Ollier. For several weeks, the Secretary to the Royal Commission, Kenneth Herde, and the French Ambassador to Australia, Louis Roche, had been discussing a joint announcement of Mme Ollier's arrest and the release of the transcript of the *in camera* Ollier hearing which had taken place in Melbourne on 20 June. Now, on the afternoon of 3 September, M. Roche invited Herde to an interview. He intended, in the light of the *Sun* story, to make a public statement on the Ollier arrest. The morning newspapers of 4 September were dominated by the Madame Ollier sensation. The first Petrov spy had apparently been caught. An enraged Dr Evatt threw himself into retaliatory action. On 5 September the front page of Australia's leading Sunday newspaper, the *Sun-Herald*, carried the story of his chivalric defence of Mme Ollier and his attack upon the dastardly conduct of M. Roche. One sentence in Dr Evatt's statement particularly stuck in the throats of the Royal Commissioners: 'Today [Mme Ollier] will find herself defamed throughout the world as a spy apparently on the say-so of the two paid informers who, on their own admissions, have been treacherous to both Russia and Australia.'

When the Commission resumed its sittings on Tuesday 7 September, Dr Evatt was informed that his leave to appear at the Commission was under consideration. How could Dr Evatt justify the gross impropriety of the remarks he had made about two witnesses appearing at the Commission? Dr Evatt explained that he had been acting perfectly properly in his role as leader of the opposition. This was precisely where the problem, according to the Commissioners, lay. Was it not becoming daily more obvious that there existed a fatal incompatibility between Dr Evatt's legal role as counsel for his staff and his political role as leader of the opposition? Even at the Royal Commission it was quite unclear whether he was appearing for his staff or for himself. He seemed, moreover, to lack altogether the disinterestedness required of an advocate. Dr Evatt hotly contested the Commissioners' arguments about his conflicting responsibilities. Nevertheless, if they required him to 'choose between his two roles' as advocate and political leader, he would unhesitatingly choose the former. While he did not apologise for his weekend statement about the Petrovs he did promise that nothing resembling it would occur in the future.

After protracted argument it became evident that the Commissioners were not to be deflected from their decision to remove him from their Commission. Dr Evatt appeared hardly able to believe what was happening. He had done nothing else over the 'last four or five weeks' than prepare for this case. Now, just as he was about to begin a renewed cross-examination of Richards, which he believed might prove decisive, his leave to appear was being threatened. Strange things, stranger than he had ever before experienced, had been happening at this Royal Commission. 'I feel more deeply about it than I appear to indicate.' Nothing other than 'an absolute determination, as far as determination of heart and head and hand can go to get to the truth of the matter' was driving him on. Was it not evident that he was not being opposed by the equal determination of Richards and—he hinted darkly—'perhaps of others' to prevent the truth emerging? With some genuine pathos he begged the Commissioners to reconsider their decision. They would not. Before lunchtime on 7 September Dr Evatt involuntarily and his juniors voluntarily had departed the Commission.

VI

On 8 September, on the day after his expulsion from the Royal Commission, Dr Evatt returned to Canberra for his first Caucus meeting in a month. Here he delivered to his colleagues an uninterrupted and highly dramatic speech (which extended to some hour and a quarter) on the Petrov affair and its historical significance. This case was, he told them, the most important of his life. It involved one of the most diabolical

conspiracies in political history. When the truth was finally
revealed the Menzies government would fall. During his discourse Dr Evatt revealed to the Caucus—as he had to the
Commission—that *News Weekly* had boasted that it had
known of the impending Petrov defection as early as January
1953. Clearly Petrov had been nurtured by security for more
than eighteen months. At least on some of his Caucus colleagues of the left and the right, the hint of some sinister connection between security and B. A. Santamaria's 'Movement',
the precursor of the National Civic Council, would not have
been lost.

According to the *Sydney Morning Herald's* source, during
his Petrov address Dr Evatt 'was trembling and almost tearful
with emotion'. Although the atmosphere in Caucus must have
been electric, he was heard out in silence. When he had concluded, well after the time the meeting had been scheduled to
end, Eddie Ward—apparently in defiance of the wishes of the
parliamentary executive—attempted to move a motion of confidence in his leadership. Caucus tensions now exploded. As
Dr Evatt tried to close the meeting, several members—including Stan Keon and Albert Thompson—rose to their feet
demanding the right to speak to Ward's motion; others
exhorted him to withdraw it. The Labor left (who enthusiastically supported Evatt's Petrov crusade) and the right (who
abominated it) exchanged abuse. Thompson and Ward almost
came to blows and had to be separated.

Uproar followed Dr Evatt from the Caucus room to the
floor of the House. During question time on 8 September he
repeatedly shouted his opinion that Australia had become
a 'police state', before the Speaker, curiously ruling such
language unparliamentary, obliged him to withdraw. Later,
during a speech by Fred Daly, Dr Evatt was observed thump-
ing the table with his fist and muttering: 'Tell 'em about the

Petrov Commission—that is what they are frightened of!' On 9 September, outraged by headline reports of the previous day's Caucus eruption, he hurriedly convened a press conference in his office. For forty minutes he shouted at reporters and denounced the enemies—'the treacherous liars'—in his midst. The story of the clash between Eddie Ward and Albert Thompson was a 'deliberate lie' being peddled by those he called paid and unpaid 'informers' inside Caucus in order to injure him. The previous day's meeting had in fact been the quietest he had experienced 'in ten years'. As he had revealed to his party the 'inside story' of the Royal Commission, this audience had been, he said, 'enthralled'. Dr Evatt ended his week by issuing a 1500-word press release which called upon Mr Menzies to dismiss the present Royal Commission and replace it with a new five-man tribunal to investigate his conspiracy charges. By now several of his Labor colleagues feared he was experiencing some form of nervous collapse. Since Sydney he had appeared 'thinner, white-faced, strained, unpredictable' and, above all else, 'fanatical on the subject of the Petrov Commission'.

On 22 September Labor's Petrov cauldron, which had long been simmering, finally boiled over. Dr Evatt's chief accuser was the member for Fawkner and once a *News Weekly* editorial board member, Bill Bourke. Bourke accused Dr Evatt of doing the communists' work for them at the Commission and of being their greatest asset. Evatt's conspiracy charges were ridiculous and would not hold water. The adulation he was receiving from the communist press was sickening. The leading communist barrister Ted Hill was merely Rupert Lockwood's junior counsel. Dr Evatt, it was well known, had even frequently conferred with Hill in Hill's chambers. Bourke spoke for some ten minutes. His words apparently shocked many of his colleagues.

Finally Bourke was speaking to a motion Ted Peters had proposed and Tom Burke seconded: 'That the Leader do not appear as a Counsel at the Petrov Royal Commission nor make any further public statements on its operation or constitution without the consent of the Parliamentary Labor Party expressed by the Caucus.'

Both mover and seconder, however, distanced themselves somewhat from the scathing tone of Bill Bourke's remarks. (The fine psychological line between those right-wingers who would split and those who would not was here prefigured.) Reg Pollard rose in Dr Evatt's defence. There were some members in Caucus, he said, who 'were not fit to lick the Doctor's boots'. Had not Bill Bourke given succour to the Liberal Party during the last election by his attack on Labor's means test proposal? Had not he and his mates 'run dead' during the anticommunist referendum? Dr Evatt could not be blamed for the content of the communist press. Bill Edmonds pushed further. He informed Caucus—which was by now in uproar—that before this meeting he had been asked to support a plot to replace Dr Evatt with Arthur Calwell. All eyes now turned to Calwell. At once he disclaimed any knowledge of this plot. Indeed, he thoroughly supported his leader's call for Ted Peters to withdraw his censure motion. Ted Peters withdrew. With several members—including the 'Movement's' John Mullens—still clamouring to be heard, Dr Evatt closed the discussion once and for all.

Tactically Dr Evatt had won a victory at the Caucus on 22 September. In August Caucus had resisted the left's attempt to have his appearance at the Commission approved retrospectively. In September it had resisted the right's attempt to condemn it. The uncompromising quality of Bill Bourke's anticommunist denunciation of Evatt—which had gone too far even for some of his right-wing friends—had most likely swung the feeling of the Caucus centre to Evatt's side. Dr Evatt, who had promised his colleagues that he would never again miss a parliamentary day on behalf of Petrov, had retained his freedom to speak his mind on the Petrov affair. He had not yet, however, silenced his 'Movement' enemies within the Caucus.

VII

At the beginning of October, Dr Evatt arrived in private at a momentous decision—perhaps the most important of his political life—to declare war upon B.A. Santamaria's 'Movement'. Most directly he was, of course, responding to the violent attack made upon him by Bill Bourke on 22 September in Caucus which, on 29 September, John Mullens, who was even more closely associated with the 'Movement' than Bourke, had tried unsuccessfully to renew. Dr Evatt was thoroughly convinced by now of the existence of some sinister connection between ASIO and his 'Movement' enemies in Caucus. Was not the *News Weekly* article of January 1953 proof of this connection and of their joint involvement in the Petrov conspiracy? In coming to his final decision Dr Evatt must have been influenced by the atmosphere within the salon which formed around him during the Sydney Royal Commission hearings, which comprised secular anti-Catholic Actionists like Leslie Haylen, and left-wing Presbyterians like the Reverend Keith Dowding and Allan Dalziel. He was certainly, too, influenced by the journalism of Alan Reid who, in the Sydney *Sun* on 21 and 28 September, had written (for the first time openly in the Australian press) about the 'Movement' and about B.A. Santamaria, portrayed by Reid as a brilliant but alien Mediterranean figure, a 'Svengali' of the ALP right or, alternatively, a medieval monk of the anticommunist crusade. Finally, Evatt was also now predisposed to being profoundly affected by the text of a most striking speech which had been delivered by B.A. Santamaria earlier that year to the 'Movement', which was circulating widely on the left in early October and which had been pressed upon Dr Evatt by one of Santamaria's targets in it, the Catholic enemy of the ALP's Industrial Groups, J.P. Ormonde.

On 5 October Evatt informed the Australian nation of the existence of a small group of 'subversives' within the Labor Party, directed from outside it and centred upon *News Weekly*, who used 'methods which strikingly resemble both Communists and Fascist infiltration of larger groups—calculated to deflect the Labor movement from the pursuit of established Labor objectives and ideals'.

'This group,' Evatt had learned from loyal supporters, 'intended to assist the Menzies Government, especially in its attempt to initiate in Australia some of the un-British and un-Australian methods of the totalitarian police state.' Their activities had caused 'a rising tide of disgust and anger' within the Party. Their activities had sapped Mr Chifley's 'health and strength'. They interpreted 'tolerance' as 'weakness'. 'A serious position' existed. Dr Evatt announced that he intended to bring this position to the attention of the Federal Executive and Federal Conference.

Dr Evatt's statement of 5 October was a direct consequence of the impact of the Petrov affair on the Labor Party—on the one hand of the genuine fury felt within the anticommunist right about Evatt's Petrov behaviour and on the other of Dr Evatt's dark suspicions about the hidden connections and purposes of the 'Movement' as manifest in the Petrov conspiracy. His statement set in train a protracted political struggle which, within a matter of months, had split the Labor Party and which, for the succeeding eighteen years, kept it from office in

Canberra. As Robert Murray, the author of *The Split*, has shown, by the time of Dr Evatt's statement, throughout the ALP—within the federal and state parliamentary parties and executives and within the trade union movement—often quite delicately balanced armies of Groupers and anti-Groupers had massed. The Petrov affair did not, of course, create these armies and was only one of the issues (which concerned jobs almost as much as values) over which they contended. It did, however, create the political condition for the Evatt statement of 5 October. In turn, Evatt's statement set these armies in motion. Irrespective of Dr Evatt's attack on the 'Movement' there would have been prolonged struggle within the Labor Party between Groupers and anti-Groupers. There may, however, have been no all-out war, and possibly therefore, no split.

In August Dr Evatt had revealed to the public the role played by ASIO and Mr Menzies in the Petrov conspiracy. On 9 October he revealed that the conspiracy extended even into the heart of his own party. His 'Movement' enemies, whom he was now referring to as the 'Santamaria–McManus–Keon' group, had for a long time been in 'closest touch' with Australian security. The sinister association had, indeed, been 'forged' in order to discredit the Labor movement on the eve of an election. Evatt now promised that 'The closeness of the link between this anti-Labor group I have mentioned and the Security Service will be cleaned up.'

Dr Evatt had, of course, first to weather the non-'Movement' storms to be expected in Caucus. Before it met on 13 October it was widely anticipated that Evatt's antics would now finally bring on the long-awaited challenge from Arthur Calwell. If Calwell stood, it was also expected that Allan Fraser—an independently-minded leftist—would put up for the deputy's position (most likely against Ward). When Caucus met, Senator Cole of Tasmania called for a spill of all leadership positions. Dr Evatt, as party chairman, refused to accept Cole's motion. Notice of such a motion was, he argued, required. Calwell—who many believed could have had the leadership that day if he had fought Evatt's ruling—once more remained silent. Strong attacks were launched upon Evatt but neither from Calwell nor from his Caucus targets—Keon, Mullens and Bourke.

During the following week support for the Calwell–Fraser leadership bid dissipated. Before Caucus met on 20 October many newspapers already knew that it would fail; some even predicted (wrongly) that Senator Cole's motion would be withdrawn. At this Caucus Evatt's 'Movement' targets now gave voice to their true feelings. Bourke outlined the Petrovian challenge he intended to argue against Dr Evatt before the Federal Executive. Keon called his leader a 'sectarian monger' and threatened him with a defamation writ. Most bitterly and dramatically John Mullens demanded to know what charges Dr Evatt—the 'smear merchant', the bogus civil libertarian— intended to prefer against him. He accused Evatt of preparing a 'Moscow trial'. Above the tumult he warned his colleagues that, if they still wanted Evatt as leader, they were 'gluttons for punishment'. An open vote was taken on the spill motion. In the excitement Evatt leapt onto the Caucus table; he and Eddie Ward began recording names. Even after five New South Wales members crossed to the anti-Evatt side in a gesture of indignation at the Ward intimidation, the Cole motion was lost 54 votes to 28.

Dr Evatt had survived as party leader. At the end of the following weeks he had won a second round of his battle with the 'Movement'. After a special meeting on 27 and 28 October, the ALP Federal Executive decided not to censure Evatt for his statement of 5 October but to conduct an investigation into Labor's Victorian branch. For this meeting Dr Evatt had prepared a 6000-word statement, some half of which was devoted to the Petrov affair and the involvement of his 'Movement' enemies in it.

> Those controlling *News Weekly* were, early in 1953, in close contact with Security and Bialoguski. It is significant that in Caucus I was bitterly attacked by W. M. Bourke for having caused Bialoguski to give evidence...Mr Mullens showed a foreknowledge of [a] confidential and supposedly secret exhibit...Those controlling the 'Movement'...hailed the Petrov case in order to advance and support their own extremist policy. It was dangerous to them if the defection of Petrov proved to be not spontaneous but part of a carefully organised...plan for election purposes.

By an exquisite irony, the Federal Executive met that day in the very hotel where, a year and a half earlier, Rupert Lockwood, Fergan O'Sullivan and Albert Grundeman had—so fatefully for Dr Evatt and his party—drunk and gossiped together. The split was now in the making. Within six months there was not one but two Labor parties in Australia—the ALP and Anti-Communist Labor, the forerunner of the DLP.

VIII

With the passage of time Dr Evatt's conviction that the Petrov affair represented one of the most wicked political conspiracies in world history seems, if anything, to have deepened. By 1955 it was the most solid and dominating feature of his inner political landscape. By this time he had, moreover, bestowed upon his 'Movement' enemies a pivotal position in the affair.

There is in the Evatt Archive at Flinders University in South Australia some rather startling documentary evidence of the atmosphere which was, by 1955, pervading the Evatt camp. Scattered throughout the archive are upward of fifty very strange speculative papers on the Petrov affair—some very short, others running to three or four closely typed pages—composed for Evatt by a gentleman calling himself 'Phil's Friend'. Clearly 'Phil's Friend' operated as Dr Evatt's private adviser on intelligence matters during 1954 and 1955. As it happens, from the evidence of the Evatt Archive the identify of 'Phil's Friend' can be determined with certainty. He was R. F. B. Wake, a former deputy to the first director-general of ASIO, Mr Justice Reed. Wake had been dismissed from the organisation, on the grounds of erratic behaviour, when Colonel Spry had taken command in 1950. He bore a deep grudge against both Spry and ASIO.

The stream of papers Wake delivered to Dr Evatt assumed, without argument, the existence of a vast international and Australian conspiratorial network involved in the Petrov affair. Wake's purpose was to uncover the chief actors, organisations and interests involved in it. From the broadest perspective Wake regarded the affair as part of some international collaboration between imperialist interests in the United States and the Vatican, whose ambition was to create conditions for a war of aggression against the USSR. Wake inquired of Dr Evatt:

> When was it that MENZIES prophesied War in 3 (three) years? In Oct. 51 General Mark Clark a personal friend of Pope Pius XII, Chief of the US Field Forces nominated as first American Ambassador to the Vatican. Kennan, head of the 'Free Russia Committee'—set up to liberate Russia from Communism—became the new US Ambassador to Moscow. At the same time 4 million copies of an American magazine dedicated to the coming war against the USSR were distributed in the USA. War against the USSR was anticipated in 1952. The point I am making in a cumbersome manner is that Menzies, the Vatican and Washington were all singing

the same tune at the same time.

Wake was also certain the Ollier case or what he came to call the 'Ollier–Roche set-up' was part of this 'whole world-wide' conspiracy in which ASIO, M. Roche, the French security service and the CIA had been involved.

While the Petrov affair, then, appeared to Wake to be part of a larger international movement centred upon a Washington–Vatican axis he was also convinced that it had been concocted by a variety of local political organisations to advance their own interests. For Wake the most important of these were ASIO, the Liberal Party, Australian Naval Intelligence, Moral Rearmament, Sir Edmund Herring's 'the Call', General Blamey's 'Association' and, of course, B.A. Santamaria's 'Movement'. The most essential ambition of the intelligence analyses he wrote for Dr Evatt was to reveal the various points at which these apparently disparate organisations were connected, especially at the personal level. In his view all these groups had pulled together to create the Petrov affair. It was a sinister and nightmarish vision.

For the role of Australian master-conspirator Wake favoured not Mr Menzies or Brigadier Spry or even B.A. Santamaria but a rather kindly Catholic writer from Adelaide, Paul Maguire, who had been from 1953 the Australian Ambassador to Rome. Wake's decision to concoct such a persona for Maguire, while absurd as a matter of fact, is not difficult to fathom. Paul Maguire was one of the very few Australians of the mid-1950s who was genuinely at home in the two social worlds from which Wake believed the Petrov affair had been conjured—establishment conservatism and Irish-Australian Catholicism. Wake assured Dr Evatt that Maguire had links with American Catholic interests through Cardinal Spellman. Even his appointment to the Vatican in

1953 (before the Petrov affair broke) seemed to Wake sinister, based upon what he described as 'an anxiety to get him out of the country during a vital period'. 'Good God,' he exploded to Evatt in May 1955, 'Paul Maqguire's [sic] involvement in this business sticks out like bubbles on a washtub.' Throughout 1955 he recommended that Evatt campaign on the slogan of the 'Menzies–Maguire–Santamaria Axis'.

In reality what Wake was feeding Dr Evatt in his Petrov papers was a quite old-fashioned political sectarianism, adapted to present circumstances. Wherever Wake peered he found the mark of the Vatican or 'Catholic Action'. One of his papers was entitled 'Extraneous Catholic Activities (State Within A State)'. It dealt with 'Catholic Action', the 'Knights of St Columbus' and 'Catholic Guilds'. On one occasion he expressed the view that 'the US and Cath. Action knew …about Petrov long before ASIO caught up on the deal'; on another that Dr Evatt's wartime typist, Frances Bernie, was a 'Catholic Action' plant on Evatt's staff and the Australian Communist Party. Even the Burgess and Maclean affair had for Wake a Vatican explanation: 'In 1939 over 40 per cent of the British Foreign Office were Roman Catholics. A recent estimate, 1954, suggests that it is now nearer 60%. Is it probable that B & McC got fed up with the RC intrigues in the show and went walkabout?'

It is not possible to know what precisely Dr Evatt made of the theories of Wake. It is clear, however, that he did not discourage him from producing his never-ending stream of Petrovian analyses and highly likely that he felt considerable sympathy at least for the general thrust of Wake's analysis of the Petrov affair. During the 1960s Robert Murray spoke to many participants in the events of the split while the memories were still fresh. On the basis of this anecdotal evidence he arrived at the following conclusion.

By the spring of 1955 Evatt appeared again to be losing control of his complex personality...He was by now completely obsessive about the Petrov affair, and there are innumerable stories of the lengthy, conspiratorial theories he would expound to often reluctant listeners in private conversations. His obsession with the 'Santamaria Movement' was by now almost as bad. Evatt was morbidly suspicious of people he believed to be 'CA' (Catholic Action) in the Party, the press, the government departments, among employees at Parliament House...He was wont to believe any story peddled to him, no matter how fantastic or how suspect the source, provided it fitted his conspiratorial vision of the Santamaria–Menzies–Petrov 'plot'.

In his pursuit of the 'truth' about the non-existent Petrov conspiracy Dr Evatt posed an even greater danger to himself than his political enemies.

On 17 February 1955 Dr Evatt despatched a letter concerning Petrov to the Foreign Minister of the USSR, M. Molotov. Why did he do this? According to one man who ought to know, his private secretary Allan Dalziel, Evatt wrote to Molotov because of the profundity of his respect for the rule of the law. Dr Evatt was, above all else, according to Dalziel, 'an eminent jurist'.

The right to enter a defence, to state a case in reply to charges...was basic to the operation of justice within the framework of the law. He stoutly rejected the idea that, because a person or cause was unpopular or the subject of general disapproval, the right to be heard in one's own defence should be suspended. For him, as a lawyer of unchallenged integrity, it was vital that the views of the Soviet Government be examined and assessed.

At this critical moment in his career, according to Dalziel, Dr

Evatt's finest instinct—his passion for justice—triumphed. While, however, soaring high above the world of petty politics he exposed himself to the scorn and ridicule of the Australian philistines who had long desired to bring him down. Here, encapsulated in Dalziel's account of the Molotov letter, is the Evatt Tragedy, or, if you will, the Evatt Myth.

It is actually difficult to imagine an explanation of Dr Evatt's motives in writing to Molotov which could be more misleading than that offered by Dalziel. Within the Evatt Archive there exists a copy of his famous, portentous letter. It reveals not a dispassionate lawyer concerned with even-handed justice but an impassioned political crusader searching even in the most implausible quarter for support and ammunition. In his letter Dr Evatt does not invite Molotov to defend the USSR against the charge of espionage—except as an afterthought. Rather he implores the Soviet Foreign Minister to lend his assistance in Dr Evatt's struggle to unmask a plot in which the Australian government and security service have been involved. Time is short. The Royal Commission hearings, he reminds Molotov, are drawing to a close. Lest this account should appear exaggerated it is necessary to quote from the Evatt letter at some length.

> I have come to the conclusion that few, if any of [the] documents were genuine but that they were deliberately fabricated in 1953 by Petrov and others for the purpose of being subsequently utilised for party political purposes against the Labor Party (of which I am Leader) in the election of May, 1954...It is plain that the U.S.S.R. authorities, especially the M.V.D., know whether for certain Petrov has been engaged in a systematic plan to cheat and defraud the Australian people...In short, your Government, or its officers are undoubtedly in a position to produce official and absolutely conclusive evidence of the fact (if it be a fact) that the Petrov

documents are fabricated and spurious…In order to expose what I believe to be a crime against humanity, I request an immediate intervention by Your Excellency as the Commission of enquiry seems to be approaching the last stage of their [sic] activities.

Dr Evatt suggested to Molotov that he might then place the matter before an 'international court of jurists' for arbitration.

Evatt's letter to Molotov must rank as one of the strangest ever sent by a responsible western politician to a Soviet leader. To speak of the Petrov affair, in the language of the Nuremberg trials, as a 'crime against humanity', especially in a letter to one of Stalin's most faithful lieutenants, was grotesque. To place weight upon the words of Molotov in an investigation into Soviet espionage was self-evidently preposterous. Moreover if details of this letter were to leak to the press or Dr Evatt's political enemies in Australia it had the capacity to do him great harm. To appear to prefer the word of Molotov to the findings of an Australian Royal Commission would certainly be offensive to a generation which still had faith in its judicial system. To call in the Soviet Foreign Minister as an ally in his battle with the Menzies government and ASIO was—especially in the political atmosphere of mid-1950s Australia—an act of potential political suicide.

The Soviet Foreign Ministry may have been genuinely puzzled by Dr Evatt's letter. Perhaps they read into it some complex trap. For six weeks there was no reply. When it finally came, despatched on 9 April 1955, it must have represented a severe disappointment to Evatt. The letter was signed not by Molotov but by a relatively junior official of the Soviet Foreign Ministry—Ilyichev, chief of the press department—who claimed to write on the Foreign Minister's 'instructions'. Its contents were bland and non-committal. Ilyichev expressed the fullest agreement of his government with Dr Evatt's analysis of the Petrov affair. It had, indeed, been staged by anti-democratic forces intent upon harming Australian–Soviet relations. The Petrov documents were, he agreed, fabrications. Unhappily, however, Ilyichev offered Dr Evatt neither new evidence on this matter nor even fresh argument. He politely but firmly declined Dr Evatt's suggestion for the arbitration of the affair before an international panel of judges. Such an arbitration, he pointed out, would have no 'subject matter'. Here, at least for the moment, the Evatt–'Molotov' correspondence rested.

IX

On the evening of 19 October 1955, Dr Evatt initiated the House of Representatives debate on the Petrov affair. In some ways Evatt had been preparing himself for this moment for the past eighteen months. He informed the House that, if permitted, he could have spoken for 'twelve days'. His deputy had negotiated with the government leader in the House for 'unlimited time'. In the end he had been allotted the far from miserly two hours. Sensing that this speech might prove of some significance to Australian history, someone in ASIO wisely decided to make a recording of Dr Evatt's Petrov address. As it turned out, it was to prove the most important of his political life.

Dr Evatt began, promisingly enough, with a passage suggested to him by his political ally, the left-wing historian and civil libertarian, Brian Fitzpatrick.

> What is the upshot of the Petrov affair? Two foreigners, the Petrovs, and one foreign born Australian spy, Bialoguski, have made a lot of money. The forum in which they appeared cost the taxpayers £140,000...The nation has

suffered heavy loss in trade, and the breaking of diplomatic relations with a great power. There has been the attempted smearing of many innocent Australians…but…no spies have been discovered. Not a single prosecution is recommended.

He moved on, less promisingly, with a passage very much of his own. One of the major issues raised by the Petrov affair, he told the House, was the authenticity of the 'Moscow letters'.

Determined to ascertain the truth of these grave matters, I took two steps, as follows: First of all, I communicated with His Excellency, the Foreign Minister of the Soviet Union…I pointed out that the Soviet Government…[was] undoubtedly in a position to reveal the truth as to the genuineness of the Petrov documents. I duly received a reply sent on behalf of the Foreign Minister of the Union of Soviet Socialist Republics, Mr Molotov.

There was within the House a pause of unbelief, and then—from that merciless enemy of the absurd—volleys of laughter. The laughter came from both sides of the House. Dr Evatt appeared momentarily surprised. 'Honourable Members can laugh and clown but they've got to face up to some facts tonight.' The House was now in uproar, but Evatt continued. Mr Molotov had claimed the Petrov documents were fabrications. Evatt attached 'grave importance' to his letter. He suggested the establishment of an international court 'to settle the dispute once and for all'.

In the printed columns of Hansard Dr Evatt's Petrovian address reads like a powerful, if fundamentally wrong-headed, attack upon the Menzies government and ASIO. However, in the House on 19 October—in the atmosphere created by his reference to Mr Molotov—it was a political disaster. A parliament which has smelt blood is a cruel human assembly. Dr Evatt delivered his speech in a flat, unworldly monotone amidst taunts and jeers. (At one point the Speaker threatened that if he discovered which members were whistling he would have them thrown out of the House.) In his Molotov references all judgment had deserted him. As he spoke, his isolation from his fellows appeared profound. By the time he had concluded, there was, no doubt, gaiety in the hearts of government members. On the opposition benches—in a gesture of wonderful eloquence—Dr Evatt's supporters held their heads in their hands.

Mr Menzies spoke in the House on the evening of 25 October. The speech he delivered—which was, like Evatt's, recorded by ASIO for posterity—revealed him at the top of his form. It is justly regarded as one of the greatest moments of his parliamentary career. Wisely, he had accepted the advice of his department. A painstaking refutation of Dr Evatt, no matter how successful and intellectually satisfying, would have been politically self-defeating. Mr Menzies' ground was not that of the advocate but the conservative elder, whose duty it was to protect tradition, institution and character from what he called Dr Evatt's 'reckless and villainous charges'.

The Royal Commission on Espionage had been established, Mr Menzies reminded the House, with the unanimous support of parliament. It had listened patiently to evidence over ten months. Dr Evatt's suggestion that the parliament could not set itself up as a court of appeal over the Commission was ridiculous, 'frivolous and offensive'. The judges who had sat upon it, whose findings were disputed by Dr Evatt and so damaging to him, were outstanding lawyers of unquestioned integrity. Two had been chosen to serve the Curtin–Chifley governments in different capacities. They had done so with distinction. All three had rallied to the nation's flag in World War I. Mr Windeyer had been in World War II a highly decorated soldier. The very name Windeyer represented 'all that is

165

best in the New South Wales legal tradition'. And as for Brigadier Spry—the central target of Dr Evatt's 'venomous' attacks' for whom Evatt had said 'peace' was a 'dirty word'— had he not been wounded on the Kokoda trail in the service of his country? (Eventually this catalogue of military virtue proved too much for one Labor backbencher who asked Menzies to outline his own military record. Menzies suggested he rather ask 'Bert and Eddie' about theirs.)

Dr Evatt's motives throughout this affair had been thoroughly contemptible. He preferred the word of Molotov to that of distinguished Australian judges. His mind was 'unbalanced', filled with 'fantasies', 'delusions' and 'obsessions'. He posed as a defender of justice; he was in reality interested only in himself.

It was a cruel, devastating and decisive speech.

On the afternoon following his Petrov address Mr Menzies announced in parliament what had been confidently predicted for the past week—there would be an early election on 10 December for both Houses. Menzies' justification was the good sense of realigning the elections for the Senate and the Representatives. His reason was the split in Labor and the quality over the past months of Dr Evatt's leadership. If any doubts existed in his mind about this course, Evatt's injection of the name of Molotov into the Petrov affair had surely resolved them. There were now, once again, rumours of moves to replace Dr Evatt. The independent leftist, Allan Fraser, had, once again, broken ranks in order to tell the truth. Dr Evatt's reference to Molotov had 'astounded' his Caucus colleagues. After the Menzies announcement of the early election, Dr Evatt threw at him a premonitory text from Corinthians: 'Let him that thinketh he standeth take heed lest he fall.' A political journalist on the *Sun-Herald* thought a more appropriate text for the present circumstances was to be found in the Book of Samuel: 'The Lord has delivered thee today into mine hand.' A landslide victory, in the lower House at least, seemed inevitable.

The overwhelming issue of the 1954 election had been the cost of Dr Evatt's program. If there was any issue which dominated the 1955 election it was his character. As one coalition advertisement put it: 'Evatt has wrecked the Labor Party. Don't let him wreck Australia.' No doubt in deference to his colleagues' wishes and fears Dr Evatt did not so much as refer to the Petrov affair in his opening campaign address. This was a telling omission. Everyone (except *Tribune*) now knew that the Petrov affair had become for the ALP an electoral liability. Whenever Dr Evatt himself raised the issue later in the campaign it was in self-defence. The cry of 'Molotov' pursued him from one election rally to the next. In May 1954 Sir Arthur Fadden had posed to Dr Evatt 'thirteen questions' about communism. In November 1955 he asked him to answer a more modest nine about Molotov.

All this was probably in the end of little account. The arithmetic of Australian politics after the Labor split was all too clear. While Anti-Communist Labor could take a substantial vote from traditional Labor and pass its preferences to the coalition, the prospects for the ALP were bleak. At the polls the coalition received 47.6 per cent of the vote for the House of Representatives, traditional Labor 44.5 per cent and Anti-Communist Labor 5.2 per cent. While the combined Labor vote (by now a metaphysical concept) was almost identical to that of May 1954, the preferences of Anti-Communist Labor (at least in Victoria where they won 15.8 per cent of the vote) proved critical. In the new House of Representatives the government had seventy-five seats, the opposition forty-seven. This was not a mere electoral victory; the Menzies era had arrived.

POL POT AND
THE INTELLECTUALS

IN MAY 1979 I read in my morning newspaper this analysis of
the Cambodia of Pol Pot.

> It will be hard to discover how many Cambodians have been
> killed. The new government has made a rough census of
> those now leading a 'stabilised life' under their control...
> These account for 3.1 millions. About half a million have
> been temporarily installed in areas where they can take part
> in the vital effort this season to get the rice crop planted...A
> few tens of thousands more are on the road, moving from
> east to west and west to east to regain their native villages
> from which they were uprooted by the Pol Pot régime. There
> are a few tens of thousands more in remote jungle areas
> where Pol Pot guerillas are active. *So the total population*
> *may be upwards of five millions out of between seven and*
> *eight millions at the time the Pol Pot forces ousted those of*
> *Lon Nol on April 17, 1975.*

The author of this article was none other than Wilfred Burchett who was, at the time, making a tour of Cambodia. Burchett's story was one of a series he was sending to western newspapers concerning the terrible crimes of the Pol Pot régime, a theme which had been utilised by the Vietnamese government since early 1978 as valuable propaganda cover during their installation and consolidation in Cambodia of a pliant, puppet régime.

Burchett, whose career as a publicist for communist movements had, as we have seen, stretched over several decades, was, if nothing else, a professional. The stories of the Pol Pot atrocities were here trotted out with the same cool professionalism with which previous atrocity stories had been either fabricated (American germ warfare in Korea) or covered over (Vietnamese massacres at Hue). But there *was* something truly unusual in the role that fate had chosen for Burchett here. For one thing, in these reports (for the first time possibly in his career) *the truth concerning communist atrocities was expedient.* And for another, the stories that Burchett was recounting here were precisely those which had just two years before been widely regarded by the 'revolutionary left' in America, Britain and Australia as the cynical concoctions of the propaganda machines of the CIA, Pentagon and big business, and for whose telling certain authors, most notably John Barron and Anthony Paul, had had their names dragged through the mud.

To recall this atmosphere I should like to reproduce a letter published in 1977 in an obscure and naive pro-Pol Pot newssheet produced in Sydney.

Dear friends,
John Barron's book *Murder of a Gentle Land*, is soon to be published and there is, of course, the same gentleman's

recent article in the *Reader's Digest*. I think it is important that the Australian people receive other opinions and reports on Cambodia, to at least give some sort of balance. According to the *Australian* (5/5/77 'Cambodia punishes lovers with death'), Barron stated at a recent U.S. Congressional hearing on Cambodia that he estimated 1.2 million of an estimated population of 7.9 million 'have been executed since the revolutionary government took control'. *Barron is therefore saying that the population is now 6.7 million.* Yet, in the *Digest*, he particularly emphasized a statement supposedly made by Cambodian President Khieu Samphan last August, that the population of Cambodia was 5 million people. Thus for, Barron, the population is 5 million in February 1977 when he wishes to reinforce his views of large scale massacres, but it has reached the more believable figure in time for the hearings in May. Indeed a remarkable feat, but even more so because, according to Barron, Cambodian lovers are punished with death!

The first thing I remember noting about this letter was its plain falsity. (There was no discrepancy in the figures at all. Barron had argued that 1.2 million people had been *executed*; the other deaths, which made a figure of five million Cambodians still alive quite plausible, were those as a result of malnutrition, overwork and disease.) But this simple error was not, of course, what made the letter memorable. Nor was it the conventional polemical sarcasm ('the same gentleman') or the absurdly inappropriate liberal cant ('it is important that the Australian people receive...some sort of balance') that stayed with me. What stayed with me was the tone of this letter, its merry, jaunty air. Here was a discussion of the possible deaths by execution or overwork or disease of millions of people in a mood that could only be described as *light-hearted*.

II

After reading Burchett's article it occurred to me that it might be worth recalling and analysing the campaign (of which this letter was a typical example) which aimed at convincing western progressive opinion that there had been no 'bloodbath' in Cambodia after the fall of Lon Nol, and that the claims of massive numbers of deaths caused by the initial evacuation of the cities, by executions and by pitiless slave labour policies, could be explained as deliberate fabrications of a corrupt and mendacious press in the service of the established order.

As far as I can tell this campaign was orchestrated and led most effectively by a remarkably few people who, for a short time during 1976 and 1977, gave it a considerable part of their energies. In the United States the most forceful campaigners were connected with the Indo-China Resource Centre, in particular a certain influential anti-Vietnam publicist, Gareth Porter, who (in collaboration with George Hildebrand) produced the campaign's major work—a book entitled *Cambodia: Starvation and Revolution*—and who put the campaign's case at the US Congressional hearing on Cambodia held in May 1977. In Britain most active was the late Dr Malcolm Caldwell (of London University's School of Oriental and African Studies) who had the misfortune to be shot in Phnom Penh (presumably by a pro-Hanoi agent) while making a tour of Cambodia on the eve of Vietnam's Christmas invasion of 1978. It was Dr Caldwell who, according to a fellow visitor to Cambodia (Elizabeth Becker of the *Washington Post*) coined the immortal phrase—'I have seen the past, and it works'— shortly before his death. The most notable figure, however, who gave his talents and energies to the campaign was, without doubt, the linguist Noam Chomsky.

The arguments used by these authors to cast doubt on the stories of mass killings in Cambodia were pitched on several levels. At their most general the campaigners sought to discredit the atrocity stories by the argument of *cui bono?* It was argued that as belief in atrocities by the Pol Pot régime served the interests of American imperialism (by introducing some sense of moral ambiguity into the assessment of former American activities in Cambodia and thus encouraging future similar actions against other revolutionary liberation movements), such beliefs were likely to be fabrications of the American established order. Thus Porter and Hildebrand argue at the conclusion of their book:

> Cambodia is only the latest victim of the enforcement of an ideology that demands that social revolutions be portrayed as negatively as possible, rather than as responses to real human needs which the existing social and economic structure was incapable of meeting. In Cambodia—as in Vietnam and Laos—the systematic process of mythmaking must be seen as an attempt to justify the massive death machine which was turned against a defenseless population in a vain attempt to crush their revolution.

Why the American propaganda machine should have chosen Cambodia as the scene for a bloodbath and not Vietnam (where the bulk of US military effort in Indo-China took place) was never discussed, let alone explained.

A similar argument also heard frequently in the campaign, and one that particularly attracted Noam Chomsky (who adopted a peculiarly unctuous and hectoring tone in his polemics) was that the stories of Pol Pot atrocities were concoctions retailed by the American press in order to disguise from the American people that the media shared with Nixon, Kissinger and the military machine *sole* responsibility for the *present* sufferings of the Cambodian people. Here is Chomsky in the *Nation* of June 1977 (in an article written jointly with Edward Herman):

> It is difficult to convey the deep cynicism of this all-too-typical reporting which excises from history the American role in turning peaceful Cambodia into a land of massacre, starvation and disease. While the editors prate about morality, people are dying in Cambodia *as a direct result* of the policies that they supported and indeed concealed.

Others, *not* associated with the campaign, like David Chandler (a former US official in Phnom Penh and now a Cambodian specialist at Monash University) who did not deny the fact of the atrocities, argued that American guilt was such that no American should speak about what was going on in Cambodia—'as a friend of mine has written, we Americans, with our squalid record in Cambodia should be "cautiously optimistic" about the new régime "or else shut up"'— and even that (an argument that seems to me almost wholly irrational) in some way American bombing in Cambodia had turned the Cambodian communists into crazed killers:

> What drove the Cambodians to kill? Paying off old scores or imaginary ones played a part, but to a large extent, I think, American actions are to blame. From 1969 to 1973, after all, we dropped more than 500,000 tons of bombs on the Cambodian countryside. Nearly half of this tonnage fell in 1973…In those few months we may have driven thousands of people out of their minds.

This was not a theme advanced by Chomsky or Porter who, in so far as they conceded that any executions had taken place in Pol Pot's Cambodia at all, explained them by analogy with the murders in France after liberation, an analogy which had the advantage of making the killings appear justified, small in scale and spontaneous—and the disadvantage of being entirely misleading on all these three points.

Having established the motive for the creation of the myth of the mass killings in Pol Pot's Cambodia, and having vested the United States with sole responsibility for whatever suffering had occurred, Porter, Chomsky et al. occupied themselves with discrediting the two most influential books concerning the situation in post-1975 Cambodia—François Ponchaud's *Cambodia Year Zero* and John Barron and Anthony Paul's *Murder of a Gentle Land*.

While the Barron and Paul book was generally treated as beneath contempt, very largely on no other basis than that it had been published by the Reader's Digest Press, François Ponchaud (a French Catholic scholar who had spent ten years in Cambodia) was treated with more respect and his book subjected to what Chomsky called 'scholarly' and Gareth Porter 'methodological' criticism.

The central 'methodological' weakness discovered in Ponchaud's book was that it was written largely as a result of interviews with refugees who had fled from Cambodia since 1975. It was argued that these refugees came only from one region of Cambodia, the north-west, and thus gave a seriously distorted account of conditions as a whole. (The reason, of course, that the bulk of refugees interviewed came from the north-west was that these provinces lie adjacent to Thailand and they were thus available for interview in 1976 and 1977. It was later discovered—when Vietnam went to war with Cambodia and when it became opportune for Vietnam to reveal their existence and allow them to be interviewed—that larger numbers of refugees had fled from eastern and central Cambodia into Vietnam. These refugees told identical stories to those who had fled to Thailand.)

This geographical distortion was compounded, according to several articles written during the campaign, by a more serious *class* distortion. While some argued that only wealthy and educated people had fled ('Peang Sophi is one of the very few Kampuchean refugees of lower class origin'!) Gareth Porter argued that only the educated, wealthy and privileged had given evidence to Ponchaud. This was completely untrue. As Ponchaud explained in the introduction to the English edition of his book.

> I...mistrusted those who spoke French, and those who came from the wealthier classes and who had too much to lose under the new régime. I was mainly interested in the ordinary people, the army privates, peasants and labourers who could neither read nor write nor analyse what they had seen but whose illiterate memories could supply exact details.

Finally, and most interestingly, Chomsky and Porter argued that refugees' accounts were in principle a suspect (if not wholly dismissible) source which had to be treated with what was euphemistically described as 'care and caution'. 'Refugees,' Chomsky argued, 'being frightened and defenseless' and 'at the mercy of alien forces...tend to report what they believe their interlocutors wish to hear...Specifically, refugees questioned by westerners or Thais have a vested interest in reporting atrocities on the part of Cambodian revolutionaries.' Porter went further. He thought the problem of 'exaggeration and falsification' so serious that he described the written accounts of life in revolutionary Cambodia given to François Ponchaud as 'the least reliable kind of documentation'. (Presumably less reliable than the propaganda broadcasts of Radio Phnom Penh that Porter used extensively in his book to establish, for example, the huge successes of the rice harvest!)

The plain words of François Ponchaud, in his short reply to the Chomsky-Porter 'methodological' criticisms, could not be bettered.

> After an investigation of this kind, it is surprising to see that 'experts' who have spoken to few if any of the Khmer refugees should reject their very significant place in any study of modern Cambodia. These experts would rather base their arguments on reasoning: if something seems impossible to their personal logic, then it doesn't exist. Their only sources for evaluation are deliberately chosen official statements. Where is that critical approach which they accuse others of not having?

Even more remarkable than the attempts to discredit Ponchaud's book on the grounds that it used the only evidence available was Noam Chomsky's subtle attempt to discredit the book on the basis of a review of it. (This is indeed a novel kind of guilt by association.) The review was written by Jean Lacouture (the hagiographer of Ho Chi Minh) for the *New York Review of Books* and it achieved considerable notice when published for the extremely poor reason that it was written by a leftist with impeccable anti-American credentials. The review was highly rhetorical, emptily self-condemnatory (in a way calculated to enhance Lacouture's reputation and self-esteem) and, worst of all, extremely careless. Lacouture in his review had made a number of crude errors, for example claiming that a quotation from a Thai newspaper was from a 'Cambodian government' source, and implying that Ponchaud had claimed that the Khmer Rouge had boasted of killing two million people. (In fact Ponchaud had not claimed this and had been careful to make it clear that it was impossible to know how many had been killed.) In replying to the criticisms of these errors Lacouture apologised contritely to Chomsky (whom he described as a man of 'truth' and 'freedom' with 'an admirable sense of exactitude') and went on to make his case even worse by putting forward the manifestly absurd proposition that it was not of central importance whether the Cambodian government had murdered 'thousands or hundreds of thousands of wretched people'.

What made this intrinsically unimportant correspondence between Chomsky and Lacouture significant was the use to which Chomsky, Porter and others put Lacouture's errors. Henceforth Chomsky in particular was to suggest not that Lacouture had misquoted Ponchaud on a few points (which was all that had happened) but rather that the 'myth' of the mass killings in Cambodia rested in fact on an *unbroken line of distortion* which began with the Khmer refugees and was transmitted through Ponchaud, Lacouture and the American press until it reached the broad American public. As a consequence, I was to hear in the next twelve months several learned references (on the ABC's 'Broadband' for instance, and at a conference of the Australian Council for Overseas Aid) to these Lacouture misquotations, which were mentioned as serious evidence for the proposition that Ponchaud's book could not be relied upon, and even that no killings had in fact taken place in Cambodia!

As an alternative to Ponchaud's book as a source for conditions in contemporary Cambodia, Porter and Chomsky were to suggest that there existed a wide body of scholarly and specialist opinion (not open to Ponchaud's 'methodological' weaknesses) which cast serious doubt on the plausibility of the stories of mass murders and deaths in Cambodia. Here are Chomsky and Herman:

> We would like to point out that apart from Hildebrand and Porter there are many other sources on recent events in

Cambodia that have not been brought to the attention of the American reading public. Space limitations preclude a comprehensive review [sic], but such journals as the *Far Eastern Economic Review*, the London *Economist*, the *Melbourne Journal of Politics*, and others elsewhere, have provided analyses by highly qualified specialists who have studied the full range of evidence available, and who concluded that executions have numbered at most in the thousands.

In some ways this assertion of Chomsky's and Porter's (for Porter referred to the *Economist* and *Melbourne Journal of Politics* as his major evidence at the US Congressional hearing) was the most extraordinary of the whole campaign. I do not know to which article in the *Far Eastern Economic Review* Chomsky referred but I have read that magazine regularly since 1975 and know that it contains article after article confirming Ponchaud's argument. On inspection, the *Economist* analysis, which Chomsky described as 'the most authoritative report so far available' turns out to be a *letter to the editor* from a certain statistician, W. J. Sampson, who left Phnom Penh in March 1975 and who, when subsequently questioned, thought that it was likely that one quarter of a million people may have died on the march out of Phnom Penh. As for the article in the *Melbourne Journal of Politics*—which is, incidentally, an undergraduate journal—this was written by someone who was at the time a young left-wing student, Ben Kiernan.

On examination, then, that broad body of scholarly opinion to which Chomsky and Porter refer as casting significant doubt on Ponchaud's book (and the stories from thousands of refugees of mass killings inside Cambodia) boiled down to an unidentified article in a weekly news review which has for four years affirmed consistently in its reports the Ponchaud analysis; a letter to the editor of a man who now believes that hundreds of thousands of deaths were directly caused by the actions of the Pol Pot régime; and a piece by an ideologically blinkered student in an undergraduates' magazine.

III

Perhaps all this is now of 'mere' historical interest. Certainly the controversy concerning the Pol Pot régime is, by and large, concluded. Driven into remote jungle and mountain country by the conquering Vietnamese armies, the Pol Pot régime is now almost universally despised and has already largely faded from memory. For those political movements which rest their legitimacy on the inevitable and benevolent workings of the laws of history it is true to say that 'nothing fails like failure'. Moreover for former Pol Pot supporters to maintain their allegiance would entail both forthright denunciation of Vietnamese aggression against Cambodia, and the belief that Hanoi had been involved in a malicious and lying propaganda campaign to blacken the name of the Pol Pot régime. With the exception of a handful of esoteric party-liners, it is just not possible that the western left, whose most recent triumph was the successful struggle against the war in Vietnam, could accept such entailments.

Nor are the 'lessons' of these controversies—that there is no régime too base to be defended; that there is no evidence that will shake the faith of its defenders; that refugees are more reliable guides to twentieth-century politics than professors— in any way surprising for someone with even a passing knowledge of the history of the relationship between intellectuals and totalitarian movements in our century. There is little new to be learnt from this aspect of the controversy.

What may be learnt (or at least reinforced) from the debate concerning Cambodia is that during the 1970s liberal anticommunism was so completely defeated in western universities and intellectual circles that one could no longer hope that arguments couched in its language would be listened to seriously. Nor, sad to say, is it possible to expect that the political self-confidence of the former supporters of Pol Pot will be in the slightest deflated by the fact that concerning their estimation of him and his odious régime they were wholly, shamefully and ludicrously wrong. Pol Pot has passed; Noam Chomsky, I fear, persisteth.

'EVEN OLD STACKS TALK': THE COMBE AFFAIR AND POLITICAL CULTURE

HOW WELL served are we by the media? Is the Australian media politically biased towards the right or the left? The question of the bias in the media can be posed in so general a way that it is hard to resist the view of the Professor of Government at the University of Sydney that there is no true answer, that to enter discussion on the bias in the media is to enter upon a hopelessly relativistic area of discourse, a sea of subjectivity in which we are certain to drown.

This chapter is devoted to the alternative proposition: that the question of the political bias in our media can be addressed objectively. Its method is the case study; its subject matter the Combe affair, probably the most important political story of 1983. Examined in detail are the performances of ABC public affairs, the two leading metropolitan and two leading national dailies, the *Sydney Morning Herald* and the *Age*; the *Australian* and the *Australian Financial Review*; the most influential weekly newspaper, the *National Times*, and the most prestigious public affairs program on commercial television, Channel Nine's 'Sunday'.

The Combe affair offers an excellent beginning point for examination of political bias in the Australian media. In part this is because it raised issues of extreme ideological sensitivity (fundamental attitudes towards the United States and the Soviet Union and towards the apparently competing claims of 'civil liberties' and 'national security') and in part because a Royal Commission has made publicly available in nearly complete form the evidence needed to form a judgment on the affair and the media's handling of it. The following is the story of what the 'serious' and 'quality' media in Australia made of the Combe affair.

THE MONSTROUS INJUSTICE

The Combe story broke in the press on 10 May 1983. On that morning the *Sydney Morning Herald* published an article by Paul Kelly which made clear that ASIO had named a senior ALP figure as a security risk because of his links with the expelled KGB agent Ivanov and that the ASIO allegations were beginning to cause 'deep tremors' inside the ALP. Although in political and media circles it was well known by now who the senior ALP figure mentioned by Kelly was, his article made no mention of David Combe.

Within the day Combe's name was out. In the parliament, the leader of the National Party, Ian Sinclair, asked the prime minister if the ministers in his government had been told not to associate with Combe. Mr Hawke chose not to evade the question. The implication of his answer was obvious—Combe was the senior Labor man of Kelly's story.

During Wednesday 11 May the government struggled to contain the issue. The Attorney-General, Senator Gareth

Evans, negotiated with Combe the wording of a statement which it was proposed Hawke would deliver that afternoon to the parliament. Both sides agreed that after Hawke's statement—which made clear that Combe was not a 'Soviet spy' but that 'he had been, or appeared to have been, compromised by Ivanov'—neither would speak further to the media. On the evening of 11 May, however, David Combe broke this understanding. At the Hope Royal Commission he claimed he had broken it because he had become convinced that Hawke's office was 'backgrounding' journalists on the affair. No convincing evidence was ever to be produced to confirm Combe's claims on this point. The truth seems simpler. On the evening of 11 May Combe, no doubt stung by growing criticism of his capitulation, decided to take on the Hawke government. His weapon would be the media.

Already before 11 May Combe had discussed his position in detail with journalist friends Laurie Oakes and Brian Toohey. In the early evening of 11 May Combe gave various journalists his interpretation of the Hawke statement. Late in the evening at a Canberra restaurant he told his tale to a group of journalists which included Michelle Grattan and Ken Haley of the *Age* and Richard Carleton of the ABC. Combe's media campaign had now begun in earnest.

The morning press of 12 May was, not surprisingly, full of stories attributed to 'close friends' of David Combe. One such story, from Ken Haley, which must have been filed shortly after his evening with Combe, began thus: 'Mr David Combe, loyal party man for twenty years, resisted all opportunities yesterday to speak out with his side of the story.'

As a consequence of Combe's breach of agreement and the obviously inspired pro-Combe morning press of 12 May, Mr Hawke had come to understand that the Combe affair could not be contained. Only a full judicial inquiry could clear the air.

From the first moment the media was supportive of David Combe and hostile to Mr Hawke. The opening volley of the pro-Combe campaign was fired by the ABC's Richard Carleton on the evening of 11 May:

> An extraordinary state of affairs exists here in Canberra tonight. A man seven years the national secretary of the Australian Labor Party, a man who is as close as close can be to the prime minister, a man who is a very, very popular figure here in Australian politics, David Combe, has tonight had his livelihood and his reputation probably destroyed by Mr Hawke.

By the end of the first week Hawke's incompetence in his handling of the Combe affair was being taken for granted; he had 'made a mess of it'. Who would have believed, Michelle Grattan asked, 'that the government's second full week of Federal parliament could have been worse than its first…But it was worse…much.' How, Paul Kelly asked, could Hawke have been so naive as to believe that the decision to place Combe under a ministerial ban could be kept secret from him or that when he found out 'he would sit put and accept it'?

While some of the tactical criticism was certainly just, the more substantive criticism was less so. Hawke's attempt to keep the details of the Combe–Ivanov relationship within the confines of the Cabinet intelligence committee was evidence for the media not of a desire to protect Combe's reputation but of his secretiveness, his 'penchant for ruling through the cabals', which was certain to arouse for the future the suspicions of his ministerial colleagues. Hawke's decision on 12 May to call a Royal Commission without consulting Cabinet was interpreted generally not as decisive leadership but as an act of panicky impetuosity, signifying a 'shoot from the hip' style of leadership. Throughout the first days Hawke was portrayed as an authoritarian and ruthless politician who had condemned a close friend and colleague without giving him any chance of a defence. Inevitably Hawke was seen as playing McCarthy to Combe's self-proclaimed Alger Hiss.

The language used in this first week to describe the Hawke government's treatment of Combe was more than a little extravagant. Combe had been 'destroyed' (Carleton, 11 May), 'traduced' (Haley, 12 May), 'pilloried' (Grattan, 13 May), 'liquidated' or, alternatively, 'dynamited out of existence' (Geoffrey Barker, *Age*, 14 May). The *Sydney Morning Herald* thought that Hawke had been 'manifestly unfair' to Combe; the *Financial Review* that Combe had received 'very shabby treatment'. Brian Toohey in the *National Times* thought that he had suffered a 'massive injustice', and Barker (whom no-one could outbid) a 'monstrous injustice'.

By and large the serious media had by the end of the first week of the affair made up its mind about the nature of the relationship which had precipitated Ivanov's expulsion and Combe's blacklisting. On 11 May Richard Carleton's commentary had suggested that David Combe had been destroyed as a result of some casual social contact with a Soviet representative in Australia: 'I have been in the Soviet Embassy here in Canberra, I have drunk their vodka more than once. But does that mean I have been or appear to have been compromised?'

The next day, however, it was generally known to the media that Combe's relationship with Ivanov went much deeper than such a comment implied. By 12 May certain journalists had acquired, from what Carleton coyly described as 'impeccable sources', considerable detail concerning Combe's relations with Ivanov. For the first but not the last time Combe, in his media campaign, had sought to defuse possibly damaging evidence by what might be called pre-emptive revelations, placing in the hands of journalists his version of the evidence he now knew (after speaking to the director-general of ASIO on 11 May) ASIO had presented to the government.

From 12 May the media knew that ASIO had in its possession transcripts of two conversations that had taken place between Combe and Ivanov. They knew that in these conversations Combe had discussed working for the Soviets; that Combe had agreed to pass on to Ivanov 'documents' concerning the CIA and 1975; and that in the second of these conversations Ivanov had suggested to Combe that due to ASIO surveillance of them they should be more discreet about future meetings. The politically crucial question was how this evidence was to be evaluated.

The journalists to whom Combe's selective revelations had been given accepted his interpretation of the evidence entirely uncritically. It was widely, for example, reported in the press that the 'documents' on the CIA and 1975 which Combe had promised Ivanov were newspaper clippings merely. Paul Kelly thought Combe may have been unfairly condemned on the basis of 'circumstantial evidence', not for what he had done but 'for what he said and what he might do'. Michelle Grattan's review of the revealed evidence left her puzzled as to why the government believed Combe to have been compromised. Stephen Mills of the *Age* thought there was 'little more' in the Combe–Ivanov relationship than 'professional dealings between an apparent diplomat and a bona fide lobbyist'; Brian Toohey thought the government did not have enough evidence 'to hang a sheep'.

Given the media's presumption of the innocence of David Combe it was not surprising that already in the first days of the affair explanations were being offered for the injustice done him. One line of explanation focused on ASIO, the other on Mr Hawke.

The *Australian Financial Review* thought the most important issue raised by the Combe affair was 'ASIO and its behaviour'. The *Review* found it 'difficult not to suspect deliberate entrapment' of Combe by ASIO. The 'crazy Left' who wished to destroy ASIO had been handed wonderful ammunition by the 'crazy Right' who inhabited it. It hoped that the outcome would be 'an effective cleaning out and reform of our security services'. The *Review* added: 'Not everything the USSR does is evil and not all contacts with its diplomatic representatives, its trade or financial representatives, *even to some extent its KGB operatives*, is reprehensible.' [my italics]

The *Review* was not alone in placing the blame on ASIO rather than the KGB for the downfall of David Combe. Brian Toohey regarded Combe as a casualty of ASIO and what was called 'the agent of influence syndrome gone mad'. So did Richard Hall, author of *The Secret State*, whom the media took up as their leading intelligence expert. (By their experts shall ye know them.) In the first days of the affair Hall explained to the listeners of the ABC's 'PM' and the viewers of 'Sunday' that the KGB was 'a bureaucracy, made up of paper shufflers' and that the idea that the KGB tried to recruit agents of influence was merely part of 'a war of propaganda' to which Combe had fallen victim.

The second line of explanation floated in the media of the injustice done to Combe focused on the prime minister. Richard Carleton, characteristically, hinted that Combe's demise might be linked to the vanity of Mr Hawke. Combe, he informed his viewers, had in the bugged conversation with Ivanov of 4 March 'drawn some rather unflattering word portraits of a number of prominent Labor politicians including the prime minister'. According to Brian Toohey, Hawke might have been particularly stung by Combe's mocking comments to Ivanov about his failed attempt to lead the Jews out of Russia. In similar vein Geoffrey Barker argued that Combe may have been an innocent victim of the deep grudge Hawke bore the KGB for its betrayal of him following his 1979 negotiations over the emancipation of Soviet Jews.

Interestingly, in the face of this media onslaught the prime minister chose to defend himself not in what he must have assumed would be the hostile environment of conventional public affairs programs but on sympathetic outlets in the popular media—the Bert Newton and Mike Walsh television shows. Hawke here sought to reassure the public that matters were under control, attacked the media for what he called its 'gratuitous rush to judgment', and, not for the last time, appealed to fair-minded people to reserve their judgment on the affair until the findings of the Hope Royal Commission.

Perhaps Hawke's plea was in vain. In politics, as in life, first impressions count. In many ways the most crucial period in the media's coverage of the Combe affair had been its first four days. In these days a remarkably durable image of the affair was set in the public mind. The first impression the Australian media created for the political nation was of a secretive and ruthless Hawke, a paranoid and sinister ASIO and a hapless and innocent David Combe.

THE VEIL OF SECRECY

The Royal Commission began its proceedings on 1 June. Within a day tentatively and within a month overwhelmingly the media had found a new theme—excessive secrecy.

The reporting of the first day's proceedings by the group of journalists who were to cover the Commission over the next five months provided a minor foretaste of what was to come. For the *Australian* Laura Veltman, the most fair-minded of the young Commission journalists, began her report on proceedings by pointing out that the federal government had agreed 'to release Cabinet documents, warrants and possibly taped conversations'. For the *Sydney Morning Herald*, Richard McGregor, and for the *Age*, Margot O'Neill, led with the opposite point, that the government had urged that a particular document which counsel for the commonwealth, Michael McHugh, had described as possibly 'the most decisive in the case' should not be made available to Combe or his counsel. Laura Veltman's article was headlined 'Combe wins access to secret files'; Richard McGregor's 'Document barred to Combe'. Paul Malone for the *Financial Review* had a different slant. He reported that the submission by Combe's counsel, Ian Barker, marked 'the break between Mr Combe and Mr Hawke' (where had he been in May?) and that there could no longer be any 'pretence' that Combe 'had accepted the statement and actions which Mr Hawke outlined' in parliament on 11 May. The clear implication of Malone's report was that the statement made to the parliament by Hawke had represented not an agreed joint statement (which Combe had repudiated) but an act of duplicity on the part of Hawke.

June was a frustrating month for the media. After its brief opening on 1 June the Commission did not sit again until 14 June and even then heard the evidence of its first two witnesses—Harvey Barnett, the director-general of ASIO, and the ASIO desk officer who handled the Combe–Ivanov case—*in camera*. The public sessions of the Commission were devoted almost entirely to legal argument, concerning such matters as the Commission's terms of reference and the admissibility of, or conditions governing access to, certain categories of evidence. Through June the media became increasingly restive. After all, for whose benefit was the Royal Commission being held? Its displeasure on the matter of the secrecy of the proceedings was directed against both the government and the Royal Commission. 'Secrecy,' an *Age* columnist reflected, was 'a bit like AIDS. Hang around a few spies and you're likely to catch it.'

At no point was the media willing to concede that genuinely delicate and difficult questions concerning the competing claims of public disclosure and confidentiality might be involved in the Royal Commission. In regard to the motives of the government and the judgment of the Commissioner the media confidently and routinely assumed the worst. Let two examples suffice. On the first day of the Commission, as we have seen, the government's counsel argued that a certain decisive document ought not be made available to either Combe or his counsel. We now know what was not known at the time: that this document was the report Combe made to the businessman Laurie Matheson on his return from Moscow which Matheson had passed on to ASIO, and that the government's motives in trying to keep it confidential were a matter of honour in relation to Matheson and prudence with regard to ASIO's future relationship with its sources. The media, however, in June, assumed the government's case rested on nothing other than chronic secretiveness.

Again, in late June, McHugh argued for the government that because of the Westminster principle of Cabinet solidarity the decisions of Cabinet should be examined by the Commission but not the individual positions of the ministers who attended the Cabinet security committee. Almost universally the press discounted the seriousness of the constitutional principle and assumed a political motive—the desire of the government to cover up embarrassing details of the 'well known' disagreement on the question of Combe between Hawke and Bowen on the one hand, and Hayden and Evans on the other.

In the *National Times* of 1 July, David Marr, who was from this moment increasingly to carry the flag for the media on the Combe affair, argued that Hope's initial decision (later reversed) to support the government's case on the question of Cabinet privilege

> makes it doubtful if there is much point going on with this branch of Hope's inquiries: what lies ahead looks a bit like a murder trial where the weapon is in full view but no one can discuss the motive…to the fiction that David Combe is not on trial is now added the fiction of the collective mind of the Cabinet.

Marr clearly could not make up his mind as to who—the government or Combe—was on trial at the Commission; his analogy suggested the government, his ideology David Combe.

In the first week of July the frustration level of the media with the proceedings of the Hope Royal Commission was high. The Commission's proceedings were, increasingly, 'shrouded' in a secrecy which 'verged on farce'. The secrecy provisions might indeed be merely 'ludicrous', the *Sydney Morning Herald* observed, if the matters before the Commission had not been so serious. Far too much time was being spent *in camera*. The Combe commission was 'proving more secret even than the Petrov matter in the hysterical days of the '50s'. The government was covering its tracks and reneging on its promise of a full inquiry. Justice, the *Age* and *Sydney Morning Herald* reminded the Royal Commissioner, must not only be done but must be seen to be done.

Mr Justice Hope was clearly by now alarmed at the growing press criticism of his Commission. On 6 July in a public hearing he expressed the fear that 'the recent media coverage of the Commission's proceedings may colour, in advance, and on only partial information, the public perceptions of what has been taking place and in that way prejudice the Commission's ultimate findings'.

He promised the media edited transcripts of evidence as

soon as practicable but explained that he regarded it as his duty to maintain the confidentiality of evidence which identified ASIO's sources, or which was obtained in confidence from other intelligence agencies, or which might reveal ASIO's methods, technical capacities or knowledge of KGB officers and operations.

Not one of the newspapers which had been so intensely critical of the Commission's secrecy thought fit to publish Hope's clear statement of the principles governing the hearing and editing of Commission evidence. Indeed the Commission was never to shrug off the bogus aura of secrecy the media had surrounded it with in its early days.

LATE NIGHT RAMBLINGS

In the *Sydney Morning Herald* of 6 July Richard McGregor observed that the government was manifestly losing and David Combe winning 'the public relations battle'. The Commission was likely soon to lift 'the veil of secrecy' which had covered its proceedings thus far. In the near future edited transcripts of evidence and the tapes of the bugged Combe–Ivanov conversations would be released. 'This might stop criticism about the secrecy,' he predicted, 'It might also reveal the thinness of the Commonwealth's case.'

McGregor's predictions had about them the quality of self-fulfilling prophecy. Who after all, other than the journalists, were going to evaluate for the public the strength of the government's 'case' against Combe? Indeed, already before setting eyes on the transcripts of the Combe–Ivanov conversations McGregor seemed to have more than half made up his mind about their significance: 'If the material in them is as bland and as trivial as has been suggested, then the Government's action against Mr Combe will appear even more questionable.' Combe's pre-emptive revelations of May were beginning to prove their worth.

The transcripts of the Combe–Ivanov conversations of 4 March and 3 April were in fact released on the same day as McGregor's article and Mr Justice Hope's expression of concern with the media coverage of the Commission. The more important was the conversation of 4 March.

The transcript showed that their conversation that evening had touched on many topics. Combe had told Ivanov of his intention of making big money as a result of his Labor Party connections and eventually of landing one of the plum 'jobs for the boys' he thought his due, possibly the chairmanship of Qantas, possibly the ambassadorship in Moscow. He had assured Ivanov that he could rely utterly on the group of Australian filmmakers which included Brian Toohey and Marian Wilkinson of the *National Times* who were making the film *Allies* and who wanted to visit the Soviet Union (to interview KGB Colonel Kim Philby on the Petrov affair). They were 'not interested in doing a job on the Soviet Union,' he assured Ivanov, but 'want to really nail the Americans'. He had expressed some sympathy for the Soviet position in Afghanistan, where 'mad mullahs' were running around, and late in the evening had given his advice on how best to treat Soviet dissidents: 'Piss them off.' Leave them 'stateless'.

Among the many topics of discussion that evening the most important and persistent concerned trade. Combe was aware of a 'brief' Ivanov had received to speak to him about trade matters. From where, Combe asked, had that brief come—the central committee or the foreign ministry? (Combe did not even consider the ministry of foreign trade.) Ivanov indicated that while it was signed by the foreign minister its ultimate source was Boris Ponomarev (a major figure in the Soviet élite; 'a relic,' as Khrushchev had called him, 'of the Comintern';

and for thirty years head of the international department of
the central committee). Combe, obviously intrigued and flat-
tered, recognised his extreme seniority. Was he not an alter-
nate member of the Politburo?

Combe informed Ivanov that he was presently facing a
decision as to whether or not he should enter on a long-term
contract with his client, the Soviet trading company Commercial Bureau. He told him that his report to Commercial
Bureau, which suggested it play a more overtly political role in
furthering Soviet–Australian relations, had raised a storm in
the company. Were the views expressed in his report about the
relationship of politics and trade accurate? Ivanov raised the
possibility of some work for Combe in the area of trade
'research'. Combe wondered whether this would create a conflict of interest with Commercial Bureau. He asked Ivanov 'to
make the decision whether I can work for [Commercial
Bureau] and for you'.

Combe expressed in the conversation of 4 March the greatest possible interest in working for the Soviet Union. He
believed 'very fervently in Soviet–Australian relations'. After
speaking to the Australian foreign and trade ministers Combe
proposed flying to Moscow for trade discussions. Ivanov
slowed him down. They agreed, however, to resume discussions in the near future.

The Combe–Ivanov conversation was introduced to the
Australian political nation by Richard Carleton on 'Nationwide' on the evening of 6 July:

> To a person not steeped in the lore of the spy industry this
> primary evidence constitutes an amazingly weak case by the
> commonwealth. Combe said some stupid things...But does
> stupidity justify sentence to loss of livelihood, a sentence
> itself that Mr Hawke originally wanted to keep secret?

Combe, Carleton suggested, might come out of his conversation with Ivanov 'smelling a little badly'. Was a man to be 'condemned' for an 'exchange of views'? Certainly Combe's bragging to a KGB agent about his influence in the ALP might be regarded as 'unseemly' or 'naive', but what was it to be a lobbyist if not to sell 'entrée and influence'? In what way did all this make him a security risk?

The morning press of 7 July carried the transcripts of the Combe–Ivanov conversations, detailed reports of their contents and injected a tedious strain of culinary humour about the code meaning of 'jelly and whipped cream', etc., into the coverage of the affair. Insofar as interpretations of the conversations were offered they followed the Carleton line. In the *Age* Michelle Grattan, under the headline 'Documents merely point to extreme naivety', argued that the tapes failed to 'support the government's central argument in the affair' but revealed Combe as 'a self-promoter, eager for dollar' trying rather to 'clinch a commercial deal' than to 'give away State secrets'. (Who had ever suggested that?)

By midday 7 July the mood of the serious media was such that on the ABC's 'World Today' Warwick Beutler asked the prime minister to 'concede that the conversation was little more than just a conversation that any people over a dinner table in Canberra...might have', while his colleague Mark Colvin 'wondered' whether the prime minister's actions in the whole affair might not have been motivated by 'Mr Combe, an old and trusted colleague of yours, being very rude about you'. Not unjustly Mr Hawke regarded Beutler's question as absurd and Colvin's as impudent. Hawke asked Colvin not to insult him by suggesting that he made his judgments concerning the national interest 'in terms of whether I have perceived that I may have suffered some personal hurt'. That evening the ABC's 'PM' replayed the Hawke–Colvin exchange under the following introduction by Huw Evans: 'Well it was quite like old times. For a minute or two prime minister Bob Hawke's short fuse appeared to have been rekindled to something like its former glory.'

On the evening of 7 July Richard Carleton interviewed David Combe for 'Nationwide' on what Combe called his 'late night ramblings'. Combe duly confirmed he had not intended to betray his country. He was greatly relieved that the tapes were in the open although 'appalled' at the portrait he had seen of himself on the television the night before. 'I guess,' he consoled himself, 'none of us is immune from indiscretion in the context of discussions we've had'. Part of the conversation was, he affirmed, 'tongue in cheek'. Late in the evening, he confessed, he was drunk. What most concerned Combe about the release of the transcripts was 'the invasion of privacy which I've suffered' although he had the good grace to acknowledge that 'in the circumstances' their release was precisely what he had wanted. (Since the opening of the Royal Commission Combe's counsel and the media had maintained an attack on the government and the Commission for their non-publication.)

On 8 July the morning press once more followed the Carleton lead with extensive interviews with Combe. In the *Sydney Morning Herald* Combe described the tapes as revealing 'someone who is human to the point of being exceedingly and embarrassingly garrulous and a trifle indiscreet when in a state of inebriation'. In the *Age* Michelle Grattan confirmed that 'late at night over a drink, or more precisely a lot of drink, David Combe is, as his friends…will recall, expansive and opinionated'.

A media image of the vital Combe–Ivanov conversation of 4 March had by now formed. In his talks with Ivanov, the media suggested, Combe had shown himself to be naive, indiscreet, greedy, drunk and garrulous. The tapes—or what Geoffrey Barker was soon to call 'those rather dreary ASIO tapes'—signified nothing more than that.

The media's assessment of the Combe–Ivanov conversations was, to put it charitably, less than adequate. No journalist asked why negotiations with Combe concerning a trade relationship with the Soviet Union should have been conducted not by one of the Soviet trade officials in Australia but by a senior KGB officer. No journalist asked why the Soviets should have been interested in establishing a trade relationship with a man with excellent political connections but no trade expertise. No journalist pondered the significance of the fact that Ivanov had told Combe that the brief to speak to him emanated not from the ministry of foreign trade or even the foreign ministry but from the head of the international department of the Soviet central committee, the department responsible for handling relations between on the one hand the Soviet Communist Party and on the other non-ruling communist parties and, wherever there appeared an opening, western socialist parties. Clearly the name Ponomarev (with the exception of Anthony McAdam in the Melbourne *Herald*) rang no bells in the Australian press. No journalist even inquired as to what precisely had passed between Combe and Ivanov before 4 March or paused to wonder what became of the talks between them which in the conversation of 4 March Ivanov had made clear were soon to be resumed. Only it would seem if Ivanov had asked Combe to spy for Russia and if Combe had agreed would the Australian media have thought ASIO's concern with the Combe–Ivanov relationship legitimate.

ON THE TRAIL OF HAWKE

On the afternoon of 14 July the special minister of state, Mr

Mick Young, offered his resignation to the prime minister. Media interest in the Combe–Ivanov affair—already intense—was heightened more than a notch or two. Although Mr Hawke announced that the reason for the resignation would not be made public until the next sitting of the Royal Commission on Monday 18 July—a decision which exposed him to yet another bout of media attack on the old grounds of secrecy—from the first moment no-one doubted that Young's resignation was the result of the improper disclosure by him of information supposedly privy to members of the Cabinet security committee. Indeed within a day an accurate account of the reasons for the Young resignation (which concerned information Young had passed to a friend Eric Walsh who was, like Combe, retained by Laurie Matheson as a lobbyist for Commercial Bureau) had become public knowledge.

On 15 July the media smelt blood. The morning press asked with one voice whether the leaks from the Cabinet security committee ended with Mick Young, and, if not, were more resignations to be expected? The question was soon more precise than this. Since May it had been general knowledge that on the eve of the Ivanov expulsion an associate of the ALP, Richard Farmer, who had been about to enter David Combe's lobbying business, had been advised by someone senior in the Labor government not to go into partnership with him. The journalists strongly suspected that Farmer's adviser was none other than the prime minister. If Mr Young had resigned over the information he had passed on to Eric Walsh might not Mr Hawke be forced to resign for the information he passed on to Richard Farmer? The Commission had become, in the image now favoured by the media, 'a time bomb' ticking under the prime minister.

A campaign of 'innuendo' (Hawke's term) whose stakes were very high indeed—the possible resignation of a prime minister—now began. Who better to initiate it than Richard Carleton? On the evening of 15 July Carleton on 'Nationwide' suggested that *the* 'unanswered question' of the Combe–Ivanov affair was 'who tipped Farmer off?' Carleton commented: 'On the answer to this question depends whether more heads will roll. It's asserted in some quarters that Farmer was tipped off either by, or at least at the instigation of, somebody senior to Mr Young.'

In the campaign of innuendo no journalist at first felt able to name names although on the ABC's 'PM' one got as far as asking the opposition leader Mr Peacock whether the man who leaked to Richard Farmer might not 'very well be the prime minister himself'.

The question of the Farmer tip-off—which Carleton clearly regarded as the guillotine suspended above Mr Hawke's head—dominated the political speculation of the weekend of 16-17 July. On the Nine Network's 'Sunday' Max Walsh announced that for legal reasons the anticipated guest Richard Farmer would not be appearing. His stand-in, Peter Bowers of the *Sydney Morning Herald*, consoled Walsh with the thought that Farmer's appearance would anyhow have been somewhat 'pointless' as 'the only question you want to ask…who tipped you off to have nothing to do with David Combe?' would not be answered until Farmer presented evidence to the Royal Commission. Bowers believed there was 'prima facie evidence' that Farmer had been told considerably more by his informant than just to 'be wary of David Combe' but, on the other hand, had a 'hunch' that 'a lot of people' who were hoping for great things from the Farmer lead were going to be 'disappointed'.

By the weekend of 16-17 July there was another suggestion in the air. Combe's ubiquitous 'friends' had reappeared in the press, now with the idea that the tapes of the phone taps ASIO had made of Combe's conversations between 22 April and 3

May 'would prove more embarrassing to the Government than to him' and may indeed contain information suggesting further 'leaks' from the Cabinet security committee.

To the suggestions that the prime minister had been the source of the leak equivalent to the one that had cost Mick Young his portfolio were now added speculations that the phone taps of Combe might contain material harmful to the government. No doubt stung by all this Mr Hawke decided to try and answer his critics. On 18 July the government counsel at the Commission, Mr McHugh, argued for the immediate release of the transcripts of the Combe phone taps. The first batch were released the following day.

For three weeks the media had been intensely critical of the prime minister's secrecy in his handling of the Combe affair, in particular for the failure to make public vital evidence. Instantly it now decided that the release of the phone taps represented a gross violation of Combe's civil liberties. The media, it appeared, was hostile to the government on secrecy grounds when ASIO's evidence was not released and on civil liberty grounds when it was.

The media's line on the phone taps was established on the evening of 19 July when David Combe on 'Nationwide' described the release of the Commission of his dinner and telephone conversations as 'the greatest invasion of privacy that has ever been inflicted upon any citizen in the history of Australia'.

The following morning Combe's judgment on this matter figured prominently in the front page stories of the *Age* and *Sydney Morning Herald* and was repeated on the ABC's 'AM'. The common view of the press was that the telephone taps provided 'no evidence that Mr Combe was a threat to national security or was compromised by Mr Ivanov' and vindicated the judgment of Combe's 'friends', or now Combe himself, that their release would do more harm to the government than to Combe.

Indeed they did. From 20 July to 23 July, in the wake of the release of the Combe telephone taps, the pressure on the Hawke government was more intense than at any time in the entire affair. The government was now unambiguously 'on trial'; its competence and in particular the competence of the prime minister, was 'shaping as the issue'. Old enemies of Hawke now emerged to suggest that the job was too big for him and that there was 'a good leader on standby' in Mr Hayden.

The intensity and quality of the media criticism of the government between 20 and 23 July is most easily demonstrated by a brief examination of the performance of one newspaper, the *Sydney Morning Herald*. On 20 July the *Sydney Morning Herald*'s report of the Combe phone taps ran under a front page streamer, 'The greatest invasion of privacy which has occurred in this nation'. On 21 July its report of the flak following the release of the phone taps was under the headline 'Labor in Revolt over Bugging'. The *Sydney Morning Herald*'s lengthy editorial of 21 July argued that the only security problem so far revealed by the Hope Commission was 'with ASIO and the Federal Government itself' and suggested an improper motive (the desire to embarrass old political foes) in the Hawke decision to release the phone taps. Two days later it suggested that even if the Combe phone taps had been published without the names of the callers (as Hawke had argued at a press conference they ought to have been) their release would still have been totally improper. In its high moral dudgeon it seemed to have slipped the *Sydney Morning Herald*'s mind that less than three weeks earlier it had chastised the government for its 'reluctance to allow material to be made publicly available' so that 'the people of Australia' could test its worth.

And what of the *Sydney Morning Herald*'s columnists? They exposed their readers to a concentrated dose of the mainstream anti-anticommunist banalities of the age. Yvonne Preston asked three times in a single column why we were all so 'paranoid' about the Soviet Union. Mike Steketee agreed. 'The whiff of McCarthyism' for so long now in the Canberra air had turned 'pungent'. Bob Hawke, he revealed, had 'strong anti-Soviet feelings—some would say a blindspot'. Combe's only 'crime' had been to take a 'relaxed view' of the Soviet Union and to prepare to make some money as a consequence. For Peter Bowers the issue of the affair was no longer security but 'the incompetence of the Hawke government and of ASIO'. Bowers characterised the government's release of the phone taps as 'disgraceful' and 'shameful'. 'McCarthyism' (again) was 'alive and well and living in Australia in 1983...The Ivanov–Combe affair has presented the Hawke government with a critical test early in its life.'

In the midst of this atmosphere, when the government was more on the defensive and Combe more on the attack than at any other time in the affair, it was indeed fortunate for David Combe that the single most damaging piece of evidence in the hands of ASIO—Combe's report to Matheson—should have been leaked to the journalist Laurie Oakes. There would never be a more psychologically favourable moment for the news of this report to be made public nor more sympathetic a journalist to break it than Oakes, whom Combe described at the Commission as 'a very close friend'.

Combe's report to Matheson, written on his return from Moscow in December 1982, had suggested that Commercial Bureau might improve its trading prospects in Moscow if it provided funds and played a more prominent role in the affairs of the Australia–USSR and USSR–Australia friendship societies; if it contributed money to the establishment of an Edinburgh University-style conference (where influential Australian and Soviet citizens would discuss alternatively in Australia or the USSR foreign policy, trade and economic questions); and if it funded and was known in Moscow to be funding Combe's work for the 'upscaling' of relations between the CPSU and the ALP.

Oakes' articles in the *Age* of 21 July (there was both a report and a comment) combined information, interpretation and special pleading. In his lead article Oakes outlined much if not all of significance in the report. (He omitted, for example, Combe's suggestion to Commercial Bureau that it should help finance the Edinburgh-style conference.) Combe's 'black-balling', he suggested, had been justified by government references to a 'mystery' document. If this was that document it would seem 'very little evidence is required to brand a person a security risk'. Combe's 'friends' had pointed out to Oakes that it had never been proposed that relations between the ALP and the CPSU should reach even the level achieved between the ALP and the Communist Party of Rumania. The much vaunted confidentiality of the report had nothing to do with Australia. There was no evidence that Combe planned to launder Soviet money to influence the Australian government on behalf of the Soviet Union. Indeed the whole report seemed to Oakes 'innocuous enough'.

The Oakes interpretation of the innocuousness of the Matheson report carried the day in the Australian press. For the *Sydney Morning Herald* Mike Steketee thought the Matheson report a slender thread on which to hang a man and saved his fireworks of 22 July for the government. The *Age*'s Michelle Grattan thought it did nothing to 'advance the Government's case'. On 'Sunday' Max Walsh's analysis of the report consisted entirely of a lengthy interview with David Combe who, unsurprisingly, concurred with the Oakes judgment of it. Walsh himself suggested that possibly 'even more important' than the content of the report was 'how it reached ASIO'. And in July the *National Times*—a veritable bull terrier with regard to evidence it thought damaging to the government— virtually ignored it.

As with the Ivanov dinner tape of 4 March the media's investigative performance in regard to the Matheson report was less than penetrating. No journalist questioned the propriety of Combe's recommending to a commercial company that it gain trade favours in Moscow by becoming involved in funding Soviet propaganda outfits or his own plans to work for the 'upscaling' of relations between the CPSU and the ALP. No journalist inquired as to what authorisation Combe might have had from the ALP leadership for his discussions in Moscow concerning the 'upscaling' of relations with the CPSU or whether on his return from Moscow he had discussed these plans with its leaders. No journalist noticed that Combe had in the dinner conversation of 4 March given Ivanov details of a report which Oakes' articles claimed was made confidential only to keep it from Soviet eyes. No journalist, finally, asked whether there might be any connection between Combe's expression in Moscow of his keenness to 'upscale' relations between the ALP and the CPSU and the 'brief' Ponomarev had subsequently given Ivanov to discuss with Combe the possibility of his playing a role in the area of Soviet trade.

With a little help from his friends Combe had cleared his most formidable hurdle effortlessly. Hawke—or so it appeared—had still to face his. The tantalising question of who tipped off Richard Farmer—a question Mr Hawke had made clear would not be canvassed until he took the stand at the Royal Commission—remained unanswered. In the final week of July the media was held in a state of suspended animation. Mr Matheson, whom the press had labelled as the 'mystery man' of the affair—was giving evidence at the Commission but *in camera*. He had arrived at the Commission tight-lipped, refusing absolutely to discuss 'the unanimous question' the media wished to ask him: 'Mr Matheson, have you ever worked for Australian intelligence organisations?' The best the media could beat up on the Matheson front was to investigate whether or not he had played a part as a naval frogman in the search for Harold Holt!

As the appearance of the star witness at the Royal Commission approached, the more detailed and damaging did the stories of the Farmer tip-off become. On the weekend prior to Hawke's appearance the *National Times* ran a story entitled 'Labor Warned—Worst is Still to Come' which included reference to a Canberra 'chain' which had passed on secret Cabinet security committee information about Combe's blacklisting. The *National Times* mentioned only two links in this chain— Farmer and the lobbyist David Barnett. On the morning of Hawke's appearance the *Sydney Morning Herald* ran an 'exclusive' story which added several more. Peter Bowers now reported explicitly (what had long been implied) that the 'chain of communication' had started with Hawke's phone call to Richard Farmer and had then passed to Richard's brother David, to David's squash partner Martin Rawlinson, to Rawlinson's business associates David Barnett and Alister Drysdale, and from one of them to another lobbyist, Dale Budd. Not only had the chain started with Hawke but, more importantly, according to Bowers' story, Farmer had 'learnt that Combe would be denied access to the Government *because of his association with Ivanov*'. (My emphasis.) If this last detail were true it was very difficult to see in what way Hawke's phone call to Farmer differed from Young's chat to Walsh. The worst might indeed be yet to come for Mr Hawke and his government.

From the point of view of the media Mr Hawke's appearance in the witness box on 3 August proved something of an anti-climax. Without demur Hawke confirmed that he had indeed phoned Richard Farmer on 23 April warning him not to go into partnership with Combe because he would be denied ministerial access, but denied absolutely that he had mentioned Ivanov or any question of security to Farmer as the reason. Hawke explained that he had no choice but to warn Farmer off Combe. To fail so to do, and to allow the partnership to be formed, would be a means of indirectly restoring Combe's access to ministers.

On the evening of 3 August Richard Carleton's hopes on the Farmer front were still high. He announced that the prime minister had 'leaked' to Farmer the news of the Combe blacklisting and retold the Bowers' tale of the morning, a tale he claimed was now 'critical to a number of reputations'. While not challenging Hawke's claim that he had not mentioned Ivanov or security to Farmer, Carleton commented sarcastically that someone obviously had 'managed to put two and two together' and concluded that 'tonight Mr Peacock is asking what's the distinction between Mr Hawke's leak and Mr Young's'.

By the morning of 4 August, however, the media seemed convinced that the prime minister, at least for the moment, was off the hook. The news divided more or less equally between Hawke's 'admission' in the witness box that he had tipped off Farmer and his evening announcement that Mr Peacock's press release equating the tip-off with Mr Young's leak was 'wrong', 'defamatory' and possibly in contempt of the Commission. While some journalists argued that Hawke's challenge to Peacock was an attempt to divert attention from the more serious questions raised by his evidence none gave real support to the opposition's call for Hawke's resignation. Michelle Grattan now thought the tip-off to Farmer could at least be 'partly defended'.

Like many other journalists, after Hawke's first day in the witness box, Ms Grattan felt more troubled about the quality of ASIO's case against Combe and Hawke's uncritical acquiescence in it than she did about the Farmer 'brouhaha'. Peter Bowers' 'hunch' had proven correct. Many of the journalists who had been following the Farmer lead on the trail of Hawke had been disappointed. From 4 August ASIO and Hawke's relations with it became for the media the central issue of the Combe affair.

BAGGING ASIO

In the long run probably the most important consequence of the Combe affair turned out to be the damage it inflicted on the reputation of ASIO. ASIO might have expected 'just a little glory' from the Ivanov expulsion. What it got was 'public rebuke' and 'ridicule'. Although as we shall see ASIO can by no means be absolved entirely from responsibility for this turn of events, the major responsibility undoubtedly rests with the Australian media.

The media's critique of ASIO began in earnest after Mr Hawke's decision of 18 July to request the Commission to release the Combe telephone taps. In the ASIO transcripts certain errors were discovered. The transcripts referred to Combe's wife as 'Nina' not 'Meena' and on occasions spelt the name of Combe with a double 'o'. The clerical staff at ASIO had failed to comprehend part of a conversation between Combe and Matheson. A few lines were misattributed, and one rendered by an ASIO clerk in phonetical gobbledygook as 'Even old stacks talk'. These errors were of course of no substance whatever but given what was at stake (and in particular given the mood of the press) they should not have been made or allowed to stand.

The media now had its opening. ASIO was mocked mercilessly. New jokes about 'old stacks' replaced the old ones about 'jelly and whipped cream'. On the foundations of 'Nina', 'Coombe' and 'old stacks', Peter Bowers concluded that 'our national security' was 'in the hands of a bunch of dangerously incompetent amateurs'; while Michelle Grattan explained that the 'old stacks' line 'encapsulates the reason why many of us distrust ASIO: a fear that its conspiratorial world encourages bungling, incompetence and an alarming ability to miss the wood while it hides under the trees'. (She did not however explain the deeper meaning of the fact of her own newspaper having, on 19 and 20 July, thrice accidentally referred to a Mr Coombe.)

In the next fortnight new details of ASIO errors emerged. In the *Age* of 29 July Laurie Oakes revealed that in the *'aide-mémoire'* Harvey Barnett had originally presented to the government on the dinner conversation of 4 March ASIO's transcripts had Ivanov commenting to Combe that if he got the Moscow ambassadorship he would have his hands on the 'files' and Combe referring to Ivanov's 'brief talk' to him about trade. The official transcript made clear that 'files' should have read 'pulse' and 'brief talk' 'brief *to* talk'. While Oakes himself did not believe in ASIO conspiracy theories he was sure such errors would lead members of the ALP to believe that Combe had been set up by ASIO in the interests of Australian conservatism. He did not mention that while one of these errors marginally weakened, the other strengthened ASIO's 'case' against Combe. Nor of course did he mention who was his source for *in camera* Commission evidence.

On the day before Mr Hawke was to appear in the witness

box details of a further ASIO error transpired. On 1 May ASIO had mistakenly reported a breakfast meeting between Combe and the prime ministerial staff member Bob Hogg. (The press, for once interested in the source of a leak, hinted it came from the Hawke camp—the prime minister's own version, perhaps, of a pre-emptive revelation.) When Hawke took the stand on 3 August he confirmed in his evidence this ASIO error and spoke of the considerable anger it had caused him. He also confirmed that ASIO had initially wrongly claimed that in 1976 the Combes had had a free trip on a Soviet cruise ship (in fact their accommodation had merely been upgraded) and that in 1982 the Soviets had paid the airfare of both Combe and his wife (in fact they only paid his).

It was plain by now that ASIO had made far too many errors. But it was also plain that the errors were of little significance to the central issue of the affair—the nature of Combe's relations with Ivanov. The most serious error, ASIO's report of the Hogg–Combe non-breakfast, had a political importance for Hawke but no bearing whatever on the Combe–Ivanov relationship. The errors concerning the Soviet subsidies of Combe family holidays were trivial. The transcription errors in the phone taps were amusing but entirely irrelevant to the government–ASIO 'case' against Combe. And the transcription errors in the ASIO '*aide-mémoire*' if anything on balance favoured Combe. Yet notwithstanding all this the ASIO errors had undoubtedly given the media a useful stick with which to flail ASIO and Mr Hawke.

The value was apparent in the reports of the first day of Hawke's evidence at the Commission. Under the headline 'Evidence deepens the mire', Michelle Grattan expressed deep concern at Hawke's 'sloppiness' in failing to 'adequately search' ASIO's evidence—at least prior to 3 May. The *Australian Financial Review* reversed chronology to point out that 'the crucial decisions' on the fates of both Ivanov and Combe had been taken by Hawke 'despite revelations of mistakes' by ASIO. And in the *National Times* David Marr now wondered whether the government's belief that the relationship between Ivanov and Combe was about to go 'clandestine', and even that Ivanov was KGB, might not merely reflect yet more ASIO errors.

ASIO was never allowed by the Australian media to forget its errors. The technique of endlessly repeating and exaggerating the significance of errors was put to most effective use against ASIO by David Combe's media supporters. Against this form of attack ASIO was certainly vulnerable although, as its counsel at the Commission Stephen Charles showed, not entirely defenceless. After a characteristically nasty swipe at ASIO from Richard Carleton, Charles called on him to 'give away the role of journalist buffoon and [to] start to listen to the evidence'. Carleton was behaving, he claimed, not as a reporter but as a 'campaigner'. 'From the start' he had 'followed a role of bagging ASIO'. It was no less than the truth.

Naturally the media critique of ASIO did not end with the exposure of its errors. Throughout the affair—but particularly after the edited transcripts of the ASIO evidence before the Commission began appearing—the media placed ASIO under investigation. For the media the evidence of an ASIO director-general and desk officer provided 'a brief but historic—and at times bizarre—glimpse' of the world of Australian intelligence. It revealed 'much more about ASIO's worldview' than it did 'about the KGB in Australia'. Indeed was it not rather ASIO than Combe that now was 'on trial'?

The ASIO discovered by the young reporters let loose upon the Commission evidence did not disappoint their preconceptions. ASIO indeed lived in a John Le Carré world of trench coats and 'tradecraft' superstitions. This was a world where the perfectly ordinary behaviour of a Soviet diplomat (like having a television blaring in his home or warning an Australian friend to be more discreet about future meetings) took on sinister meanings about neutralising bugs and pushing relationships onto clandestine paths. ASIO read straightforward boozy conversations as if they were in code. They jumped to conclusions about the KGB status of Soviet diplomats, and jumped to yet further conclusions about KGB objectives. If Ivanov was KGB this had to mean for ASIO that the cultivation of a friendship with Combe had a recruitment intention and that its purposes were illicit.

According to the journalist who made most of the running in the media on this matter, David Marr of the *National Times*, the trouble with ASIO was that it could not distinguish between 'fact' and 'inference'. Nor, it would appear, could he. In the course of his campaigning for Combe, Marr, on the basis of the flimsiest reasoning and most circumstantial evidence, concluded that Combe had been used by ASIO as a 'dangle' to lure Ivanov to indiscretion and expulsion; and Matheson employed by ASIO to set Combe up. Marr argued further that Combe had actually suffered by *not* having been 'targeted' for surveillance by ASIO before 22 April. (If he had been placed under full surveillance many of ASIO's errors in its initial presentation of the case to the government might have been avoided.) Marr's logic, then, came to this. ASIO was willing to set Combe up and use him as a 'dangle' to catch Ivanov without placing him under surveillance. The ways of ASIO were mysterious indeed.

According to the media ASIO was, however, prone to more than bungling, wild deduction and conspiracy. They were also ideologically suspect, 'cold war warriors', unable to transcend the outmoded *Weltanschauung* of the 1950s. Michelle Grattan put the general view succinctly: 'From what we have seen revealed of its counter-espionage work, [ASIO] still operates on many of the Cold War assumptions about international politics. ASIO, for example, seems to have been quite preoccupied with Combe's anti-CIA views which it equated with being anti-American.'

For the *National Times* and David Marr, in having put Combe's (supposed) 'bitter anti-Americanism' to the government as a factor in the Combe–Ivanov case, ASIO was establishing an insidious 'loyalty test' for all Australians. Marr's suggestion here (and he was by no means alone in it) was that ASIO regarded in the case of Combe and regards in general the expression of anti-American opinions as matters in themselves of security concern. In fact—as ASIO at the Commission made clear—what was of concern was not Combe's anti-American opinions but the encouragement they expected the expression of them to Ivanov would give the KGB in their cultivation of Combe.

'Absolute understanding of the KGB,' Marr reported ironically was 'the rock' on which ASIO's case against Combe had been built. In response it must be said that a near-perfect innocence about the KGB was the rock on which the media built their defence of him. Margot O'Neill of the *Age* thought the Cheka-NKVD-KGB self-description as 'the sword and the shield' of the Revolution an ASIO invention. Her colleague, Michelle Grattan, was gently amused at the ASIO belief that Australia had any secrets of interest to the KGB. (Strangely enough it took the American anti-CIA campaigner, Victor Marchetti, who had been brought to Australia by Combe to give evidence on his behalf, to convince one member of the Australia press that we did.) In the *Australian Financial Review* Anne Summers reflected that Mr Hawke's evidence to the Commission was 'quite plausible...if one has sympathy at all for the notion that the KGB is active in western democracies such as Australia'.

If? Between 1974 and 1983 over 300 KGB or GRU (Soviet military intelligence) officers—many caught red-handed in acts of military or industrial espionage—had been expelled from scores of countries including almost every western democracy. Did Dr Summers really not know this?

And, most importantly, time and again throughout the Combe affair Richard Hall emerged to argue in the media that the idea of the 'agent of influence' was a 'slippery and vague notion', invented by western intelligence services to broaden their warrant for surveillance over the lives of innocents like David Combe. Hall showed no knowledge of the recent cases where 'agents of influence' had been uncovered (like the cases of the journalists Pierre-Charles Pathé and Arne Petersen, the former of whom published *Synthesis*, a pro-Soviet newsletter in Paris, under the guidance of KGB officers working in the Soviet Embassy or the Soviet delegation at UNESCO; the latter of whom conducted various operations in the Danish press under the direction of KGB officer Merkulov). He also showed no interest in ASIO's quite precise definition of the concept as outlined at the Royal Commission:

> At least some intelligence services, and particularly we are talking about the KGB, have also a strong interest…in influencing the course of events, and one of their means for doing so is to recruit persons who do not have access…to secret information at the time but who can, because of their standing in their own community, have an influence on either government views or public opinion…With KGB control and input, that influence can be turned to the use of the Soviets. The danger is, of course, that the source of the inspiration, if you like, is concealed.

Hall's own claim that certain people mentioned in the

Petrov documents—like Senator McCallum or Arthur Calwell—'could be defined' (by whom?) 'as agents of influence' was based either on a complete distortion of the notion of 'agent of influence' or a total misunderstanding of the proceedings of the Petrov Royal Commission. (Certainly at least in part the latter. Hall mistakenly took the 'John Pringle' of the Petrov documents as the John Douglas Pringle of the *Sydney Morning Herald*, a mistake suggesting he had not even read the Commissioner's report.)

It was perhaps fortunate for Mr Hall's self-esteem that he decided to decline an invitation to give evidence at the Hope Royal Commission. He thought, as he told the *Sydney Morning Herald*, it useless to appear given what he called Mr Justice Hope's 'ineradicable psychological disposition' to believe that 'agents of influence' exist.

Throughout the Combe affair the media showed itself not only ill-informed about the KGB but not even vaguely interested in it. Whereas articles and programs repeatedly placed ASIO under the microscope, I came upon not one single article or program (with the exception of B.A. Santamaria's columns in the *Australian*) which provided an international perspective on the KGB. A search for material on the KGB's espionage activities or disinformation campaigns in the western democracies or on its historical role in Stalin's mass murder (as the NKVD) and present function in the crushing of dissent inside the USSR was a search in vain. This ignorant uninquisitive provincialism was the single most astonishing and disturbing fact in the entire story of the coverage of the Combe affair. In the Australian media the KGB appeared merely as a spectre in the Cold War fantasies of ASIO.

THE MERCILESS DISSECTION

In his press conference of 21 July—when pressure on him was at its most intense—Mr Hawke urged the reporters to suspend judgment on the Combe affair until all the evidence had been heard. Only then, he argued, would they be able to assemble from the fragments of evidence 'the total picture—the total mosaic' of the Combe–Ivanov relationship. From that moment members of the press waited irritably for Hawke's promise to be fulfilled. In late August David Combe took the stand at the Commission. For those with an interest in the truth this was undoubtedly the critical moment in the proceedings of the Royal Commission. As a result of his testimony—and in particular as a result of the cross-examination of him by Mr Charles for ASIO and Mr McHugh for the government—the total mosaic took shape.

In the late winter of 1982 Valeriy Ivanov—who Combe at the Royal Commission conceded was indeed a KGB officer—began cultivating the friendship of Combe. In September, when Combe still barely knew him, he visited the Combes' Canberra home bearing gifts. At the same time Ivanov was responsible for having Combe chosen to represent the Australia–USSR Society (hereafter the AUS) at a major international conference in Moscow of Soviet friendship societies. At the Commission Combe claimed at first that he had been chosen by the society itself without the intervention of the embassy. When, however, confronted by some secret evidence (presumably a phone tap of a conversation between Ivanov and an officer of the AUS) he agreed that Ivanov had indeed made the choice. Ivanov was involved in the Combes' travel arrangements (David insisted on being accompanied by his wife, whose fare he paid) and the two of them dined with

Ivanov (at Ivanov's expense) in October.

In the Soviet Union, at least in the latter part of his trip (Combe felt the atmosphere in relation to him changed halfway through it), Combe was involved in a series of meetings with senior Soviet officials. At the Commission Combe denied believing Ivanov responsible for arranging these meetings. He could not understand why he had said to a journalist friend on 26 April that Ivanov 'had helped me get some meetings I wanted when I was over there'. With Mr Smelyakov, a deputy minister of trade, Combe claims to have discussed the affairs of Commercial Bureau and agreed to organise (in obvious violation of existing post-Afghanistan sanctions) a delegation of Australian businessmen to visit the USSR and inspect advanced Soviet technology. With Mr Parasteyev, the head of the English-speaking section of the Friendship societies, Combe agreed to help organise (again in obvious violation of sanctions) an Australian equivalent of the Edinburgh University Conference. According to Combe, Parasteyev offered him free medical treatment. Combe also met with three members of the international department of the CPSU central committee—Messrs Sharif, Lagutin and Kudinov. The most extensive discussions were with Kudinov, the Australian desk officer, with whom Combe discussed, according to his account, relations between the ALP and the CPSU and once more the Edinburgh Conference idea.

On his return to Australia Combe prepared the report for Commercial Bureau (which Oakes had written about in July) urging Matheson to fund his decision to work for the 'upscaling' of relations between the ALP and the CPSU and to contribute money to the Friendship societies and the proposed Edinburgh University Conference. According to Combe he asked Matheson for $10,000 for this project; according to Matheson, $50,000.

On 15 December Combe spoke to Ivanov (whom he had told Kudinov he wished to work with in Australia) on the telephone. According to the ASIO summary of this conversation Combe spoke of his eagerness to play a liaison role in relations between the CPSU and the ALP and of 'lots of undertakings' given him by Parasteyev and Kudinov while in Moscow. He also referred to certain other matters best not discussed on the phone. The pair agreed to meet in the near future for a 'long, long session'. At the Commission Combe claimed that, apart from a short visit Ivanov had paid the Combes at Christmas to present them with a gift of vodka, he did not meet Ivanov again until the Combes dined with him on 7 January 1983. His mention of matters best not discussed on the phone was a ploy to end the conversation. He could not for the life of him recall what (apart from Parasteyev's offer of medical treatment) were the 'lots of undertakings' he had mentioned to Ivanov.

On 4 March—as all the world now knew on the basis of the transcript released on 6 July—Combe had dined at Ivanov's home. As we have seen the conversation centred on the 'brief' Ivanov had from Ponomarev to discuss the possibility of Combe playing some role in Australian–Soviet trade. Combe had left to Ivanov the decision as to whether or not he could work for both Commercial Bureau and the Soviets. Ivanov had also made clear that before negotiations could progress further he would have to put some formal proposition to Moscow for approval. 'We have a practice,' he told Combe, 'that we should send our official proposition to Moscow and then we receive a reply and then we work it out.' On 6 March Ivanov visited the Combes bearing gifts of champagne, chocolate and cigars. He told Combe he did not predict any conflict of interest if Combe agreed to work for Matheson. On 15 March he phoned Combe. Could he come to see him? He had some news. Was it, asked

Combe, good or bad? Not bad. Combe warned him that from 8.30 p.m. he would be watching *The Dismissal* on television. Could he come at 7.30? He came.

At the Royal Commission Combe claimed no recollection whatever of the news Ivanov brought him on 15 March. He thought it might have concerned Ivanov's telling him that a rival trading company, Pactra, was defeating Matheson's Commercial Bureau in the race between them for Soviet trade. But was not this news, Mr Justice Hope asked, wholly bad? After reflection Combe agreed it was. What news Ivanov brought Combe on 15 March was never to be clarified at the Commission.

On 16 March—the day after Ivanov visited Combe—Combe spoke to a New South Wales trade adviser, Jay Alparslan. According to Alparslan, Combe told him he had been 'appointed as a representative of the Soviet central committee' and was 'liaising with the political officer of the USSR Embassy here in Australia'. Combe did not deny discussing Soviet trade with Alparslan on 16 March but hotly denied using any such form of words to him. He agreed with the government's counsel that if he had used them it would have been totally 'destructive' of his 'credibility' in the affair.

On 21 March Combe returned a phone call from Ivanov and agreed to meet him that day at a Canberra restaurant. At this meeting, according to Combe's account, Ivanov offered Combe medical treatment in the USSR, mentioned the possibility of a Black Sea coast holiday and repeated his interest (apparently first expressed on 4 March) in receiving material from Combe on CIA involvement in the 1975 dismissal of the Whitlam government.

On 3 April Combe arrived unexpectedly at Ivanov's home. (The tape of this conversation was of course also long known to the world.) Although it was five in the afternoon Ivanov was in bed, apparently with a hangover. After turning on the television, Ivanov accepted legal documents from Combe concerning Matheson's trade rivalry with Pactra. Combe promised future 'documents' from Brian Toohey on the CIA and 1975. Combe maintained throughout the Commission that the documents he had in mind were merely newspaper clippings which were to be supplied to him by Toohey. Toohey, however, had made no mention of his role as Combe's source of newspaper clippings in the article he published on 13 May defending his friend. Toohey was the man who boasted on 6 May in the *National Times* of having in his possession 'thousands of pages' of secret intelligence documents.

Once outside the house Ivanov told Combe that he expected he might soon be expelled from Australia and that he had information which suggested that Combe's phone had been tapped by ASIO after he had returned from Moscow in December. They should not phone each other. According to Combe's evidence at the Commission Ivanov told him that in future they should make contact only by private visits—to Combe's office or Ivanov's home. According to Matheson's evidence Combe had told him on 6 April that Ivanov had said that Combe should keep a low profile and wait for Ivanov to contact him. Combe was absolutely certain Ivanov had not used these words. 'This is the one matter you have a clear memory about?' Mr Justice Hope asked drily. Why, ASIO counsel asked, had Combe not alerted someone in the Labor government to what Ivanov had told him. If what Ivanov told him were true, was it not 'outrageous' and would it not give Combe a splendid chance of 'shafting' ASIO? If it were false did it not raise serious questions in his mind about the game Ivanov was playing?

Throughout the Commission Combe denied knowing before his expulsion that Ivanov was KGB. In response to this, cross-examining counsel confronted him with the evidence of Matheson who had claimed Combe had told him that Ivanov was 'more than he appeared to be'; of the journalist Ken Haley who after speaking to Combe on the evening of 11 May had written that Combe 'always suspected...Ivanov as being a KGB officer'; of a friend of Combe's to whom Combe had said on 26 April that he had 'always assumed' Ivanov to be KGB; and of the director-general of ASIO who had given evidence that Combe had indicated to him that he regarded Ivanov as KGB. Combe at the Commission claimed that if he had known Ivanov to be KGB he would not have dealt with him. Yet—as cross-examining counsel pointed out—Combe had drunk with a Soviet Embassy official (Koshliakov) whom he assumed to be KGB before setting out for Moscow and had requested a meeting while there with another old acquaintance (Raina) whom he had long believed to be KGB.

Combe also argued at the Commission that after 15 March he had come to resent Ivanov's attentions and had come after 3 April to regard him as a 'creep'. Nevertheless, as cross-examining counsel showed, he had returned Ivanov's phone call of 20 March promptly and immediately arranged to meet him, had dropped in unexpectedly on 3 April and had then suggested a future meeting between the two of them and Mr Hayden. After the expulsion order had been announced Combe had thought of inviting Ivanov to his fortieth birthday celebrations and after the expulsion had occurred mentioned at no time—either in public or in private—a rift in relations. In his numerous post-expulsion media appearances Combe had consistently referred to his 'close friendship' with that very 'charming man' Ivanov. In answer to all this Combe claimed, at the Commission, that his attitude to Ivanov had 'softened' after his expulsion was announced and that he was, despite being a bit of a 'creep', 'charming in an ongoing way'.

Although on 4 March Combe had placed the question of the propriety of working for both Commercial Bureau and the Soviets in Ivanov's hands, and although on 6 March Ivanov had assured him there was no conflict of interest, Combe consistently claimed at the Commission that after mid-March his Soviet trading ambitions were completely satisfied by his contract with Commercial Bureau and that he had now lost all interest in playing an independent role in the area of Soviet trade. He could not really explain why his two potential business partners—Richard Farmer and Bill Butler—had both claimed in evidence to the Commission that Combe had spoken to them on 22 April of the fortune he hoped to make from Soviet trade or why two of his media supporters—Brian Toohey and Richard Carleton—had filed stories in mid-May (after discussions with Combe) in which Combe's trade hopes with the Soviet Union were emphasised. Nor could Combe satisfactorily explain why trade negotiations should have been authorised by the head of the international department of the central committee and conducted in Australia by a senior KGB officer, or what he—a former prominent political figure but self-confessed ignoramus in the area of trade—had to offer the Soviet Union.

Finally Combe had considerable difficulty at the Commission in explaining aspects of his relations with his old party. Combe, as we have seen, had discussed a 'liaison' role for himself in relations between the ALP and CPSU with both Kudinov and Ivanov and had sought funding for it from Matheson. At the Royal Commission he thought it possible he had discussed this matter with an assistant secretary of the ALP, Ken Bennett, but could not be certain. He said he did not consider it needed to be raised with the party's parliamentary leadership. But why, he was asked, when troubles had blown up, had he not mentioned his proposed liaison role in his

statement to the government of 11 May? Combe claimed he
had intended to annex to his statement to the government a
copy of his report to Matheson which would have made his
liaison-upscaling ambitions clear. Why, then, had he not
included a copy of the Matheson report—which had been
preying on his mind in early May as open to 'misinterpreta-
tion'—in his statement? Combe claimed his solicitor had
warned him that to include it would involve a breach of the
confidentiality he owed his client Matheson. Had he attempted
to clear the matter with Matheson? Combe admitted he had
not. If he was so concerned about the confidentiality of the
report why had he shown sections of it to Farmer and Butler
on 29 April? And if he was so concerned about the interests of
his client why had he outlined its contents to Ivanov on 4
March in a way almost certain to damage the trading
prospects of Commercial Bureau?

Combe left the stand emotionally shattered, or, as his
defender David Marr was to put it in his book on the affair,
'one of the walking wounded', his credibility as a witness and
a principal in the affair torn to shreds. If justification for the
ordeal Combe had been put through by Charles and McHugh
was needed it was that by September 1983 at stake in the
question of the Combe–Ivanov relationship were the reputations of both Mr Hawke and ASIO.

What, then, did the media make of the devastating and
decisive cross-examination of David Combe? Very little
indeed. By the time Combe took the stand the media had
begun to lose interest in the increasingly complicated details of
the affair. Only one journalist, David Marr, in a story subtitled
'the merciless dissection of David Combe's life', revealed even
a rudimentary understanding of what had taken place at
the Commission between 30 August and 12 September. While
Marr tried as best he could to shield and comfort Combe he at

least outlined the kind of case that had been put to the Commission by Charles and McHugh.

From ABC public affairs there was virtually nothing. On the first day of Combe's cross-examination Richard Carleton reminded his viewers on 'Nationwide' that Stephen Charles was the man who had called him a 'buffoon' and then proceeded to prove Charles' point by a commentary restricted to admiration for Charles' 'Perry Mason' style of advocacy. Of substance on the first day of Combe's cross-examination there was nothing from Carleton. And after the first day nothing at all.

In the newspapers daily reports were filed but these reports in general showed little grasp of the significance of the evidence being outlined and were often concerned with matters at best marginal to the substance of the affair. The headlines of the stories written by Paul Malone for the *Australian Financial Review* during the period of Combe's cross-examination are some indicator of the quality of at least his reports. 'Judge appears to lose his patience with David Combe' (1 Sept.); 'Cameron tried to "heavy" him to make statement—Combe' (2 Sept.); 'Combe reveals antagonism for Federal Govt over treatment' (6 Sept.); 'Cross-examination torturous [sic] Combe tells Hope inquiry' (7 Sept.); 'Ivanov nominated Combe for Soviet trip Commission told' (8 Sept.); 'Combe to enlist the help of ex-CIA man' (9 Sept.); and 'Govt handled Combe-Ivanov affair badly: Labor MP' (13 Sept.). During September, the young Commission reporters, Malone, Margot O'Neill of the *Age* and Richard McGregor of the *Sydney Morning Herald*, all published feature articles highly critical of ASIO based on interpretations of the ASIO evidence presented to the Commission. Not one, however, published a story interpreting the Combe evidence. At the time Mr Justice Hope was preparing to listen to counsels' final submissions and then retire to write his report, David Combe could, despite his ordeal in the witness box, at least console himself with the thought that he had thus far won the battle for the media handsomely.

HOPE—AND ITS CONSEQUENCES

The Royal Commission report on the Combe–Ivanov affair was tabled in parliament on 6 December 1983. In it Mr Justice Hope argued that there was absolutely no doubt that Ivanov was a KGB officer who was cultivating Combe and that before 4 March Ivanov had received written instructions from 'the highest level' in Moscow to ask Combe to work for the Soviet Union. Hope was also convinced that Ivanov's purposes in the cultivation of Combe were 'illicit'. Ivanov as a KGB officer had in Combe as promising a target 'as he was ever likely to get'. Ivanov was not a trade official. 'The Soviet Government did not require the intervention of a KGB officer to further its legitimate trading interests.' The offer of trading work was 'a bait' in the cultivation process; Ivanov's misinformation of 3 April about ASIO's tapping Combe's phone was 'typically part of a process of recruitment'. He thought it likely that the ultimate intentions of Ivanov were 'if possible to use Combe to obtain and to hand over to him information and documents illegitimately, and in the interests of the Soviet Union, and to act, wittingly or unwittingly as an agent of influence'. Recent Australian experience, he reflected tartly, reveals how easy it is for someone outside government 'with the right connections' to obtain confidential information.

> The view that Australia has no secrets that the KGB would wish to acquire, and that the KGB would not seek to influence those in this country who would reject an overt

approach by its officers, can hardly stand with the continuous KGB presence and activity in Australia.

David Combe, Mr Justice Hope reported, 'at the least' believed that Ivanov 'was probably a KGB officer'. On his return from Moscow in December 1982 he had already suggested in his report to Commercial Bureau a role for himself which would have made him in effect 'an overt agent of influence'. He had responded enthusiastically to Ivanov's offers of work for the Soviet Union and had, despite believing him probably to be KGB, 'proposed to accede' to Ivanov's suggestion that they should meet in the future 'in such a way as to avoid surveillance'. Hope regarded Combe's claims that his feelings for Ivanov had soured after 3 April and that after mid-March he had lost interest in the Moscow proposal to work for the Soviet Union as clear and deliberate falsehoods. He had no doubt that Combe would not have agreed in April 1983, if asked directly, to spy for the Soviet Union. However he did have doubts as to 'whether Mr Combe could have withstood a long and subtle process of cultivation and whether he appreciated the dangers inherent in his relationship with Mr Ivanov'.

> His ambition overriding his judgment, he allowed himself to be led into a position where his loyalty could become suspect. The consequent danger was certainly apparent and probably real. The extent of the danger turned on his ability to perceive it and extricate himself before it was too late. Mr Combe may well have done this, but there was a reasonable chance, obviously perceived by the KGB, that he might not.

In all major matters Mr Justice Hope approved the Hawke government's and ASIO's handling of the Combe affair in which he had no doubt there were 'serious implications for national security'. His report was tightly argued, extremely fair-minded and revealed a mastery of the evidence which had been presented to him over four and a half months. The soundness of his central conclusions will, I hope, be evident to readers of this chapter.

In general—with the notable exception of the *Australian Financial Review* which attacked the Hope report as 'thoroughly unsatisfactory'—the press on 7 December commented upon the report untendentiously and reported its findings accurately and in great detail. According to the editorials in the *Sydney Morning Herald*, the *Age* and the *Australian* the Hope report fully justified Mr Hawke's confidence that his government's treatment of Combe would be vindicated when the 'total mosaic' had taken shape. On 7 December in these newspapers no serious criticism of the report or its findings was offered. The journalists did not try to disguise the harshness of Hope's findings in relation to Combe. It was generally agreed that it was 'a devastating report for Mr Combe'. Combe's statement attacking the report as 'a whitewash' was covered accurately but not highlighted. Hope's minor criticisms of the government and ASIO were analysed but, apart from the *Australian Financial Review*, placed in perspective. Criticism of Mr Hawke was confined to entirely reasonable questioning of his decision to restore Mick Young—who had not escaped the lash of Hope—to Cabinet.

In the media's coverage of the Combe affair 7 December stands as an entirely exceptional day. The Hope report had acted on the media like a flash of lightning at midnight. For one brief moment an entirely unfamiliar landscape was brilliantly and precisely illuminated. But within a day the memory of the report had begun to fade. One day's illumination could not withstand six months' misreporting. By 8 December the press was at it again.

Let us see how some of our old friends interpreted the Hope

findings. In the *Australian Financial Review* of 8 December, in a remarkable article entitled 'Combe sunk by "Might Haves"', Paul Malone implied that the opinions of the New South Wales Council of Civil Liberties and the findings of Mr Justice Hope (who had examined the Combe affair over six months) were of equal status. 'On the spectrum of findings open to the Commission,' he wrote, 'Justice Hope's report is at one end and the Council of Civil Liberties' conclusions are at the other.'

Malone argued against the view of the KGB as 'an all pervasive sinister body'. He was of the opinion that Ivanov might have developed his relationship with Combe 'to collect information legitimately'. He was also of the opinion that Ivanov's proposal to Combe for meetings outside ASIO earshot might merely indicate that Ivanov 'legitimately believed that Mr Combe's phone was tapped'. The implication of this presumably was that Malone saw nothing illegitimate or sinister in a KGB officer suggesting to an Australian citizen meetings designed to evade ASIO surveillance and nothing improper in an Australian citizen acceding (as Combe admitted in evidence he had) to such a suggestion.

In long articles in the *National Times* and the *Sydney Morning Herald* of 9 December, David Marr and Paul Kelly supported Malone's view that Combe had done absolutely 'nothing' and had been condemned (i.e., denied ministerial access) merely for what he 'might have' done. Marr called the whole affair 'outrageous' and spoke of Hope's 'savage' 'attack' on Combe. Hope's 'exercise' had not 'turned on evidence'; his 'homeground' was 'the field of remote possibilities'. For Kelly the 'most enduring impression' left on him by the Hope report was of the 'ruthless cynicism' of the Hawke government. He explained the 'brutal' assault on Combe in part by the government's determination to 'prove its reliability to the power centres normally suspicious of Labor...business, the United States and the intelligence world' and in part by a 'personal antagonism towards Combe from within the Government'. In the *Age* Michelle Grattan wrote of Hawke's 'intolerance', 'insensitivity' and 'contemptuousness' as revealed in various stages of the 'the seven month destruction of Combe' while one of her colleagues, Kenneth Davidson (a newcomer to the field), likened Combe's position in relation to Ivanov to a Belgian employed by the Australian government to represent our interests at the EEC, and chastised Hope for making 'no attempt to try [sic] to view the relationship as simply a commercial' one.

Of the mainstream political commentators only Geoffrey Barker of the *Age* accepted the basic thrust of the Hope report. In May Barker had believed Combe had suffered 'a monstrous injustice'. Now Barker believed Combe had 'only himself to blame for the grave personal and professional damage he has suffered'. He also now believed ASIO had served the new Labor government 'with distinction' and had shown itself 'sensitive' to Combe's rights. But there was yet another, third, Barker to come. In June 1984, in reviewing David Marr's book *The Ivanov Trail*, Barker wrote of his 'concern' at the quality of the case ASIO presented to the government, of ASIO's 'talent...for investing seemingly fatuous remarks with conspiratorial significance' and of ASIO's 'paranoiac worldview'. After a brief flirtation with independent-mindedness, the *Age*'s associate editor had reverted to type.

By the time of Barker's review the memory of the Hope report had more or less entirely faded. While in December 1983 those who sided with Combe at least felt obliged to attack Hope's findings, by middle 1984 they were able to put it around in the media—without any apparent opposition— that Hope had 'cleared' and totally 'exonerated' David Combe.

CONCLUSION

During the course of the Combe affair Mr Hawke contended that in his public life he had never come upon a more glaring instance of journalistic laziness, unprofessionalism and bias. Readers of this chapter may not find it difficult to agree with Hawke's judgment. What may cause disagreement is why this was so. I have two suggestions to make.

The first concerns the peculiar kind of relationship which existed during 1983 between the reporters and David Combe. In evidence to the Commission Combe denied that he had orchestrated a media campaign in his defence.

> *Charles:* Would you describe the process of taking your side of the case to the media and what has followed as not being a campaign, Mr Combe?
>
> *Combe:* Well it was not a planned, carefully orchestrated campaign, Mr Charles. But yes, I made a lot of comment to the media.
>
> *Charles:* Not a planned and carefully orchestrated campaign?
>
> *Combe:* I would say it was not, yes.
>
> *Charles:* Do you really regard that answer as honest?
>
> *Combe:* Yes, I do. I did not run away from media interviews. I saw no reason why I should.
>
> *Hope:* But you sought them, did you not?
>
> *Combe:* No, I did not seek them, your Honour.

After the Commissioner's report Combe made no such pretence. On the ABC's 'Tuesday Despatch' of 12 June 1984, in a program which brought David Combe, David Marr and Brian Toohey together to discuss, without any opposing voice, the problem of reporting 'the truth' of the Combe–Ivanov affair, Combe described his media campaign clearly:

I think I had a very deliberate strategy very early on…and that was to realise that the lawyers wanted to play the particular game of conducting all the proceedings in secret…But one thing I said to [Ian Barker] was that I regarded the whole thing as being totally political, and that he was being engaged to handle the quasi-judicial, or the quasi-legal side of it but that he had to accept that as far as I was concerned there would be a second stream and that would be a public campaign which I would run through the media and through the Australian Labor Party to familiarise people with just how outrageous it all was…Had it not been for that determination on my part to make the thing public, by encouraging journalists to comment upon proceedings, by feeding stuff out to the media, then our case would have been dead and buried, and I with it, by the end of June.

The journalists in the Combe affair kept confidential from their publics the fact that the source of much of their inspiration and information on a matter concerning the reputation of David Combe was Combe himself. Although there is nothing unusual in this, it is an interesting reflection on our age that certain journalists, who regard the confidentiality of their sources as an ethical absolute, were openly contemptuous of the government and Mr Justice Hope for attempting to safeguard the confidentiality of an ASIO source, Laurie Matheson. More importantly several journalists in the Combe affair also kept from their publics knowledge of their close personal and political associations with Combe. As we have seen, some of the most sensitive material in the affair was first reported and analysed by Laurie Oakes. Oakes was a very close personal friend of Combe. There is more than enough evidence to suggest that Combe put to excellent use his many journalistic contacts. At points in the Royal Commission proceedings Combe spent 'a couple of nights' a week at the National Press Club discussing his media campaign. After the Commission he praised the *National Times* and Paul Malone of the *Australian Financial Review* for their work on his behalf.

It is not my intention to moralise at Combe for his attempt to manipulate the media in his favour. What I am concerned with is the willingness of journalists, ostensibly reporting objectively, to campaign for Combe, to disguise from their publics what they were doing, and to strive consciously to shape opinion on a question where issues of national security were concerned and where the reputations of the prime minister and of ASIO, as well as the reputation of Combe, were at stake.

Far more than the factor of personal and political friendship is, however, needed in order to explain why so many journalists were unable to report the affair objectively. To explain this it needs to be understood that the Combe affair was the most recent chapter in the long, complex and bitter struggle in Australia over attitudes towards the United States and the Soviet Union. During the 1950s ideological hegemony belonged to those who regarded the United States as a benign democracy which led the free world in the struggle to contain Soviet-communist expansionism. During the 1970s this worldview came under persistent challenge from a sector of the intelligentsia which viewed the United States as an imperialist power, the CIA as its ruthless instrument, and anticommunism its ideological façade. In the 1950s when the left was more marginal to the political culture, the attitude towards the United States was a function of pro-Sovietism. In the 1970s this was reversed. The attitude toward the Soviet Union was now primarily a function of anti-Americanism.

In the view of the anti-American intelligentsia Australian conservatives had used American connections, the rhetoric of anticommunism and, on occasions, ASIO to maintain political dominance over a gullible population and a Labor Party split by anticommunist elements. For them the 'coup' of 1975 was overwhelmingly the central event of the decade—an event in which Australian conservatives and, they suspected, the CIA had conspired to destroy a progressive Labor government.

No figure in the Labor Party more personified the anti-American worldview or its possible consequences *vis-à-vis* the Soviet Union than David Combe. No figure in the journalistic world more personified it than Brian Toohey. It was not at all surprising that when Combe's association with a KGB officer landed him in hot water his old anti-CIA political confederate should have launched a campaign on his behalf or that many young left-wing journalists should have joined the campaign. What is slightly more surprising is how thoroughly a version of the anti-American worldview had captured cynics (like Richard Carleton), centrists (like Michelle Grattan) and economic rationalists (like Max Walsh).

Mr Hawke's decision to ban ministerial access to Combe on the grounds of his dealings with the KGB officer triggered a series of Pavlovian responses throughout the media. Outrage at what was seen as the 'McCarthyist' treatment dealt out to Combe roused the passions of the journalists. The Hawke–ASIO–Hope concern with national security left them cold. ASIO was seen to be staffed by 'Cold War warriors' whose worldview (because it suspected the KGB was up to no good) was 'conspiratorial' and 'paranoiac'. The KGB was given the benefit of the doubt and of ignorance. 'Cold War attitudes' towards the Soviet Union were, after all, impermissible. The KGB was not to be seen as the secret police arm of a totalitarian state. The word 'legitimate' attached itself more naturally to the KGB than the word 'sinister'. ASIO words like 'clandestine', 'agent of influence', 'recruitment' caused journalists to wince or snigger. Many found it genuinely amusing that

Charles had suggested to Combe in cross-examination that he had a patriotic duty to report evidence he thought he had of KGB penetration of ASIO.

The depth of feeling against Mr Hawke, as seen in the reporting of the Combe affair, needs additional explanation. For much of the intelligentsia—the class to which journalists belong—the Hawke Labor victory in 1983 was at best a mixed blessing. (Combe's attitudes as expressed to Ivanov on election eve are, once more, typical. The Labor Party under Hawke was trying to prove it was as 'conservative' and as 'right wing' as its opponents. If the Australian people face 'a principled socialist alternative,' he explained to Ivanov, 'they send you down the tube. It's a terrible reflection on the sort of society in which we live...terribly depressing.') While during the election campaign Hawke could not resist playing to the press gallery on the anticommunist issue (with his decisive 'reds under the beds' joke, a joke which by an exquisite irony Richard Farmer had coined) for those in the know Hawke was unsound on the American issue and had a 'blindspot' where the Soviet Union was concerned. Hawke, moreover, was not preoccupied with 1975 and was openly contemptuous of the anti-ASIO, anti-CIA brigade in his own party. For the intelligentsia, Hawke's handling of the Combe affair confirmed their worst fears. Hawke had made his peace with the old world of ASIO and anticommunism, his pact with the devil. For the intelligentsia Hawke was now a traitor.

If there is doubt about my central point here—that the systematic media bias in favour of Combe was a reflection of the prevailing anti-anticommunist worldview of Australian journalists—let me try to convince by analogy. (Like all analogies this one is far from perfect.) Let us imagine that in March 1983 Mr Fraser and not Mr Hawke had won the election. Let us suppose that after it he was approached by ASIO concerning a former senior figure in the Liberal Party who it was believed was being cultivated by a member of the South African Embassy whom ASIO had identified as a senior officer in the South African secret police, BOSS. Let us imagine that our prominent Liberal (Smith) had met with our BOSS agent (Kruger) a number of times, had been chosen to represent Australia at a Friends of South Africa conference in Capetown, and—while there—had had discussions with senior officials of the South African government and the ruling party. Let us imagine Smith had discussed in Capetown ways of raising money for a pro-South Africa university conference (and on his return had approached business for money to fund the idea); had while there discussed ways whereby sanctions forbidding sporting contacts might be evaded; and had (unbeknown to Mr Fraser) discussed in Capetown the upscaling of relations between the National Party of South Africa and the Liberal Party of Australia. Let us imagine that on his return to Australia Kruger had offered Smith work for South Africa and had discussed with him ways of meeting in the future so as to avoid ASIO surveillance. And let us imagine, finally, that when all this was brought to the attention of Mr Fraser he was to decide to do nothing other than expel Kruger and forbid his ministry to deal directly with Smith's new lobbying business. Is there anyone who seriously believes that after this began to come to light the Australian media would spend six months championing Smith as a civil liberties martyr, vilifying the prime minister and bagging ASIO? I for one do not.

WRITERS AND COMMUNISM

No ONE will argue that we have now witnessed the decisive end of the communist experiment in Europe. We can now look upon the period 1917–91 as a completed chapter in European history—although it is clearly incomplete in Asia and Africa and may be so in Latin America. Communism—as a cultural, political, intellectual force in western societies at least—is dead. What did this strange chapter signify? Where has it, as it were, left us? And in particular, what meaning does this episode contain for our understanding of the literary intelligentsia?

I am assuming that I no longer have to argue for my premise, that is, that communism was, for the European countries over which it established its hold, an almost unmitigated calamity. In the Soviet Union since 1917 and in Eastern Europe since 1944 communism caused the deaths of tens of millions of innocents; perpetuated one or other form of economic misery or hardship over the generations; alienated peasants and farmers from the soil; turned the most straight-forward aspects of daily life—like shopping or medical care—into drudgery, or adventure, or worse; made talk of democracy a form of cant disguising vicious personal dictatorships or immobilist gerontocracies; perverted a radical version of the ideal of equality into a cover for the class rule of privileged strata of party bureaucrats, the *nomenklatura*; stifled national self-determination for scores of ethnicities from Central Asia to Central Europe; destroyed all concept of the rule of law; injected fear and, then, cynicism into the souls of generations of Soviet and East European subjects; turned art into propa-ganda; and confronted artists with the choice between self-exile or hackery. Apart from its capacity to extract high proportions of gross domestic product for the armed forces, to win Olympic medals and to maintain large masses of people in attitudes of submission over long periods of time, it is gen-uinely difficult to credit communism with any cultural achievement.

And yet—and this is really my starting point—for several generations communism acted as a magnet of attraction for many of the outstanding writers of our century—for Maxim Gorky, Georg Lukacs, George Bernard Shaw; for Heinrich and even Thomas Mann; for Bertolt Brecht; for the Americans Upton Sinclair and John Dos Passos in one generation and, in a different sense, for Susan Sontag and Mary McCarthy in another; for Romain Rolland, André Gide, Jean-Paul Sartre, Maurice Merleau-Ponty, Louis Althusser; for Pablo Neruda and Gabriel García Márquez—and for literally thousands of lesser known figures. Perhaps even more significantly, for every unambivalent anticommunist among the literary intelli-gentsia—like George Orwell or Raymond Aron or Sidney Hook—there were a dozen others who would have agreed with Jean-Paul Sartre's description of the anticommunist as a swine. Only with the recent revelation that more than 90 per cent of the people of Eastern Europe and the Soviet Union are heartfelt anticommunists has this atmosphere collapsed. I have observed of late an epidemic of cultural amnesia. We are, to paraphrase Sir William Harcourt, all anticommunists now. Even ten years ago to be an unambivalent anticommunist was, in cultural circles, distinctly unfashionable.

There are a number of reasons why writers in our century have been drawn to communism and viscerally hostile to anticommunism. Some were attracted to communism as a consequence of reflection on the horrible slaughters of World War I, which came to seem to many of them—influenced by both the Leninist and Luxemburgist brands of Marxism—a grotesque fruit of late capitalist economies. Some were drawn to communism because of the charm of theoretical Marxism and its apparent capacity to extend to its initiates the key to history's meaning. Some were drawn to communism during the Great Depression which seemed to prove—as it turned out, falsely—that Marxism had correctly diagnosed the unavoidable tendency towards the immiseration of the proletariat and the self-destructiveness of the capitalist economy. Some were drawn to communism because of the rise of fascism and, then, Nazism because communism seemed, until the Nazi–Soviet pact, its only resolute enemy. Some were drawn to communism through a yearning for authority or utopia, in the insecurities of a post-religious age; some because of the secret attractions of régimes where the intelligentsia appeared, finally, to hold the whip. Some were drawn to communism because of a profound contempt for the hypocrisies and sterilities of bourgeois civilisation or, in a later age, because of European repugnance at the materialist vulgarity of American—Coca-Cola—civilisation. Some were drawn to communism because of the illusion that this movement represented the culminating moment in what might be called the Enlightenment project—the victory of rationalism and scientism against old prejudice and authority, irrationalism and obscurantism. Some, more recently, were drawn to communism because of a shame at the European treatment of the peoples and natives of Asia and Africa, seeing in communism—*pace* Pol Pot, the boat people and Colonel Mengistu—a form of Third Worldism. And some—*pace* Solzhenitsyn's great classic *The Gulag Archipelago*—were drawn to communism because of a genuine, if terribly misplaced, sympathy for the downtrodden.

What lessons may be learned from this long and strange flirtation between writers and communism in our century, this tragi-comic tale of protracted misunderstanding? The experience raises, firstly, a serious question about the capacity of the literary intelligentsia for political judgment. Political judgment—the capacity to judge rightly of political matters in the totality of things—is clearly a quality quite distinct from, say, poetic imagination or theoretical originality. Indeed one is tempted to wonder whether there is something non-accidental about the calamities which occur when the writer of heightened sensibility or conceptual brilliance is let loose on politics. I regard George Orwell as one of the greatest political writers of our century. However it is also clear that he altogether lacks a poet's imagination or a philosopher's theoretical stamina. What he possesses in abundance is high-order sanity; anti-metaphysical, temperamental scepticism; an ear for cant; an understanding of power and its corruptions; a suspicion of utopianism; a feeling for the meaning of pain and deprivation; an instinctive love for established ways of life. No doubt Lukacs or Sartre could put Orwell to shame with their philosophical grasp. No doubt they would find his political writing, at best, simple-minded and banal. Yet it was he, not they, who

was able to grasp the nature of communism. In 1940 Orwell
wrote in a letter to a Dickens scholar:

> The thing that frightens me about the modern intelligentsia
> is their inability to see that human society must be based on
> common decency, whatever the political and economic forms
> may be...Dickens, without the slightest understanding of
> socialism etc., would have seen at a glance that there is
> something wrong with a regime that needs a pyramid of
> corpses every few years...All people who are morally sound
> have known since about 1931 that the Russian regime
> stinks.

The failure of political judgment in parts of the western
literary intelligentsia is one lesson of the long flirtation with
communism. I can see no reason to believe that now that communism has collapsed the political judgment of the literary
intelligentsia will improve.

I come now to the question of responsibility. It is a well-
known fact that those few writers of the first rank who were
implicated with Nazism—for example, Martin Heidegger, or,
on a lesser level, Paul de Man—were deeply embarrassed
about their pasts; tried, as far as possible, to dissemble about
it; and, once discovered, were fatally affected in their reputations by the world's knowledge of their personal histories. It is
an equally well-known fact that writers who were even closer
to Stalin than Heidegger or de Man were to Hitler, who sat at
Stalin's feet for a generation and sang his praises without even
a touch of irony, are scarcely adversely affected at all. Some of
the figures I have in mind remain among the intellectual
heroes of our age. Few of their peers—except perhaps the East
Europeans—would shun them because of their associations
with the crimes of Stalin. It is not necessary to believe there to
be a full 'moral equivalence' between Hitlerism and Stalinism

to find this fact puzzling. Why are Stalin apologists still not shackled with the kind of cultural shame visited, quite rightly, upon Nazi apologists? Is it because, whatever the terrible reality of Stalinism in practice, in theory it belonged to the Enlightenment and not, as with Nazism, to the Anti-Enlightenment? Does the new crime invented by the Nazis—genocide—place this movement in a different moral universe from the Stalin régime, which nevertheless despatched tens of millions of differently chosen national, social or ideological victim groups to the grave? Does an assumption about ideological rectitude or generosity of heart absolve Stalinist intellectuals— in the eyes of their peers—from all guilt? I do not know the answers to these questions.

There are, too, other puzzles about the relationship of writers to communism which occur to me.

The most precious resource of the writer is language. And yet, manifestly, no political movement has more abused language than did communism. The deadest of dead metaphors; stereotyped, reified and stale Marxian historical theory, producible on tap as required; morally simple-minded manicheanism; vindictiveness; hyperbole; catechismal self-certainty combined with the authoritarianism of secular papal bulls—are at the essence of the language of communism from the mid-1920s until its demise. Political discourse—language—was one of communism's victims. Why, then, did so many writers—for whom language is life—so willingly accept, and even reproduce, the linguistic barbarousness of communism? Why could they not hear the crackle of the gunfire or see the barbed wire of the labour camps behind the language of communism?

I have suggested that one of the many reasons for writers' support for communism was the belief that this movement represented the fulfilment of the Enlightenment project.

However one aspect of that project was, of course, a faith in the absolute value of untrammelled thought and a fundamental hostility to all forms of imposed orthodoxy—to all forms of intellectual popery and censorship. In modern times, however, no political movement—even including Nazism—has been more hostile to freedom of thought, more prone to political censorship or more caesaropapist in spirit than communism. No political movement has humiliated its writers more comprehensively and bound and gagged them more effectively. And yet many writers, who must have known all of this in the greatest detail, still flocked to the movement or found justifying reasons to explain away such unpleasant facts. What was the source of this estate masochism?

It is, finally, one of the paradoxes of the relationship I am describing and, indeed, one of its most dispiriting aspects, that in general the western literary intelligentsia were most strongly attracted to different communist régimes at times when their totalitarian aspect was at its most forbidding, when the pyramids of corpses were mounting most rapidly. It was under Stalin, not Khrushchev or Brezhnev, under Mao Tsetung, not Deng Xiaoping, that Soviet and Chinese communism proved most entrancing to sections of the western intelligentsia. Even the murderous agrarian bolshevism of the Khmer Rouge or the xenophobic Balkan Stalinism of the Albanians had their enthusiasts. For all I know there are still some westerners for whom the Shining Path of Peru offer hope and spiritual sustenance. From what dark corner of the twentieth-century soul does this pursuit of frozen, terroristic, pseudo-egalitarian utopias arise?

There is some reason to believe that since the collapse of communism in Eastern Europe the political labels which have served us as rough signifiers since the French Revolution—the labels Left and Right—have been so emptied of meaning as to become virtually useless. There is a certain cogency to this view. Consider the following examples. In the west a radical free-market advocate is generally regarded as a right-winger. In the Soviet Union someone arguing precisely the same case today is generally regarded—certainly by the media—as a leftist. Or to turn the glove inside out: the Marxists who survive in Eastern Europe are now described as right-wingers while those who survive in the west are seen, and see themselves, as the left. Never before has geography determined our political taxonomies in quite this way.

It seems to me, however, altogether too early to abandon the old left-right distinction. While across the Cold War barriers the old labels have now become hopelessly confused, and may remain so until post-communist societies come to resemble western societies more closely (as they may or may not), within western societies the old labels, by and large, still do their work. Or to put the matter more precisely, so long as we do not expect conceptual clarity from these terms they continue to tell us in shorthand a great deal about an individual's attitudes across a surprisingly wide range of apparently unconnected areas of contemporary life. Let me be parochial for a moment. If I tell you I am a leftist, your predictions as to whether I favour mining at Coronation Hill; oppose abortion; favour censorship of hardcore pornography; support a republic; would like to privatise Telecom; and whether I supported the recent Gulf War, will most likely be accurate. Within western societies we still know what we mean by left and right or, more precisely, we at least know what belonging to the left or right involves. Accordingly, we can still ask how has the collapse of communism during the 1980s and early 1990s affected the western left?

On this huge topic I will fire only one parting shot. Despite the recent epidemic of cultural amnesia I mentioned earlier, it seems to me that the well-known, long association of a considerable part of the intelligentsia with communism or anti-anticommunism has inflicted real harm on both the reputation and the morale of the western left. The left seems to me at present quite bereft of any plausible ideas about the management of the economies of welfare-state capitalism. Having tied itself for so long to the radical anti-capitalist program of Marxism, and having observed the popular repudiation of 'really existing' Marxian economies throughout the Soviet bloc, the western left lacks, at present, an economic program, a social vision and even a plausible critique of welfare-state capitalism. Environmentalism, feminism, gay liberation, multiculturalism are theoretically still tied to Marxism. Moreover they do not add up to an alternative socio-economic imaginary.

To a surprising extent the rout of the left has passed all ideological initiative to the advocates of the free market. Today the *laissez-faire* right alone possesses self-confidence and social vision. Adherents of the doctrine of *laissez-faire* are almost as devoted to Adam Smith as the left once was to Karl Marx. They regard the Market with an awe socialists once had for the Plan. Some seem almost as immune to the consequences of market failure as the left once was to the human disasters of communism. To put the point simply, the ideological vacuum created by the collapse of the Marxian socialist vision has been filled by a new historical and economic triumphalism on the right. This seems to me, in general, an unhappy turn of events. The present atmosphere is helping to avert our gaze from the psychopathic elements of social life in western societies: the breakdown of community and family; the rise of savage crime; social anomie in the forms of drug dependence, sexual barbarity and suicide; the emergence of the idea of the underclass and acceptance of the idea of permanent unemployment. The left is paying the penalty for its long flirtation with communism by being no longer listened to outside its bastion, the universities, and even more radically, of having nothing to say.

INDEX